THE NEW BOOK OF THE SPIRITS

Karine CHATEIGNER

Editions Cercle Spirite Allan Kardec

David Eckersley (Translator)

On the cover : Mediumnic painting "Platon"
© Copyright Cercle Spirite Allan Kardec – 2017
All Right Reserved
ISBN: 978-2-9543869-4-2

Spiritualism is a book without end, written by the spiritual and universal hand of the spirits to help man to understand both his origins and his future

MY JOURNEY TOWARDS THE DOOR INTO THE AFTERLIFE

Death is a subject that I have been concerned about from a very early age, like most of us I suppose. I very clearly remember constantly asking questions to which I never got any answers.

As a child, I used to go to my nanny's every day. On the way there was a cemetery in front of which I would stop for a few minutes, wondering about all this death laid out before me. "Where are you?" "What are you doing?" I would ask. But no answers came of course.

Like many other children, I went to church until my communion. I was born "by chance" into a catholic family. The only notion I could not forget following my brief encounter with the church was that of God. This idea of a Father of creation suited both my mind and the way in which I observed the beauty of the heavens. I was comforted in the thought of this eternal and benevolent presence.

Time passed and I turned from a child into a teenager......but I still had no answers to my metaphysical questions. This teenager advancing toward the adult world became less of a dreamer. Like most children, I was taught the principles of a life that would fit into the society in which I lived.
Grown-up children unconsciously follow an "invisible path" that has been marked out for them. Their thoughts, ideas, goals have been pre-planned and any revolt against this is quickly obliterated "for their own good".

I soon understood that my metaphysical questions concerned a subject that should not to be spoken about: death. The religion that had welcomed me into this world provided a few vague answers but these were not enough for me. I needed to know more. And it was through speaking with various people and reading that I discovered another avenue, that of spiritism. When this word is pronounced, most people smile ironically (if they are frank) or laugh to themselves, thinking you are mad, possessed or naive (if they are hypocrites). This mockery is often the result of misunderstanding or of fear.

But before getting to that point, my question "death and what comes after?" led me to experiment in many directions. The death of certain members of the family regularly made my questions resurface and so I decided to try to "contact" them. With a few friends we did an experiment with a table. We all placed our hands on the table top, curious and apprehensive as to what might happen. After several minutes the table suddenly moved upwards and hit me in the chest. Needless to say, everyone was very surprised but also frightened. Whatever the explanation for this, it is staggering that a table can defy the laws of gravity and move by itself. Following this experience, I kept in contact with this "moving object" for several years.

I was very rarely at the table with the same people as I was often asked by others to establish a contact. At that time I did not know what a medium was, believing that people's presence and wishes were sufficient to obtain results. It was only when I was told by others that they could not get any concrete results if I was not there that I began to realise I had a gift.

Despite proof that spirits did indeed exist, I was not particularly happy with my relationship with the afterlife. I wanted something more "serious", more philosophical.....more religious perhaps......I often criticised people for the futility of their questions and for their flippant behaviour. These seances for me were not a game.....it was serious, almost solemn. Little by little I stopped using the table as it was time consuming. I began using a glass on the table top that moved towards the letters of the alphabet to spell out the message.
I believe I can say with hindsight that during these seances, we received a number of messages from beyond the grave. Both words and ideas occurred that I did not know. The subject matter could only be understood by the person for whom it was meant. On several occasions the table refused to answer, moving towards an "undesirable" member of the group while the rest of us simply watched on.

A while later I discovered that there was a spirit group in Nancy. As I no longer wished to play at being the "sorcerer's apprentice" I got in touch with this group in 1982. This was a revelation for me, learning about people such as Allan Kardec, Gabriel Delanne, Léon Denis and many others as well as discovering what it is to be a medium. In short, I talked about spiritism with people who were knowledgeable, convinced and adamant.

That very day I became a member of the Allan Kardec group. I can clearly recall the feelings I had during that rather special day. I had just discovered what I had been seeking for the last ten years. I was sure I had just met the people I had been looking for. I had finally found the path towards what I call "my true life".

So, here I was, a spiritist. My new life was about to begin. I was soon invited to my first seance, a ouija board seance (an official version of the glass and alphabet). I noticed how serious and solemn the atmosphere was compared to what I had known before. Emotional, happy and impatient I sat down at the table. The medium placed his hand on a wooden board, closed his eyes and covered his face with his other hand. The board began vibrating then moving quite quickly. Another person began reading out the letters, struggling to keep up. I was amazed and flabbergasted and despite my years of experience felt like a child on the first day at school: the school of the spirits.

My second cause for amazement was the message: it was totally coherent although I could not understand a word as the letters were read out. The medium went back to work......the board vibrated again and moved towards me, meaning that the message was for me. The letters were dictated as I was wondering where the message might come from: my grandmother? an uncle? a deceased husband? I was impatient to know. The end of the message was signed Gabriel Delanne. I could not have imagined he would visit me as I did not know him but I have come to know him well since that day. He was a pioneer in spiritism and wrote many books on the subject. He is one of our "teachers from beyond the grave". In this message he confirmed that I was gifted as a medium and invited me to develop this within the group in Nancy.

In fact, wasn't this was what I had been looking for? Wasn't this the perfect opportunity to experiment?
Of course it was and I willingly accepted the invitation.
It took me roughly a year of weekly seances to develop this skill and then to put it to use within the group.
Following this invitation, I never missed any of the weekly, experimental meetings. As I began receiving messages via automatic writing, I started to read books dealing with the subject. These gave me valuable insight into the field: *"Research into Mediums"* by G. Delanne and *"Spiritism and Mediums"* by L. Denis.

First of all, I needed to understand and assimilate the way in which a medium becomes a go-between for the spirits and also because I have always thought that this subject is too serious to be taken lightly. If it is indeed possible for spirits to communicate with man in an intelligent and coherent manner, these spirits need to find the tool that best suits their requirements. For this, potential mediums gradually need to learn how to make their mind blank, to forget themselves and to free their subconscious. Through sometimes lengthy experimentation, the psycho-affective or emotional load or overload of a medium will be removed. Their subconscious will be unloaded in the way surrealist painters used art or poetry to do the same thing.

I began and continued working within this protected environment and one year later, via the contact that an operational medium, Michel Pantin, had with the spirits, I was informed by them that my apprenticeship was over and that I should perform official weekly séances in which each message would be heeded by its receiver or by the group, depending on its content.

This invitation to perform so-called official seances, surrounded by other spiritists,
worried me. As I said above, this subject is too serious to be taken lightly and now I had a responsibility toward the others in the group. The first few months of my activities as a medium were certainly the most difficult. Up until then I had not been worried but now I was anxious at every seance. I was no longer an apprentice but was now the worker, except that I had not learned how to handle the tools; I had learned to BE the tool that the spirits would use.

Despite all this, I was in fact rather lucky not to have been the first person to have gone down this road. My friend Michel and the spirits themselves gave me precious advice. All this provided me with answers to my questions. Having become a spiritist and a medium, I was on the path to a wonderful adventure and still am to this very day. By wiping out the frontiers of death we have been able to establish a dialogue and to obtain a number of answers to our questions. You will find these answers in the following pages.
We have spent a long time conversing with death to discover that in fact, it does not exist.....

PREFACE

A man called Hippolyte Rivail became known as Allan Kardec for spiritual reasons and wrote *"The Book of Spirits"*.

The Book of Spirits: a simple title meaning answers given by the deceased to all the questions we put to them.

Who, in spite of their religious beliefs and ideas, has never felt the urge to communicate with the deceased?

Allan Kardec believed and supposed that it was possible to communicate with those who had gone before him at a different level. Our parents, our friends, spirits.....and he succeeded.

Of course, science was immediately opposed to this and hence it became impossible to say that the spirit could communicate with man, even if it was true and had been proven.

Today, this work is being continued as man has always believed in life after death.

Death....and what next? Is there life after death? The question is this......and quite rightly so.

The answer is *yes*. We can say that there is life after death. No one is forced to accept this, of course, but we feel obliged to answer the messages and manifestations. And this book is here to continue to give answers to questions that are constantly being asked.

Our aim is not to convince you, but merely to give evidence and say that there are people who believe that death is not the end and have communicated with the deceased in order to be sure of this.

There is no question of religion here, simply research made up of numerous experiments. This research which began 28 years ago has led us to the same conclusion as Allan Kardec. The spirit indeed continues to live after death. Those that you loved can hear you, understand you and most probably send you a sign which can be a knock, a visible manifestation or a dream. No matter what it is, it is their way of getting in touch with you. This book, the follow up to the Book of Spirits, continues to tell us what they think, what they know and what they are.

We hope that you, the reader, will receive it in that way. This book is a gift......the answers that lie in its pages come from those you have loved, from those you continue to think of and who continue to live inside your hearts and minds. Everything here is factual and has been experienced.

The word death remains a difficult word because of what it implies. It is something we find hard to accept. But there is another life, another voice which says that there is no death.........

Michel Pantin

FOREWARD: ALLAN KARDEC

It is often said that spiritism began in France. This is both right and wrong. Anglo-Saxons may well reply that it began in the USA.

In fact, experimental spiritualism began both in America and in the whole of Europe around 1848 (especially with the Fox sisters in Hydesville).

However, spiritism was given its definite form and direction by Allan Kardec when he published *The Book of Spirits* in 1857.

He was the first to completely define the major metaphysical questions in the light of answers and messages he received from the spirits through various mediums.

He questioned the deceased in order to elucidate the great mysteries of life and obtained important answers. He studied the channels that enabled messages to be received from beyond the grave, differentiating the mediums according to their skills and faculties.

The word spiritism was chosen by Allan Kardec to differentiate it from spiritualism in general. One of the basic tenants of this doctrine is that of reincarnation which is present in many ancient and modern philosophies. Spiritism reveals this is true and proves that it is one of the essential characteristics of humanity.
The solution to many intellectual and moral differences is to be found in this principle. Man now knows where he comes from, where he is going, his part in the great design on this Earth and why he often suffers in life.

Allan Kardec has replaced the principle *"No salvation outside the church"* – the cause of so much bloodshed – by the spiritist phrase *"No salvation without charity"*. This implies equality of man in the eyes of God, tolerance, freedom of conscience and mutual benevolence.

Instead of blind faith which destroys freedom of thought, spiritism says *"Unshakeable faith is that which can look reason in the face at any age of humanity"*.

Allan Kardec died of a stroke on the morning of the 31st of March 1869. He fell suddenly uttering no words. Dead. Hearing the cry of the maid and assistant, the caretaker picked him up. Alexandre Delanne massaged his heart in an attempt to revive him but in vain. His life was over ......yet everything continued.

The Passage of Allan Kardec

Posthumous account of his passage (Allan Kardec, incorporation 1990):

"I embodied myself in order to remember a passage that is essential for all human beings.
In March 1869 I was looking through several spirit magazines that were to be published the following month. I was living with Emily, my wife, in St Anne passage, Lecourbe Street. Suddenly I felt a violent pain in my chest and I fell unconscious to the floor. I continued looking through the magazines as if nothing had happened. I began feeling lighter and lighter and finally I saw my earthly body on the ground, lifeless.

At this supreme instant I can still see my friend Alexandre Delanne attempting to revive me with magnetic passes.

The sight of my lifeless body did frighten me somewhat, an obvious and natural anxiety that each and every one of us feels when we leave our earthly bodies. I soon realised that despite the efforts of Alexandre, it would be impossible for me to return to that body. At that moment I could clearly see a shining cord linking the plexus of my earthly envelope to my fluidic double. A hole was clearly visible in this shining energy, a cut that left no doubt as to my new disembodied condition.

So I rose up into the air and left the room, entering a long, wide tunnel where I was sure to find those who were waiting for me, my parents, my spirit friends and all those who, by power of thought, had managed to bring Bach's "Jesus, que ma joie demeure". into this tunnel that lead to the afterlife,

At the end of this tunnel in a deep blue atmosphere I recognised my disembodied parents and all my spirit friends who had died before me. A little further on, dressed in their white robes were my friends from the past, the druids of the invisible, former Breton druids who had come to meet me.

And above them I saw my guide Zephir who repeated "My brother you are free, you are free and you can see that because you always knew: everything goes on".

At that moment however, and despite this warm welcome, my thoughts went to the Earth and to those I had just left. All the other spirits had understood this and asked me to attend my own funeral, which I did.

Following the funeral procession next to my wife, I observed all the people present, all the friends who followed my coffin to the cemetery of Montmartre (he was transferred to Père Lachaise one year later).

I can still see the spiritists and mediums of **The Union.** *One medium then decided to call on my spirit and I quite naturally answered his call to give a message to all those who were gathered together. This message was that of unity, of progress and of the desire to maintain a coherent and efficient Spiritist Union in France, a link between all the existing groups. Unfortunately, due to greed, to a lack of commitment and audacity, things did not turn out that way.*

The Grave of Allan Kardec

Even to this day, Allan Kardec's grave continues to be covered in flowers.

As is the case for many graves in Père Lachaise, numerous passers-by gather around the tombstones, intrigued by the legends within this cemetery.

Besides the real and sincere spirits that visit the site, the tombstone of Allan Kardec is prone to a certain number of rituals which greatly anger the writer of The Book of Spirits.

Here is his posthumous declaration (November 1986):

"Friends and brother spiritists, in this earthly autumn my grave in the east of Paris has never been decked out with so many flowers, has never witnessed so many visits, so much prayer and so many requests. Should my spirit be pleased about this as I come before you?

No my friends, my spirit can not be pleased with such visits, prayer and requests. They all come before my grave to ask for a better material future, a more satisfying love life, seeking answers to questions related to problems in a physical world. But I am a spirit, we are immaterial beings!

My tombstone is the object of much devotion, of much superstition. Most of the people who come regularly to visit have never known me and will never know me.

If my tombstone is a symbol, it is the symbol of the Celtic tradition. It is the symbol of a human reasoning that hopes to encounter a state of spirituality that will prove the soul lives on after death. The fact that this tomb has become a pretext used by certain fortune tellers to satisfy the requests of their clients is very upsetting for the spirit of Allan Kardec.

The answers given by Allan Kardec will never be in contradiction with spirit philosophy"[1]

---

[1] I have been to Père Lachaise several times to pay tribute to the person who has become our spiritual guide and one of the main actors in our Spirit Group. As there were so many people gathered around his tombstone, laying flowers or touching his bust, I decided to ask a few questions about Allan Kardec. The answers were always the same. He is considered either as the man who might make wishes come true, as.the one who listens to our requests, who is a healer, who can cure our ailments by magnetism. Very few people actually know the life of the man and the reason for the epitaphs. Very few have read his writings. Devotion and superstition are stronger than reason, thought and knowledge. This is a great pity, both for this tombstone and, in fact, for others.
Many people come from South America, from Brazil especially, astonished to find that Allan Kardec is much less known in his own country than in Brazil where there are streets, squares and building s that bear his name.

WHY "THE NEW BOOK OF SPIRITS" WAS WRITTEN

The creation of our group

On his death in 1869, Allan Kardec left behind him a wealth of literature that interested many but also gave rise to great successors.

Men such as Camille Flammarion, Gabriel Delanne and Léon Denis continued to follow the thoughts of the master and to perpetuate the spirit philosophy in their writings.

Unfortunately, things did not turn out that way in the organisation of spiritism in France. Indeed, the French Spirits Association had helped a number of mediums throughout the country to develop so that a comparative study could be made about increasing spirit manifestation.

It was agreed that the mediums should perform certain tasks within their association. However, a number of mediums were soon seen to making a business for themselves out of their skills rather than developing them. What is more, certain groups wanted to be more independent and in doing so destroyed the unity that the Master had taken so much trouble to build.

Consequently and despite the keenness of the theorists and experimenters, the organisation of spiritism in France on the lines envisaged by Allan Kardec was reduced to rival factions that were soon to move away from the original message.

The great French spiritist movement gradually died out, leaving behind it only negative interpretations of what it was meant to be. Spiritism had been tarnished and brought into disrepute.

Today, as in the past, many people are interested, curious or sceptical about paranormal phenomena and manifestations from the invisible world. Many novices have tried to experiment haphazardly. Some have obtained results, others have not and the results obtained are often directly proportional to the interest and attitude expressed. Performing an experiment seriously will certainly provide better results than one undertaken as entertainment during a dinner party.

Generally speaking, we must not forget that scientists and researchers have studied these phenomena before us and have written a great deal about them. It is only by being totally conversant with these writings that the science and philosophy of Allan Kardec can come back to life.

At first, our group was formed because we were inquisitive about paranormal phenomena but given the messages we received our meetings soon turned into research. This was in 1974 and there were very few members. Allan Kardec was quick to manifest himself during our initial seances. This left the members puzzled as they did not know who he was. In the message received via the alphabet and the box of matches (ouija), Allan Klardec told the two participants to go to Père Lachaise in Paris.
In this cemetery they discovered the tombstone of the master and this sentence inscribed on it: *"birth, death, rebirth and constant evolution, this is the law"*

Following this visit, they got to know Allan Kardec better by reading his writings and learning the basic laws of the spirit philosophy and science.

It was Allan Kardec himself who asked them to create a group in Nancy in 1977. In a very moving message he pointed out the dilapidated state which the few remaining elements representing the spiritist ideal were now in. Allan Kardec was both serious and deliberate when he insisted that a new group be created which was to be responsible for a new and structured lease of life for the movement.

As the participants had chosen to accept the invitation, the spirit of Allan Kardec was regularly present as a moral support for the development of the group that he was so anxious to see reappear.

It was in this way that the Allan Kardec Spirit Group of Nancy came into being. After 28 years the group has become very rich in knowledge, experience and revelations. The group possesses a considerable number of important messages obtained via various forms of contact with mediums. This is explained below.

Indeed, the contact that we have with the invisible take place using different means:

-**Automatic writing**
-**Magnetic sleep**
-**Ouija board**
-**Trans-mediumship**
-**Medium clairvoyance**

AUTOMATIC WRITING

is well known in the history of spiritism. The medium lets his/her hand be guided by the spirit which will transmit its written message. In certain cases the handwriting is similar to that of the person when he/she was alive.

MAGNETIC SLEEP

consists in putting the medium to sleep using a series of magnetic passes which are called "longitudinal passes". The passes are followed by a placing of the right hand on the forehead of the medium whilst the left hand is placed in the nape of the neck. After about 10 minutes, the spirit of the medium (along with the perispirit) can travel through time and space and can tell what he/she hears and sees.

THE OUIJA BOARD

is a small board in the shape of the hand that is placed on a larger rectangular board. Upon the latter are all the letters of the alphabet and numbers from one to nine. The medium places his/her hand on the small board and the hand is guided automatically (in a similar way to the writing) towards either the letters or the numbers to form messages. It must be made clear that the medium does not know nor see what is going on during these seances and must therefore be assisted by someone who can write down the messages as they arrive.

TRANS MEDIUMSHIP

is a relatively rare phenomenon. In this case it is not a part of the body that is used by the spirits but the whole body. As two spirits can not live inside the same body, the spirit of the living medium will find itself without its earthly envelope for a short time. In this way the spirit of the deceased will be able to use it to express itself. The voice is no longer that of the medium but of the person who appears identified. It is quite common for certain entities to appear speaking the language of their previous (re)incarnation. We have thus received messages in English, Italian, Russian etc. All our seances are recorded onto cassette and kept as documentation.

MEDIUM CLAIRVOYANCE

clairvoyance is a faculty that enables certain subjects to obtain images, information or messages from a particular support. Clairvoyance has the character of a medium when it is used in relation with the deceased, with their photographs. It is possible to discover their condition, their occupations and their wishes.

We hope not only to update spiritism in the 21st century with this *"New Book of the Spirits"* but also to perpetuate the work of Allan Kardec, Gabriel Delanne, Léon Denis, Camille Flammarion, Gustave Gelay and many others. We will not refer to the important work or research done, to the conclusions drawn in the past which all exist as proof and certain knowledge.
We therefore invite anyone who is not familiar with these authors and their writings to read some of them before delving into the areas we are studying at the present time.[2]

---

2 For the history of our association refer to :
« A la Rencontre des Espirts » (meetings with the spirits) by Jacques Pecatte

GOD

God is an infinite sphere whose centre is everywhere and whose circumference does not exist.

Blaise Pascal, Pensées

God is not outside this world, he is latent in humanity and in each and every one of us. In him we have movement, being and life.

Saint Paul

God made man in his image, says the Bible. Philosophers do the opposite, they create God in their own image.

G.C. Lichtenberg

We feel God with our heart and not our mind

Pascal

As God is the cause of all things, the hinge on which all creation rests, it is important to consider this element above all.

Allan Kardec said: *"all intelligent events must have an intelligent cause."*

When we see a work of art we wonder who its author might be and we recognise the presence of man by his work.

When we look at the work of nature do we not see the presence of its creator: God?

Those who disagree say that nature is the product of material forces, that the stars are formed by molecular attraction, moving under the effect of gravity. They give all sorts of explanations to light, heat, electricity and the like.
All this is true, but whatever forces exist, these things must have a cause. They are created, distributed and appropriated for the needs of all things by an intelligence that is not that of man. The usefulness of these forces is an intelligent effect that indicates an intelligent cause.

Ever since man has been able to transmit his ideas, either by engraving them on stone in hieroglyphics or by writing, he has always acknowledged the existence of a superior being. He has always believed in this without being able to study it. Throughout history we have witnessed a very large number of religions in all civilisations.

The centuries have passed and science has progressed along with customs and societies. But man has not done away with his God. No conclusion will ever be drawn because God is an intrinsic part of each and every one of his creatures. Only time will favour his recognition, his understanding and the gradual application of his love.

The initial cause: God

What is God?

If we had to give a definition of God, it would be incomplete but it would be this:
a loving and creative spirit, omnipotent and omnipresent with no beginning nor end. A spirit that is one with its very creation given that the universe and the Father are a single entity.

How does God reveal himself?

God constantly reveals himself throughout the whole of the Universe. He may be likened to a radiant and incandescent stone that never ceases to spread the fluid of life like an infinite wave in space.

Multiplication then arises when this life is split into individual parts, becoming consciousness and thereby giving birth to personalities and types.

It is in this way that plant life began, that animal and human life began. The fluid took on many different individual forms, the greatest of which is the human form because the physical fluid of this projection contains the secret of free choice and hence of conscience.

Where can we see the existence of God?

God is the quintessence of the Universe. He is in the heart of all living beings as all that has life is spirit. God is the Infinite and the Eternal. He is the blue in the skies that have no limit. God is not something apart from the Universe......he IS the Universe. God is not one life, he is ALL life. Everything that reveals life reveals God.

Which of these questions seems to you to be the most appropriate:

"Who is God?" or "What is God?"

Without a doubt the question: "What is God?" Religions have always wanted to see God as a supra-natural entity, a sort of grandfather of humanity. It would be misleading to think of God in this way. God is not A spirit, he IS **Spirit**. God is not one life, he IS **Life** itself.

But man has tried so hard to give a precise meaning to the word God that he has created confusion and atheists are so right to criticise this Man-God, this superior man, a master judge or charitable entity depending upon his mood. God is not some form of being hidden in a given part of the universe, he IS the Universe.

How should we consider God?

You should consider God as a goal to be reached, the goal in this case being perfection. By perfection I mean truth, justice (not the justice of man of course), charity and love for one's neighbour. In a few words, I have already mentioned more than human nature can accomplish.

What about the intuition that each human being carries the existence of God within him?
God is eternal thought, creating future eternities that will have the character of the Father if not the perfection. Our instinct constantly reminds us of our spiritual birth as man was born out of this thought. On the curve of evolution, the memory of our origins returns to us and our lives are transformed.

How is God perceived throughout evolution?
God is perceived in the way that Christ defined him when he came onto the Earth. He is perceived as a Father, an eternal Father who is not an authoritarian power but a power than gives, that shares. A Father who is not proud but loving.

We do not all feel this paternity in the same way but almost all of us are aware of it, except those who are troubled or disturbed.

We perceive this paternity as a perpetual presence. We ask nothing of it as we do not feel the need to ask. We do not ask of he who constantly gives.

Catholic thinking deforms the divine father when it constantly suggests that followers ask things of the Creator. We know that it is important to act therefore we expect nothing.
God *is power, knowledge and love* all in one. If we wish to speak of a trinity then let us speak of the trinity of these three qualities that we as individual minds can not possess. God, in his power and his greatness possesses all three in his one, single entity.

Where is God to be found?

Do not seek God, my friends, look for him in man. All joy and suffering is the presence of God. God has been over-defined but never sufficiently loved. To love God means to love man and the divine condition is a goal to aim for by believing that each human being carries a fragment of love within him. Jesus proved this. He is an example to be followed.

The Intentions of God

Are the past and present natural disasters on earth a part of God's plans?

Man has often asked himself the following questions:
-why has God allowed this earthquake?
-why did God allow this cyclone, this tidal wave?
-why did God let this drought develop?
In fact, man in his ignorance (for which the Church is largely responsible) has not understood that there is no connexion between God and these events.

It will take a long time for the conscience of man to admit that he is responsible for all of this.

Human thinking is simply the reflection of a somewhat negative human evolution overall. The blue planet may still be considered as an "inferior" planet. Thought is a fluid which becomes evil if it is the vector of pride, of hate and of all the despicable acts related to inferiority.

If man can elevate his thought he elevates the planet and changes his environment.

All the disasters that the earth has suffered are in line with its degree of evolution. Thought must therefore convey new elements:

Love and strength in constructive ideas

"In order to change his earth and his sky, man must first change himself without blaming God"

Léon Denis (from a message received 19/01/1986)

Did God want man and the spirits to meet and communicate?

Spirits manifest themselves by nature and by essence. No entities, whatever they are, will contradict the Creator by revealing themselves to man. In this, the reciprocal presence of spirits and man remain the fact of one single and eternal God.

GENERAL ELEMENTS OF THE UNIVERSE

*The Universe is rhythm. In all its parts there is a
music of the atoms as there is a music of spheres.*

J.P. Luminet

> *Our whole Universe is nothing more than the action of the spirit of God on matter*
>
> G.C. Lichtenberg

CONCERNING THE UNIVERSE

Anyone who dares to claim that the Universe has its limits rejects the notion of infinity and can not answer the requirements of true science.

Being a scientist first of all means admitting that man knows very little, not within a vast Universe but within an endless Universe.

Being a scientist means admitting that we still need to learn, without a school, without a definition, without prejudice and without material definition.

Being a scientist means admitting that there is no limit to the miracle of life and hence not cursing he who believes in the spirit and who is closer to the truth for having transcended matter.

In the true sense, being a scientist is more a state of mind than a level of knowledge. Knowledge is a tool. It is not everything there is to be known.

Love, combined with intelligence is stronger than all the faculties of the Earth put together.

Paul Langevin (1985)

THE UNIVERSE

What is the Universe?

The Universe is an enormous computer whose stars are the integrated circuits. It records all sound and visual memories. The electromagnetism that travels through inter-sidereal space is a telepathic current which transports thought in infinity.

Man, in his incarnation exists within a finite appearance limited to his body. He nevertheless possesses the idea of infinity because he originates from this same infinity.

Was there a beginning to the Universe?

There was no beginning to the Universe. Astro-physicians speak of the Big bang, suggesting that nothing existed before. The Universe has neither beginning nor end. Man only speaks of what he can observe.

Is the Universe expanding?

To suggest that the Universe is expanding is as absurd as saying that it is retracting. The Universe is infinite and as such it is not possible to apply finite observations to it. I can therefore confirm that the Universe is in *effusion*.

What is cosmic energy?
The origin of cosmic energy is twofold: it has both a stellar and a spiritual source. What is cosmic energy? could it be the result of the vibrations of all these invisible and thinking disembodied forces?
There needs to be a support for this disembodied thought. This support is itself the result of a wave-like process that will give rise to what you call light.
Each planet, each star is in fact a reserve of cosmic energy and this is infinite.

If man could accept that the source of light is called the spirit, then he could enter into contact with the solar system and radiant matter so as to better control it.

Victor Hugo had sensed something like this during his contacts in Jersey and those who made fun of him are totally ignorant.

How does the rotation of light arise? (black holes)

Black holes[3] remain an enigma for man and more especially for astrophysicians. The only observation they can make about this phenomenon concerns the intense gravity fields surrounding black holes.

Man is mistaken in thinking that a black hole is the final stage in the development of a disintegrated star. Even if the energy inherent in black holes reveals distinct particles it is not necessarily the result of disintegration.

A black hole enables us to pass from one universe to another, from one galaxy to another. The gravitational field of a black hole comes from the thought of spiritual forces. The energy produced at the black hole is thus a spiritual energy. The attraction of the black hole forces this energy to take on a circular form and in doing so creates a strong gravitational effect.

---

[3] *Scientific definition of a black hole: a black hole is nothing more than a cosmic object in the same way as our earth or sun . The difference lies in its density which is billions of times greater tha all the bodies we know. Gravity is so great on the surface of these « objects » that the speed required to get free of this power is roughly that of the speed of light i.e. 30,000 times greater than that required to get free from the earth's gravity*

Is Jean-Emile Charon[4] correct when he says that eons (intelligent electrons) are mini black holes?

The comparison is very interesting but does not hold. The energy around a black hole in space and time can not be compared to the energy of an electron.

The black hole shrinks. The black hole enables us to pass from one galaxy to another but no thought, psychic or even spiritual element whatsoever is involved in this. There is nothing to make us think that this very same black hole could be of a spiritual nature.

As for the electron referred to by J-E Charon, it is true that as the energy of the perispirit is both within and around it. It can only heed one command and take on one direction. The latter is that of the spirit that inhabits the body, that balances and structures it, that of the spirit without which the body would not exist, without which the electron would not exist. We must remember that the structure of the human body and the minute structure of a perispirit body are only real to the extent that these very same structures are inhabited by an indestructible and perpetual individuality.

---

4 J-E Charon : French physician author of « This Unknown Spirit », « I Have Lived for 15 Billion Years », Death You Have been Defeated », « Science and the Spirit ».
« We are all spirit and matter and as such are a unit. To my mind, we urgently need to have some notions about the basic problem of the spirit that are as scientific as those we use when we speak about the science of matter ».

The Comets

What is a comet?

The space between galaxies is extremely cold. Inside the cosmic vacuum, considerable blocks of ice are formed from elementary molecules. These move in an elliptical manner around suns belonging to the billions of solar systems in the Universe.

There are several comets around your sun. Haley's Comet is one of them. It turns around the sun in an elliptical movement over 76 years. When it is closer to the sun the ice block melts by a diameter of around 6 kilometres. This melted ice breaks into billions of crystalline particles that form the tail of the comet.

Do comets have an influence on the earth?

Comets have an influence which acts both physically and mentally.

They can have certain radioactive effects that may affect harvests. Anyone who works the land both organically and magnetically will most certainly manage to avoid this influence. However, those who use artificial growing aids to improve the harvests will find themselves under threat.
Comets also have a magnetic influence on the sea beds, especially that of the Atlantic Ocean.

Comets also have an influence on morale. Why is this?

Everything in the Universe is in vibration. Vibrations take on various facets depending on the elements of which they are composed. Lunar light is also a vibration that acts on the human psyche. The reflection of this lunar light on Halley's comet for instance will become a new form of light transmission and will affect human behaviour. There will be crowd movements in tropical areas and revolts will arise in certain parts of the world.
Written message obtained on 22/10/1985:

"My name is Harold. I fought against William, Duke of Normandy at the battle of Hastings in 1066. I remember the anger of the men. I remember the cruel battles and fighting. I remember the heads that were cut off, the arms and legs that lay around on the floor and the blood on our swords. In fact, the battle of Hastings took place at the very moment that the comet appeared in the sky. We went into battle with a fury and rage that I had never before witnessed. It was not a fight but pure butchery of indescribable violence. This is my testimony."

Why does a comet give off radioactivity?

The block of ice does not only form an ellipse around the sun. This block revolves on itself at high speed, giving off a force of attraction. This means that the block is not composed simply of ice but of rock that is the result of this attraction. This rotation attracts cosmic dust and forms radioactive rocky masses.

SPIRIT AND MATTER

Organised matter is simply the result of the creative movement of the spirit.

Allan Kardec

In each particle, each atom, each molecule, cells of matter live and work in hiding. This is the omni-presence of the Eternal and the omnipotence of the infinite.

Teilhard de Chardin

We are born of matter and spirit. We are a single unit. To my mind, we urgently need to have some notions about the basic problem of the spirit that are as scientific as those we use when we speak about the science of matter.

J.Emile Charon

Matter constantly advances in the form of millions of molecules in the ether of the infinite Universe. Matter in its unique and perpetual movement is in constant reaction depending on the spirit that transports it and inhabits it.

The *spirit* is source of all sources and crosses through all living matter throughout the Universe.

The spirit can never take on any material form and therefore pushes its surrounding environment forward in its constant evolution.

Matter and life:

The cell remains the unit of life. Its double power enables it to use energy to live and also to reproduce itself identically.
The psychological dynamic of the spirit establishes its presence in each of the cells.

Matter, organised into a living process, displays the symptoms of intelligence and creative impulse even at its most elementary level.

The core of the cell contains the history of this impulse in its genes, made of molecules. The latter carry information that comes from the spirit:

desoxyribonucleic acids (DNA)[5]. These very same acids come directly from an impulse of the perispirit (the double of the physical body).

Hence, energised matter is the result of a constantly repeated spiritual process in the genesis of the Universe.

Matter is thus the result of a deliberate act that takes place in an intelligent manner. It is technically very complicated but natural.

No accident, nothing left to chance....simply the wonderful mechanical architecture of our psyche[6], in direct line from God.
How could we humans, whose body is made up of matter, imagine the spirit if we were not ourselves a product of it?

---

5 DNA. Desoxyribonucleic acid constitutes the essential chromosomes which are the vehicle for heredity.
6 Psyche: from the Greek word «psukhé» meaning soul. A set of psychic phenomena considered as making up an individual human unit.

Matter

What is matter?

Matter is the result of an atomic agglomerate. Radiating energy is the result of a cluster of energising specks. What I call radiating energy can be compared to structure of your perispirital double, a radiating and energising double, made up of a cluster of energising specks. Each particle making up this double is a thinking and active particle. When Allan Kardec spoke of "the vital fluid" in his *"Book of the Spirits"*, he had already felt what was later understood by scientists, i.e. the reality of energy, the existence of a very small structure that is organised in ethereal matter.

What is the principle of the unit of matter?

As was revealed in the *"Book of Spirits"*, the principle of the unit of matter is an unchanging and universal principle. Whether matter is vegetable, mineral or organic it responds to a principle of units of atoms which is the result of a universal, rotational movement[7].

What is the structure of matter?

The structure of matter is the result of gravity, whose source is spiritual in a third zone that I will call the "thinking deuterium"[8] close to the electron.

---

7 Over a century ago, within the spiritist movement presided over by Allan Kardec, the unitary nature of living matter was asserted by the spirit. Much later on, man confirmed what the spirit said following rational and scientific research.
8 Deuterium: a heavy hydrogenisotope the size of an atom. A gaseous body obtained through the decomposition of heavy water.

What difference is there between living matter and inert matter?

Living and inert matter both have the same structure. From dust to rock there is no difference in structure and from dust to man it is the same.
Matter is born from what the spirit wants it to become. Matter is an elaborate construction of intelligent thought.

Will matter as we know it always have a reason to exist?

Metamorphosis is the future of matter. The spirit enters into it, condenses it over a period of time, understands it and goes on to master it. At a later stage, it can be reactivated so as to recover its true energising power.

This reactivation bestows another tone on matter. We will no longer be in the world of curves but in that of irrational force, a force that can not be measured by the earthly physician. An energising force it is true, but one that derives its essence from the spiritual and from your Creator himself.

What is the role of neutrons, protons, electrons and quarks inside an atom?

The role of protons, electrons and quarks is to guide the energy of the universal fluid into the components of matter[9].
In its living and tangible appearance, matter divides itself up according to these elements that would not even experience this movement if there were no vital fluid or spirit as its source. The spirit is in each particle of matter. If it can be said that the spirit exists in these particles, then it can be said that it is projected and that it is produced by each cell.
Inert matter exists on the same principle: thought energy passes through its basic molecules. The physician can only understand the vibratory movement of the electron, the proton, the neutron and the quark if he admits that there is an energising presence of a spiritual nature within these very same elements.

---

9 *Universal fluid: the vital energy that moves the length and breadth of the universe and is the source of all life*

Science places the quark in the proton, the spirits locate it in the electron. Are these the same elements?

It will always be about the atomic structure of matter. The spirit will always wish to assert that the quark is an elementary particle dependent on the electron.

For the sake of quantum physics, it is worth clarifying that the quark belongs more as a sub-particle to the hadron than to the electron. It is worth saying here that the hadron which is also an elementary particle, is opposed to the lepton in its atomic make-up. They are in opposition in the sense that they can not transfer energy.

The quark, an elementary particle, and sub-particle of the hadron, really belongs to the electron and in this respect we are not be in agreement with the current definitions of quantum physics. It must be made clear, however, that the physicians of your Earth do not agree on this point.

Can man, by investigating science, penetrate some of the secrets of nature?

The Father is an eternal loving unit whose thought spreads across space creating individual minds. Science can not accept this simple truth as it is basically atheist and materialist. It can be envisaged if an intelligent spatio-temporal environment is recognised.

The spirit can never be explained as a secretion of Matter however complex it may be. Behind each work of art there must be an architect.

J.E.Charon
from «The Spirit of this Unknown Being» p.136

The Spirit

How can the creation of the spirit be explained? How did the spark arise?

God who is eternal thought, creates future eternities. These will have the character of the Father without necessarily having the perfection.

As the spirit of the Father is eternal, spirits have always been created. The human being is not yet able to comprehend infinity.

What is the spirit?

Originally, the individual did not exist as such. Born of God, it became a spiritual atom before becoming a spirit.

In order to evolve, the spirit could not remain alone in space. It entered the universal fluid to give birth to perispirital matter, the essential element required for incarnation.

How can spirits be defined?

Spirits are incredibly numerous and are the creation of God. They inhabit those zones "beyond" materiality and are different depending on their evolution.

Are spirits constantly created?

The creative process exists and will never cease as it is infinite. When your spirits attain purity and once they have transcended matter, others will be born in space and will follow the same path. Such is the cycle of God.

Are all spirits created similar to each other at the moment of the divine impulse?

At the moment of the creation of life, the infinitely divine, intelligent and loving force that organises all of this creates simple and individual spirits in raw form. Each one can then develop and evolve. However, at this stage, God created individuality and this individuality is planned to progress and evolve slowly via a number of reincarnations all of the same nature. The all powerful Father wants each person to be different. The creator is a source of harmony and the laws of harmony require differences.

What are these differences?

They are not evolutionary differences but differences that belong to you. It is possible to belong to a world of colour and not have the same colour. No colour is superior to another.

One may belong to a world of forms but not have the same form. Each spirit bears the stamp of God. You are all unique and children of the Father.

Oh how the words of Jesus the prophet were misinterpreted in that respect!!

What takes place at the moment of divine creation?

There was no beginning to this loving force but there is a beginning to our respective individuality. There was a supreme moment in the creative energy of a God in his Universe. Was this one day? Was it at a particular date? Was it at a particular time? Should it be measured?
No. This was and will always be.

So the spirit slowly awakens to the rhythm of an awakening nature. The spirit in the ether of the Universe gradually finds its form through the impulse of the creative spirit. It then takes on its future form from the fluid of life. This form will follow it along the different stages of its incarnation. This process is known as the construction of the periphery of the spirit, i.e. the perispirit.

When God creates a spirit does he know how it will develop?

This is not possible for the divine force. God is understanding and knowledge which can only exist in relation to what is and not what will be.

Life is a constant call from the Paternal force but this force is unaware of the path that any human being will follow in answer to the call itself.

Is there an awareness in the incarnation of the flesh?

The spirit will eventually reach another form of vibration as it is transported by semi- matter. Its instinct will push it toward this new and different edifice that has been built for it as the children of God do not evolve in dangerous or risky forms. The flexibility of the material that has been taken from the depths of the universe will enable incarnation to take place via the magic of love.

What happens at the moment of incarnation?

The spirit shrinks inside the ether-like, perispirital material. It becomes the tiniest speck that joins the physical body thereby accompanying the initial incarnation process. It enters, becomes flexible and slowly awakens inside the fertilised egg or ovum. Its basic life instinct leads it towards the first brutal and unrefined-looking planet.
But this is the first step into life and is the beginning of a future freedom.

Do spirits die? Do they in fact belong to a grand whole or do they retain their individuality?

All spirits permanently retain their individuality.
One day beyond the flesh, beyond the vibration of the perispirit, the spirit in its grandeur will experience non-matter because this was its original condition. Reincarnation will no longer be necessary as the spirit will have returned to God in his understanding.

Can physicians who are in a situation of constant research accept the spirit, not because they have discovered it but because they have witnessed it?

On the Earth, physicians have made enormous progress. Their constant research into the tiniest state of the particle has led to a new form of reasoning that is closer to that of Christians.
Discovering the notion of God in the energy of life, in its movement and its different forms will be the aim of physicians in the future. They have already guessed that there is a creative force at work, responsible for organisation and harmony in nature. The idea of a quark will then be outdated. Further ahead, the physician will be able to observe the behaviour of nature, from its pre-existing energy to its organised matter: perispiritual energy.
The diffuse link between the spirit and the most infinite condition of the physical structure of atoms will be discovered. Once this mechanism has been uncovered I suspect there will be futurist schools that will gradually enter into metaphysical thinking and those of the past with fixed ideas who refuse any notion of the spirit on principle.

Charles Rydsberg (1985)

What connection is there between spiritism and science?

Spiritism is a science which highlights the spiritual reality of the spirit in its perispiritual behaviour in the phenomena that it creates. Without the study of this matter, without the study of this energy it would be impossible to accept the idea of materialisation, levitation or incorporation.
Spiritist investigation in its scientific history will always retain this extraordinary truth of having been able to bring to light an unknown force in spite of occult or magical explanations and scientist or positivist negations.

Charles Rydsberg (1985)

CREATION

When Man observes the perfection in the creation around him he is forced to feel the immense joy of a son who has just found the trace of his father.

Frederic Ozanam

Love everything God has created, without exception down to the tiniest speck of dust. If you love all things you will understand the mystery of God in things.

Fedor Dostoievski

Do not speak of the Universe......speak of universes....

The Formation of Worlds

Can we learn how worlds were formed?

"All we need to do is think"...goes the saying about truth. Thought is not always the act of will but is more an expression of power. It is the power of imagination, the way in which the spirit expresses itself in its moments of elation. Faith, over and above its usual forms, can truly transport intelligence, gradually turning it from ideas into desire.

Does God create worlds alone?

Life already existed in many areas of the universe well before man appeared on this planet. Spirits were incarnated in many spheres, some of them having already experienced a very long cycle of existence. As their consciousness was open to divinity they were capable of many things within universal creation. Some of these entities even took part in this creation, especially with regard to the terrestrial globe in its temporal metamorphosis.

Is there a creative, spiritual source that creates the seas and the oceans?

There is a spiritual source that has created all types of terrain. There is a spiritual source that has created all types of nature. These creative pulses belong to a divine, universal process.

Thought vibrates and worlds are created because thought freezes. Many elements have contributed to the creation of these worlds, of this matter. Superior powers project their thought, their images, their colours, shapes and materials. New worlds are formed out of this pure and extraordinary thought, shaping the lands, giving birth to the oceans and forests.

Can the creation of suns be attributed to particular spirits?

Pythagorus observed and discovered the mathematical side of the Universe. He concluded that there was a divine harmony in nature and that there must be an intelligence that created your physical world. God imagined the Universe.....with no beginning or end.
In the law of evolution, certain spirits have returned to God in a state of perfection. This state is far from being one of beatitude. These spirits then participate in the creation of a universal balance and of new worlds.

Suns escape this law. When the Egyptians spoke of the sun god Ra, it was not that they assimilated the sun to a god but that they had implicitly understood that the sun was the result of the thought of a spirit. In this they were correct.

The Birth of the Universe

With regard to the birth of the Universe[10] and of the earth, scientists do not have much certainty. The Universe is said to have begun between 9 and 20 billion years ago according to different articles and opinions.

---

10 It has been stated by various scientists that there are believed to be 100,000 billion stars and one million billion planets in existence. It has to be said that these figures make us feel dizzy rather than providing us with information as to real numbers. In my view this dizziness nevertheless provides some answers. How can we claim, rather pretentiously that life (as understood by our scientists) only exists on this round, blue ball surrounded by other universes? Such a claim is devoid of all reason. We need to begin with a hypothesis to be able to arrive at a conclusion. Some people do this, others do not. There seems to be a continuous battle raging in the scientific field between the progressives and conservatives. However it was believed in the past that:
- *the earth did not turn around the sun*
- *it was mad to think that steam could create power*
- *electricity and lightning conductors were ridiculous inventions of the human mind*

It is said that at the time of the big bang (what provoked this?) matter was concentrated into a very dense ball of fire. The latter suddenly exploded (for what reason?), projecting enormous masses of matter into space.

Each one of these masses became a galaxy with a multitude of stars and planets. The galaxy in which the sun, the earth and the planets (Mars, Jupiter, Saturn etc) are to be found is called the milky way.

Creation and birth of the Earth

There was a time when all was silence. Silence is often assimilated to death. Here it was not death but simply an absence of life.

In the absence of life, the word of God developed matter. The word of thought, the word of a concept; the word of the spirit that thinks and creates has shattered empty space so that novas will explode. These gradually became entire galaxies with solar systems.

This list could be extremely long. The bottom line seems to be that as soon as origins or futures are talked about, man quickly becomes strangely sensitive. In all fields of discovery and invention, people ahead of their time have always been ignored or disowned by their contemporaries.
Sometimes the most well laid-out explanations and facts have been obstinately denied because they went against common belief. As Voltaire used to say "An old custom is so sacred, especially when it's a bad one". The scholar should refer to the thinker more often because when the former says: "how?", the latter says "why?"
The scholar may be a thinker and this was no doubt the case of Camille Flammarion whom I will quote regarding the subject of planets: "planets are made to be lived upon like rosebuds are made to blossom".
Before the planets were formed, the galaxies were made up of vague collections of matter and gases. In the densest areas (more matter and more gas), particles of matter came together to form the first stars.
After the formation of the stars, the Universe filled up with enormous clouds of dust gas composed of known chemical elements. One of these clouds gave birth to the sun and the planets. This cloud was revolving on itself in the Milky Way about 5 billion years ago. Under the effect of this movement its centre became denser than its perimeter and the temperature became higher. Little by little the centre of this nebula turned into a star: the Sun.
Scientists estimate the birth of our sun to have been 4.5 million years ago, the earth appearing about 4 million years ago. The cooling of the earth brought water in the form of vapour which condensed to cause torrential rains that gave rise to the oceans.

Through the power of the Word, through the power of thought with neither beginning nor end, another system was created amongst the billions of existing systems. This was the system in which the "blue planet" was created, with its blue waters but where man did not yet exist..

When did this creation begin?

The scene is six billion years ago. Everything is pitch black. All around me there is only empty space. In the distance I can see several dots of light. I am in the restricted area in space that is going to become our galaxy, our solar system.

At the same time I become aware of the afterlife. I can see human shapes, pure spirits. They are only light forms. Bright rays of light shine forth from their bodies, suddenly lighting up my darkness. These pure spirits think matter and think shapes.

What becomes of this thought?

I can hear a distant roar. The noise gets louder and louder. I can see an enormous ball of fire travelling through space and it is growing bigger and bigger. The noise increases and gradually becomes unbearable. The ball explodes with a tremendous bang. Millions of balls fly in all directions with a whistle. All these balls continue to break up and form new planets. Big, incandescent meteorites flash by. Everything is lit up in an enormous scene of fire, with some balls seeming to take up a position but remaining incandescent. They are spinning very quickly. Other balls take up a position in their turn, spinning on their axis.

There is music. The roar dies down and the spinning movement slows.

Can you see the earth........what does it look like?

The Earth looks like an enormous incandescent sphere. A whitish gas surrounds its fire and this fire is turning into a tremendous magma.
The planet is totally covered in hot and reddish lava. The spirits are still present, continuing their role as creators. Blue, fluid rays flow outwards from their thoughts, moving towards the hollow area of our star.

The Earth is a ball of lava that seems to curl up on itself. Gigantic holes, several kilometres deep are formed and the magma slowly filters inside them. A thick white smoke surrounds the globe and this smoke condenses. Enormous vapour pockets appear around the planet and torrential rains fall all over it. The lava now hardens at the surface, forming a hot core of several thousand degrees.

The clouds grow ever thicker, the rains ever heavier. Little by little the vapour subsides and the globe turns blue. All I can see is water, everywhere...

> Exist...why exist? To do what? If only to love, for this is answer to the origin of life: God is Love

Life appears

The planet Earth is an immense ocean. The scene is 4 billion years ago[11]. Above the waters I see entities. Above these entities is an intense, moving light that beats like a heart. The spirits are listening to this living light and direct their thoughts toward the waters of the Earth.

I can see small, crystal-like limpid bubbles that are falling into the waters of the Earth. I can see the bed of the oceans and all these little moving bubbles. Some of them join together and form living clusters. Simple forms spring from these clusters, triangular, long and transparent: amoeba.

Condensation is everywhere and in everything. It is hot, very hot. The amoeba group together to give birth to new life forms.

A gigantic prayer surrounds our planet, representing the chain of superior creative forces. The rays from this prayer go through that which has already penetrated the depths of the oceans to accelerate the law of attraction.

---

11 *The solar system, born 4.5 billion years ago, is said to come from the condensation of a revolving cloud of gas and dust. This mass is said to have come together into small celestial bodies, forming planets when heat-generating collisions took place. The central area contracted to form a sun. On cooling, the planets were heavily bombarded by meteorites. Those that have been found on earth date back 4.5 billion years, indicating the age of our solar system.*

Another roar is heard and everything trembles on the beds of the oceans. An enormous explosion takes place at the core of the planet.

The solidified magma rises up and pierces the surface of the oceans. A granite-like crust solidifies. The waters everywhere are invaded by the magma which rises up at the centre of the planet. Rifts result from these terrific explosions and I then see underwater mountains.

I can feel wind, a strong and violent wind. The surface of the planet trembles, the earth cracks and vegetable life is beginning to appear.
Semi-material and invisible spherical shapes float above the globe. These are the perispirits of a primary life that are falling onto the blue planet.

Everything looks enormous, gigantic; the trees are over 70 metres tall and 3 or 4 men could lie lengthways on their leaves.
Again I can see perispirits take on an increasingly material form.

On the beds of the oceans, saurian life appears. I see large lizards. The Earth appears to be hot, very hot. Gigantic water snakes emerge from the waters, gripping the rocks and the trees.

The Earth is one, big virgin territory.........6 to 8 billion years ago[12].

Everything changes and I am transported elsewhere. I see another sphere......the planet "Subtrion"[13] and its gigantic white balls that I watch die one after the other. I see these spheres open wide, setting free their double that was inside. They then rise slowly into space.

I see the shining hands of the spirits held out as a welcome to these inferior beings. "Great apes" already live on Earth in the regions that today are Russia, Siberia, Egypt and Canada: the pithecanthropes.

---

12 This accelerated, pictorial account of the formation of the earth leads us to note a number of correlations with the results of present day research on cosmology and anthropogenics (the study of the origins and evolution of mankind). The point of convergence would seem to be the recognition and acceptance of a God
13 Subtrion: an inferior planet. One of the first planets to evolve, it enabled spirits belonging to the human reign to develop. Of course, it is not the only one, but the description was given to us so that we might better understand the genesis of the spirit and its slow evolution.

Subtrionese will be incarnated in all these regions so that man can evolve. They will use the mating of the great apes to give birth – their ethereal bodies within a body - to a different being and this will become the human body.

For now, their double will not change its spherical shape. In the afterlife, benevolent spirits send mental images to these inferior spirits so that they can leave their form to create a new one. They will then be able to take on a humanoid form.
Like a shower of new existences, like a shower of new races, perispirits fall towards the Earth. They blend into the animal mating that will produce the first man........6 million years ago[14].

The history of man is the history of a perpetual birth within an ever-increasing conscience.

---

14 Dating methods showing that the earth was formed together with the other planets of the solar system, 4.5 billion years ago. In the beginning, the surface of the planet was apparently subject to a great upheaval due to volcanic activity, to bombarding from outer space. Then the atmosphere was completely modified by biological activity. A chemical analysis of the oldest rocks (3.8 billion years) suggests the presence of a biological, photosynthetic* activity. So there was life on the earth 3.8 billion years ago : an « auto-trophic » life that could create its own basic molecular components using the carbon gas in the atmosphere in the same way as certain contemporary plants and bacteria. Therefore, it is now believed that life sprung from the earth about 4 billion years ago.
*Photosynthesis: the production of glucides by plants and certain bacteria using water and carbon gas. This can then be fixed thanks to chlorophyll and energy provided by the sun. Adjective: photosynthetic.

The history of Man

When did Man begin to inhabit the Earth?

The human condition is an evolutionary necessity. Shape and form came into being thanks to the material available on the terrestrial globe. Humans thus adapted to the pre-existing environment based upon animal flesh. This was 7 million years ago after the most primitive life forms, after the brutality of animal expression, after the harshness of the vegetable and mineral expression in an indispensable harmony of reigns. It is necessary to have already lived to continue coming to live on a planet that is still evolving[15].

Where did these living beings (Man) come from?

It was via the mating of the great apes that the first human beings appeared. There has been a slow evolution of the perispirit via the impetus of the spirit from the pithecanthropist to homo-sapiens.

The harmony of the bodies has perfected itself over millions of years.

Basically, there is only one race: humanity.

Jean Jaures

What was the original pigmentation of man's skin?

Human nature has developed from animal nature. Originally, therefore, there was no difference in the pigmentation of the epidermis. In fact, it has been the different nature of the climates on the earth that has brought about the differences in the pigmentation of the skin. In this, we agree with scientists and the biologists.

---

15 In the scientific chronology of the history of life, between 6 and 8 million years ago, the common ancestor, the missing link appeared. This was the period where there was a separation between the panidae and the hominid (the ape and man).

What types of changes will come into effect when homo-sapiens disappears?

The transformations will become apparent to some of you who are still on the Earth. There will be both behavioural and physical changes.

In 40 to 50 years man's skin will certainly alter as will his bone structure, his cellular make up and his vital organs......his sense of sight, smell, touch and taste.

Beyond these physical senses, man will naturally develop certain psychic skills such as telepathy. Man of the future, Man after homo-sapiens will generally be taller and with a darker skin. The heart muscle will be larger and will beat more slowly (50 beats per minute). The fingers will be longer and wider whereas the feet will be longer but narrower. This Man will be able to stand for longer periods and will age much more slowly.

Is the human condition very different from the animal condition?

Flesh goes to flesh, but following the logic of intelligence, the spirit was not the result of the animal instinct[16]. However, there is a common point in

---

16 From the primates to Man. What is a primate?
The primates make up the zoological order grouping about 200 species of mammal such as lemurs, tarsus, apes and man. The evolution of the primates, to which man belongs displays two main trends:
the modification of the members and the development of the skull. Roughly 35 million years ago, the great apes began to differentiate themselves from the hominoids. The majority of them remained arboreal and their arms and legs developed accordingly to enable them to jump from tree to tree. Some of these primates can be placed on the evolutionary line that lead to man, e.g. the egyptopythec, (20 to 30 million years ago), the ramapithec (12 to 14 million years) and the australo-pithec who is said to be our common ancestor. It was at this point in time that the spirits brought in the Yeti and many other names depending on the regions. Yeti comes from the Tibetan yeh (unknown animal) and the (rocky area). This was the name given by the Nepalese to the "abominable snowman".
The australo-pithec is said to have slowly evolved to eventually give birth to man, whilst at the same time continuing its animal origins. Hence the Yeti. Scientists have nevertheless been perplexed about this for many years. For some of them the existence of the Yeti has been proved (DNA study). The hypothesis has been advanced,

divine creation between the instinct of the eternal companion of man and his superior intelligence, i.e. the similar and unitary material that is to be found in your bodily existence.

somewhat timidly, "Is this Yeti the missing link between the anthropoids and hominoids?"

THE THREE KINGDOMS

*It is sad to think that nature speaks
and that human beings do not listen*

Victor Hugo

Nature, why have you created such elaborate shapes?
Why this green grass and this yellow spring daffodil?
Why this saving warmth and the blue summer skies?
Why is the structure of this snow crystal so beautiful and so intelligent?
Why does this leaf, like the parchment on which knowledge is written, fall to earth,
yellowed by the autumn?
Why these cycles? why this eternity? why all this repetition?
God the creator.....the creator with no bounds .....

Is there a distinction in the kingdoms at the moment of divine creation?

The energy that exists in all our lives, in all living organisms comes from God. It is dependent upon infinitely superior intelligence that organises the harmony of all life and all spheres in the infinity of the Universe. Each life must distinguish itself, each life must find its form and shape, its differences and its reason within a given sphere in differing harmonies of universal creation. The kingdoms were imagined and were created. Consequently, their origin is the result of the thought of God who wanted them to exist in this way.

Do different kingdoms have the same evolutionary aims?

The kingdoms move forward on parallels and evolve toward the same goal......that of the perfection of God.
At the omega point, everything in nature will come together, whatever its form and advancement[17].

Nature has infinite possibilities.
Aldous Huxley

---

17 The reign of endless happiness will come when mineral, vegetable and animal come together in an ethereal metamorphosis. Here, the greatness and wonders of nature will embrace the very form of the spirits in total happiness and harmony. Telepathy between beings will become a communion between all living things.

The Mineral Kingdom

Granite

Granite is a noble material but man has not really understood just how important it is.

In the beginning, the earth was a ball of fire resulting from a cosmic explosion planned by the higher spirits.
The fire created in space gradually became the waters of the oceans whilst the granite became the continents.

It took millions of years for this change to take place.

The creation of the granite shell is therefore the result of a thought process undertaken by higher, invisible forces whose mission is to constantly create new worlds.
Fire, water and stone are so often referred to in mystic and esoteric symbols. They were the essential stages in the methodical construction of Planet Earth.

The mineral supporting structure of the earth gradually grew solid in the ambient temperature of intersidereal space and the fire created particles of quartz, mica and biotite. Crystalline rock was about to come into existence and the joining of these particles was granite.

The molecular density of these three components was not spread evenly over the earth and some areas received more granite than others. In France, for example, the Alps and the Armor zones whose underground rock layers have great quantities of granite, are both subject to intense earth movement.

The light of the stars penetrates the biotite, fixes itself in the mica and reflects in the quartz. This process is called telluric energy. Simply observing granite geology is not sufficient to bring telluric energy to light.

The Druids had understood that there was a force stronger than matter in the formula of granite. This knowledge about the energy contained within granite did not come from simple observation but from impressions gathered by touching the rock surface.

Each time a human being places his hand on granite he is touching his past, his genesis. He receives the loving and spiritual force of the invisible creators of the planet earth via the rock and its particles[18].

Walking in nature is like being in an enormous library where each book only contains essential words.

Robin Christian
« La lumière du monde » editions Gallimard.

The Vegetable Kingdom

How is it possible to talk of spirits where plants are concerned?

The vegetable kingdom is a parallel world that is part of nature and is included in the harmony of life.

We can not speak of spirits where plant life is concerned. It is more appropriate to speak of psychic manifestations.

For thousands of years, the psyche has been present in the seeds of the vegetable kingdom.
The gradual manifestation of the psyche within the vegetable kingdom gave birth to grass, to leaves, flowers and trees. This process is semi-conscious.

What is a semi-conscious state?

Regarding the vegetable psyche, it is not likely that the whole of its physical existence is the result of a conscious intelligence.

---

18 *We have not gone into sufficient detail in this area using the question and answer process. All the minerals belonging to Mother Nature no doubt have their function. Much research has been done in this area to discover the virtues of various stones so they may be used for the well-being of mankind.*

However, it is plausible that in the Universe there is a basic and essential programming that gradually gives birth to forms. This means that, to give birth to suitable life forms, the primary psyche needs the input of the divine spirit.

How does the vegetable kingdom evolve?

The vegetable kingdom surrounds man because it is essential for his daily life. Did the hyacinth, the poppy, the daisy or the buttercup exist more than 20.000 years ago?
I do not think so. Will these flowers exist in 20.000 years time? I do not believe so. Why? Because the vegetable kingdom changes in the same way as animals or humans. In its entirety as in its numerous differences, it is inhabited by a divine force that is by nature in constant evolution.

There is no inter-penetration within the kingdoms but this does exist within a single reign, meaning that grass can turn into a flower and that a flower can become a tree.

Is the flora of the earth under threat?

Plant life is under threat from pollution. Man's attitude should be one of moral responsibility in the face of this situation. He should prevent galloping urbanisation based on the principles of production and profit.
The immediate danger is for the roots because roots are the main artery of the earth. Without roots, the microscopic life in the soil would rapidly disappear.

In the areas where the sun shines strongly the earth becomes sandy. Where the rain falls heavily, cracks form in the earth creating landslides and future earthquakes. It is extremely urgent that man plants more trees, mainly oak and beech.

Plant life on earth is not simply the artist's decor, but is also the food of mankind.

Can we speak of suffering when we cut down a tree or a flower?

You are asking whether suffering exists in the plant kingdom because of an act of man.
Nature also attacks plant life, vegetable and mineral life without man being involved.
There is suffering and reaction. And the type of reaction this is seems to have been revealed. Suffering can not be compared to that defined by human morals and philosophy. It is a reaction of the vegetable instinct that is suddenly and brutally halted in its evolution.

But plants function like animals. Suffering is only relative according to the function of this realm.
This is why it is so important to take care of your environment without necessarily ceasing to give flowers or to cut down a fir tree for Christmas.

The animal kingdom

Is there a spiritual individuality in life forms such as the insect?

Certainly not. At this level we can only speak of spirituality that tends towards individuality. Spirituality can manifest itself in the mineral, the vegetable, the single cell and the insect but here it means a life-giving fluid, a divine element that exists in all living nature and inside each kingdom.

Does this living nature evolve?

This form of life follows the basic law of palingenesis, hence it evolves.

How does an insect evolve towards its individuality?

One day, an insect will find its true conscience and its true individuality within overall animal evolution. The insect dies and is reincarnated very quickly and repeatedly. In this way, the insect develops via a set of disembodied psychic faculties that are still part of the insect species but which are also part of a more advanced nature of the animal species. This would mean that a simple wasp can gradually evolve to a mammal thanks to reincarnation and evolution. This evolution nevertheless requires a long, hard and considerable effort.

How does the animal kingdom evolve?

The animal kingdom has had a similar evolution to that of man. Nevertheless, reincarnation is quicker in animals in that when man is reincarnated 100 times, an animal will be reincarnated 200 times. This means that by the time their evolution is complete, an animal will reach its ethereal form as will man. Within the perfection of God, the two kingdoms will blend into one.

Does metamorphosis take place on earth?

There is no change from one species into another on the earth. But there is change on an inter-planetary scale. An insect will remain an insect on the earth but will take on a more elaborate form on other planets.

Do animal hypnotizers exist?

All animals without exception are healers. Natural hypnotism in the animal kingdom reveals itself in many forms and within plant life there is a hypnotism that is particularly efficient in self-healing.
Animals heal each other. They have a sort of magnetic reflex or instinct that helps them heal through rubbing, blowing or licking.

Does an animal have any conscious awareness of its former life?

No animal type has the same memory. To answer your question, we will say that pets or domesticated animals can remember their masters and other animals that were around them on the Earth. Consequently, a certain psychological behaviour may result from this, as is the case for man.

Do any animals have the faculties of a medium?

The faculties that mediums have do exist in the animal world but in a more subtle form which is that of telepathy. In your world, animals are instinctively telepathic. They have particularly developed senses and animals such as the dog and the cat can see the spirits. The animal world is therefore the extra-sensitive part of your globe.

Can an animal be a medium or be embodied?

Most certainly. The spirit of an animal can enter the body of another animal. Within this kingdom there are many subjects that receive the spirit of their fellow creatures.

When we say that a dog is howling at the moon, is there a meaning to this?

Most certainly. When a dog howls at the moon it is because it can feel death telepathically. The dog can detect the smells that are being released from the physical bodies of human beings and animals. This is why the dog's howl does not necessarily mean the death of his master, neighbour or another human being. It may be another dog or animal. The howl is their way of saying "goodbye" and is a manifestation of essential love.

How should one behave with a pet?

What you call a pet is spiritual nature, reincarnated in an individual or a group. This manifestation of love requires respect, feelings and fervour from you because you are aware that animals are part of the harmony that we cannot do without.
A cat purrs to show it is contented. This purring has a calming effect on humans and those people with a heart condition would do well to have a cat.
The animal kingdom has a vital, therapeutic function that creates a balance in each and every one of you.

Does the spirit of a domestic animal seek its masters in its next reincarnation?

The spirit of a domestic animal does not spend much time in the ethereal life as it is reincarnated almost immediately. The spirit of the animal can recognise the ones it loves and it indeed tries to reach them. But, and this is of the utmost importance, it also tries to reach those who are in need of its presence and contact as well as those who are not yet aware of the sensitivity of an animal. Such contact is vital for the development of their conscience as they will need to look after the animal.

Is it possible to forecast and avoid Earth tremors?

This question is linked to the last one. A spirit is tempted to say to you: "just ask your dog, your cat, your horse or your weasel if you want the answer because the answer to this is to be found within the extra-sensory perception of animals".

All animals, whatever their species, can feel and anticipate what is going to take place on the planet via the vibration of the earth's crust. This can also be explained by the fact that many species of the animal kingdom are in direct contact with the earth itself.

> *In the hierarchy of artists, birds are the greatest musicians on our planet.*
>
> Olivier Messiaen

What is the role of birds in the creation of the Earth?

Birds play an essential role in the balance of nature. Certain species are threatened with extinction and should be protected. Birds have a positive effect on harvests as they destroy certain insects.
But their song is a vibration, a natural mantra that is good for all human beings. If song birds disappeared there would be many more nervous illnesses, breakdowns and depressions.

The song of the bird comes to your ears without you even realising it. Because we hear it every day it has become something banal. Birds are the emotional consciences surrounding man. They put the music of their love into daily existence

An animals send good or evil fluids?

Most certainly. The animal kingdom is based on the law of evolution within an ambivalent morality, i.e. between good and evil. Certain animals are not as advanced as others and as such can sometimes emit negative elements.

Do animals pass through the tunnel when they die?

For all living matter, death is a turmoil that implies the gradual passage from matter to spirit. Animals are not exempt from this law and they too go through the tunnel leading to the ethereal world. Animals have their guides, their enemies and their feelings.

Are animals aware of turmoil?

No. The passage from the physical to the spiritual life for animals is logical and natural and is accepted as being part of the laws of nature[19].
Hence, there are no particular problems regarding death for the members of this kingdom as they all proceed to the invisible world very easily.

What do animals do in the afterlife?

Animals have an important place in the world of the spirits. Their very presence is loving and faithful.
Animals have an important role to play for the spirit of children who are still in turmoil and who are both happy and reassured to see them. Their role is important for the balance of the ethereal nature of the afterlife. Their destiny is similar to that of man in that it is constantly changing.

Are the animals that we eat aware that they are going to be slaughtered?

When a pig, a cow or a calf is taken to the abattoir are they aware of what awaits them there? The answer is "yes".
Is this cruel? The answer is "yes".
Is this wrong? The answer is "no". Certain species of animal on Earth are there to provide food and there should be no hypocrisy in this.
Is this situation permanent and irreversible? The answer is "no".......the answer lies in evolution. The nutritional part of the animal world will gradually decrease on the earth and the spirits of these animals will not return. They will be guided towards other planets. This implies that the way in which people eat will change and this change will take place over a period of approximately 40 years. New species of plants will appear on the

---

[19] *If this passage implies natural turmoil, it does not mean that this condition is a permanent one.*

earth, bringing with them an increased amount of vitamins that are vital for the human body. However, this body too will undergo changes.

Between the years 2030 and 2070 homo-sapiens will evolved towards a new body.

Do Yetis exist?

The Yeti existed shortly before Man was incarnated on the Earth.
For science, the Yeti has disappeared. For us, he continues to exist. This animal basically lent its earthly envelope to the human being and continues to exist. Its morphology is very close to that of prehistoric man, developing a particular form of intelligence. He knew how to use stone, to make tools and make living quarters out of straw or wood but he does not have the same autonomy as man. In fact he does not have the spirit of man.

Is the Yeti an animal or a man?

The animal has been labelled an animal, close to man in its physical make-up and doted with a superior instinct.

Does the animal kingdom have any missions?

Yes. Some animals have a protective role whilst others receive information from those who have died. Some are responsible for taking care of and curing others. In certain species, the mission is simply to protect the existence of that species whilst others study migrations.

Do animals have a guide?

Yes their guides are other animals. This changes much more quickly than in the case of human beings as animals are reincarnated more rapidly. Protection rarely lasts more than one year.

Are man an animal reunited in the afterlife?

Certain human spirits are accompanied by their pets in the afterlife. They are happy. It is possible to say that some people have understood the meaning of death when they are reunited with those who died before them: their animals.

Does the giant ray of Djibouti exist?

This animal indeed exists, in the same way as many others continue to exist on your planet. The giant ray of Djibouti can be compared to the animal that dwells in the depths of Loch Ness, not in shape and form nor in its intelligence and spirituality, but in its existence and its life.

Jacques Cousteau, a remarkable man, scientist and explorer has studied the behaviour of the so-called giant ray. Hiding this from you would mean hiding knowledge from you. The most surprising thing is that we, the disembodied are obliged to come and inform you of this (11/10/1987)[20].
Jacques Yves Cousteau

---

20 At the time of this message J. Cousteau was still alive. He died 10 years later on 26th May 1997, manifesting himself during a spirit seance on the 25th November 1997. Here is what he said: « if my family and my friends are honest, then the truth must come out. The truth is to be found in my films that have been hidden away until now. I can confirm that the giant ray exists and I want this to be known. My films are a legacy. I want this to be known so help me to let the truth be told. I am very grateful to you.
Jacques Yves Cousteau

This message was heard during a TV programme called "From one world to another" to which the Allan Kardec Association represented by J. Pecatte and C. Antoine had been invited. This invitation was the follow up to a T.V. report in which there was a ouija board seance that had included the message of J.Y. Cousteau.
The following day a witness telephoned to express his surprise at Cousteau's message. This man, Alain Tournier, was in the army in Djibouti in 1981 and heard about one of commander Cousteau's expeditions into the Gulf of Goubet. During a press conference he had heard Cousteau speak of a marine "monster", saying that all would be revealed after his death. "Cousteau is now dead" he said " and we are still waiting for the truth to be told".
Mr Tournier was very surprised to hear the truth be revealed during a seance of spiritism. Eighteen years earlier he knew that a secret would be revealed upon Cousteau's death. And 18 years later he saw a spirit group on TV receiving a message

What is the future of the animal kingdom?

Matter has taken on many forms on this earth and the spirit is present within them in many different ways. But there is an essential difference between you and the animal kingdom. This difference is necessary, complementary and harmonious.

Both receive from each other. The law of a God includes the need to differentiate between various forms of intelligence in the world so that they may perhaps meet up in the next world. Advancing together in the parallel of ever-changing lines, they will eventually join and be one.

Does the animal world have an ultimate meaning?

The animal world is necessary for the harmony of nature. It brings a balance to the whole entity. The psyche and thus the spirit that exists at this stage, as well as the law of evolution are present in the animal kingdom in the same way as the human kingdom.
Although on apparent parallels, the animal and the human kingdoms will converge towards a more ethereal type of life, meaning toward your final evolution in God.

---

from Cousteau in which he asks that the truth be told about the giant ray. Another witness, apparently from the same regiment as Cousteau, confirmed his colleague's story. He added that he visited the exhibition organised by Cousteau in which there was a photo of a cage that had been crushed and mangled. This special "anti-shark" cage with titanium bars had been placed on the ocean bed with a dead camel inside. The next day the cage was pulled from the sea, empty and crushed and mangled.

INHABITED WORLDS

Too little of a firmament for millions of stars

Louis Aragon

The stars are made to be inhabited like rose buds are made to open.
Camille Flammarion

A proud earth turns on itself, perpetuating its ridiculous conviction that it is the only one of its kind

Allan Kardec

The day the Earth is in harmony, we will be able to enter into contact with inhabitants from other planets who travel around infinity.

Charles Fourier

SO MANY INHABITED WORLDS

The existence of extra terrestrial life is something very obvious and logical for spirits and spiritists. The forerunner of spiritism Allan Kardec and the forerunner of modern astronomy Camille Flammarion had no doubts whatsoever that planets either similar to or radically different from ours are inhabited.

In Allan Kardec's *"Book of the Spirits"*, the spirits talk about other worlds that are more or less advanced than ours, from the most primitive to the most ethereal. In these worlds, spirits are reincarnated according to how far they have evolved.

This vital principle of spirit revelation does not stop at general ideas. Detailed descriptions have been given by the spirits.

A message from Camille Flammarion on 15/10/1989:

Today's astrophysicist must return to the romanticism of the 19th century astronomer. Today's astronomer must be humble and must explore the possibility that many worlds may be inhabited at the same time. The modern astronomer can no longer believe in a single world with a single life form in an infinite universe.
The existence of many worlds is a source of transformation and metamorphosis. Any man living on Earth can no longer think in the same way when he realises that he has brothers living on other planets. It may well be this line of thought concerning life on other planets that governments and military powers wish to hide, minimise and get away from.
Extra-terrestrial life is a scientific fact on Earth. However, it is hidden from the general public. Taboos are there to be lifted.....an audacious revelation should be planned concerning modern day research in the field of space. But for now there is silence and the media either distort or misinform any messages.
One day, mouths will open, books will appear and scientists will finally rise up against this taboo surrounding life on other planets".

If the universe is infinite, is there an infinity of worlds?

Yes. Within the Milky Way for example, approximately one billion solar systems have been counted and within this billion there are 25 million planets equivalent to the Earth. Two hundred inhabited spheres have experienced a similar genesis to the Earth.
Concerning space, the infinite force of the creator implies an infinite number of systems.

Is D.N.A. vital for all life forms?

DNA is a vital acid for all the forms of life that you can imagine. Is DNA universal in nature?
Is it found in infinity? The answer is yes.

DNA meets all the requirements of life but it is not always suitably adapted to life in certain areas of infinity. This means that certain planets, on which you can not live due to the limits of your physical bodies, are inhabited by reincarnated spirits based on the DNA principle. However, this DNA has had other acids added to it to suit the surrounding elements. It can thus be said of DNA that it is the basis for life even though it is sometimes incomplete depending upon the immediate environment of the life forms in question.

As physical worlds are not all the same, are they organised in a different manner?

The phenomenon of life is suited to the reincarnation of the spirit. Spirits adapt according to the planets, to their climate and terrain. The biological nature of these reincarnated spirits varies according to where they are.

Are there planets that do not have day or night?

Certain planets are heated through their earth, others through their atmosphere. They do not belong to a solar system and therefore do not have any daylight. The inhabitants do not suffer from this.

We wish to note in passing that the term "inhabitant" and "habit" are from the same family.

Other planets that are closer to their sun and which have learned how to protect themselves from it know only daylight. The cycle of sleeping hours/waking hours does not exist on these planets where the ethereal condition is much more advanced.

Which other planets of our solar system are inhabited?

In your solar system there are very few inhabitable planets. The chain of life familiar to the human mind has developed a form of life peculiar to your system. This life form does not exist on the chain of planets that make up the solar system from Mercury to Pluto.

Titan, a satellite of Saturn, receives both the force of the sun and that of the ring. This provides enough energy to bring to light the existence of the DNA chain and this is a source of life on this satellite.
Life in a very primitive animal and vegetable form will come to Venus. At a later stage, other forms of life will come to this planet.

In inferior worlds do not forget that you must constantly purify yourself.

Inferior planets

What does life look like on inferior planets?

These planets are the first stage of evolution after the divine creation. They receive entities that have found it hard to take on life in the flesh. The result is ill-defined shapes that are enormous, very dense and not clear cut.

Do the spirits embodied on these planets have a guide?

Guides on inferior planets can not be compared to those on the Earth in the sense that each spirit embodied on an inferior planet does not have an individual guide. Several entities decide to protect groups and communities, to manifest their power and their fluidic presence on these planets.

How do these guides influence the inhabitants?

By the power of thought. The material density of the world is extremely high on these planets. And despite this density, spirits manifest themselves from time to time by clairaudience (the hearing of voices) and flashes of light.

What sort of influence do they have?

They can prevent hatred and lower instincts from developing. They can prevent the crimes, murders and cannibalism to which this type of spirit is often attracted. The spiritual guides on these planets are a sort of monitor or regulator that maintains an equilibrium vital to the evolution of the spirits that inhabit them.

Are these spiritual guides numerous?

For a planet with roughly one billion embodied beings, about 100 guides have a very long, hard and arduous task.

You revealed to us the existence of inferior planets including Subtrion, Nobos, etc.

Are these planets numerous?

There are many planets inferior to the Earth. They are located on the same evolution curve which places your planet second on an evolutionary scale. There are also sister planets to the Earth on a spiritual level.

Do good and evil co-exist on other planets?

The more developed a planet, the less the differences between the two are apparent. A very large number of remarkable individuals have lived on your planet with the aim of opening people's eyes to the notions of peace and injustice. These individuals have provided you with the tools for thought, reflection and action. Good is embodied on so-called inferior spheres to create awareness, transformation and metamorphosis.

Do all spirits reach this goal?

All spirits, whoever and wherever they are will one day experience the light of God, the love of our invisible Father. All spirits will one day experience this supreme metamorphosis that will turn them into a perfect being within the eternity of love.

Can planets be destroyed? How does this happen?

Yes and for two reasons:

When life has returned to its creator, when matter in all its forms has reached a state of perfection then the kingdom of the spirit in God, in love and in thought has arrived.
Certain planets have attained this stage and have completely disintegrated as their inhabitants had attained such a high ethereal level that matter was no longer necessary.

Conversely, inhabited planets may be totally destroyed due to the low level of life that is on them. On certain globes, inferior life which is also a form of thought penetrates the terrain, the underground and the climate of these planets. These elements are transformed and provoke their total destruction. On other spheres, low life can reveal itself in other ways, for example in warfare and military behaviour. On certain planets, nuclear warfare has taken place and totally destroyed them.

Is the Earth capable of this?

At the present time, planet Earth is capable of destroying itself 400 times due to the power of its armaments.

There are many dwellings in the house of my Father.

Jesus Christ

More developed Planets

Is there permanent communication between the embodied and disembodied in these more developed worlds?

Communication is indeed permanent in these worlds because spirits are completely accepted there. Therefore there is no longer an artificial barrier between them and us as there is between you on Earth and us.

How do certain extra-terrestrials experience time compared to us?

As our extra-terrestrial brothers are embodied entities, the notion of time is familiar to them. If some of them remain subject to temporal occurrences within relativity, they do not necessarily experience it in the same manner.

This difference in appreciation of time is due to the notion of speed. On the earth, speed is seen as an effort in relation to mass and an effort against light. It is not seen in this way on some other planets that have managed to go beyond this notion. Light travels at a speed of 300,000 km per second. This speed does not pose any problems on a galactic level.

This is why it is relatively easy for a space vessel that has chosen the moon as its base to reach the Earth's environment.

Are there greater evolutionary differences between individuals on more advanced planets? Do rape, suicide, crime and handicaps exist there?

Certainly not rape, suicide, handicaps or crime. There are differences on planets that are more advanced than yours, but they are not as great as on planet Earth.

Can you describe the process of disembodiment on planets that are more advanced than ours?

When the spirit leaves the body, matter gives in and gives way. On your Earth, all matter is subject to the irreversible ageing of cells.
By acquiring knowledge, by mastering the force of the spirit and by the use of magnetism, this process differs on planets that are more advanced than yours.
There are other globes where the spirit knowingly leaves the body, abandoning matter so as to be able to continue its universal cycle.
There is no sadness or regret as it is easier for the spirit to assert its presence in these worlds. The body must nevertheless be buried for reasons of hygiene.

At what stage is life on Venus?

The physical crust of Venus has had a similar evolution to that of the Earth. Until now, Venus has only known vegetable life but is currently beginning to receive physically embodied forms and not only at the animal stage, contrary to the planet Earth. Venus will receive both animal and embodied spiritual life simultaneously. This new life in your solar system is beginning in relative time.

Do the spirits that are being embodied for the first time on Venus come from a low level planet?

Many spirits have decided to reincarnate on the planet Venus and many of them are advanced spirits. This means that the planet will welcome spirits having already accomplished a significant spiritual journey in palingenesis.

What are conditions like on Venus given the extremely high temperature on this planet?

Life exists on many planets. It extends as far as infinity and inside your small solar system, especially on Venus.

You speak of a temperature that may seem very high to you. We have spoken with Camille Flammarion about a hairy being with a very thick outer layer protection. The biological make-up of this being would need to be understood as well as the true temperature of his physical body. The living conditions of this sphere also need to be known.

The temperature is certainly high compared to the temperatures that you are used to. An inhabitant of Venus must adapt to his climate, to his terrain, to his circumstances and to the cycle within your planetary system.

It must be understood that life adapts itself to its incarnation and that this is the case for the whole of the Universe.

When Allan Kardec was alive, Victorien Sardou, a painter/medium, received a drawing showing life on Jupiter. What is there to say about this?

The difference between a concentration of spirits on a globe, giving rise to a spiritual sphere and the incarnation of a number of entities on another globe, in turn giving rise to an extra-terrestrial world must be made clear.

Sometimes the answers given by the spirits in the *"Book of Spirits"* have been too short or incomplete. They have nevertheless tried to tell the truth. There are worlds where spirits gather and thousands of entities come together in certain places such as the planet Jupiter.

THE PERISPIRIT

*Borrowed from the ethers, fluid of all matter
vehicle of my soul, the result of your great plan
and of my memory, the tool to attain the most distant corners
of life.*

The concept of the perispirit is not new. Somewhat imperfect descriptions of it can be found in the history of the oldest religions. All primitive religions have given an ethereal envelope to the soul. Confucius described the spirits of the dead clothed in an invisible envelope.

It was not until later, and the emergence of contemporary religions, that the notion of a pure spirit came into being. This concept was to remain until the spirit revival with Allan Kardec which clarified the existence of the perispirit.

The fluid and yet semi-material perispirit is invisible in the same way as other fluids that we know exist but that we can not see.

It accompanies the spirit in its successive lives, a sort of vehicle for it.

The perispirit forms and develops the different vital organs. The flesh builds itself around the structure of the perispirit.

The perispirit has no intelligence of its own as it is merely an intermediary between the spirit and the body.
It perceives our feelings, sends them to the spirit and keeps our memories. It is connected to the body throughout a person's life but nevertheless remains somewhat independent from it. This means it can express itself whilst at the same time maintaining contact (via sleep, leaving of the body). As such, it is flexible.

Upon death, it leaves at the same moment as the spirit, creating a spiritual body which keeps the physical properties peculiar to each individual in the afterlife.
Because the perispirit exists before our incarnation on the earth, all we have acquired from our previous lives is passed on to us. As it can not be destroyed the perispirit keeps all the positive elements we have acquired before dying.
Due to it substance it is also via the perispirit that the spirit manifests itself in disembodied life, displaying its own physical characteristics that enable it to be identified. It can and will penetrate all forms of matter without altering or modifying them.

Depending on the wishes of the spirit, it may undergo alterations that make it perceptible to the eye either by condensation or by a modification in the molecular structure. Hence, it may occasionally take on a tangible, solid and palpable appearance only to return to its ethereal and invisible state (like steam that can go from being invisible to being misty, then liquid, then solid and then back to being invisible).

Its material changes and maturity are directly related to the moral advances of the spirit until it attains the stage where it blends into the very essence of the soul when the latter has attained a state of perfection.

The importance of the peri*spirit*:

The perispirit is extremely important.

it is the intermediary between matter and the spirit
it evolves and progresses with the spirit
it preserves individuality and progress made
it serves as a mould or a substratum for any new incarnation
without the perispirit (without the spirit) the result of fertilisation would be a shapeless tumour (a clear egg)
it is not imprisoned by the body. It shines outwards to a greater or lesser degree (the aura) and is also able to travel (through sleep and dreams)

What is the origin of the perispirit?

Divinity in its creative energy has made different individuals with free spirits out of each and every one of you. The love involved in this means you are all unique.

This "me" created by the heavenly forces suddenly found itself propelled through the Universe. This individual needed an initial guide and this guide was his first meeting with the cosmic world which involved billions of fluid and physical forces. A cosmic world in which the spirit discovered its dwelling place via the perispirit that came to join its spirit after being created by the force of a God. The perispirit was born of cosmic forces and existing physical forces which are eternal.

Where does the spirit's semi-material envelope come from?

In the ether of the Universe, the spirit gradually finds its form thanks to the love of God. It then borrows its future form from the fluid of life, or *"universal fluid"*, a form that will exist during the sequences of its incarnation.
This perispirital matter has a permanent existence in the infinity of the Universe. This invisible plasma, this invisible yet real matter, this substratum of matter creates what will be the vector of the spirit, its vehicle through a succession of experiences in the flesh.

What is the perispirit composed of?

This part of the spirit is physical in nature. It is made up of a set of electronic, cellular forces. The main advantage of these cells is that they are able to record. They have a capacity for memory.

What happens to this perispirital memory during the succession of lives?

The spirit is incarnated in order to gather the experience necessary to increase its awareness. This awareness can not grow without an acquired force and this force can only be acquired through the ability of the principal matter to record.

The spirit is successively reincarnated with this evolutionary goal in mind. It instinctively knows how to use this memory induced in its perispiritcal body.
Hence the faculty acquired in previous lives follows the spirit throughout its entire experiences.

Can we speak of density concerning this double, this perispirit?

The average density of an ethereal body is roughly ten grams. These ten grams correspond to a structure that is made up in the following way:

-2g of manganese
-2g of nickel
-3g of radioactively radiating subatomic radium
-3g of basic D7 fluid

What we call D7 base fluid corresponds to the deuterium subdivided into 7 elements unknown to the science of man. The whole entity forms the perispirit, the vehicle of the spirit and the vector of your conscience.

Has science already revealed the perispirit?

The perispirit is invisible and impalpable. The instruments currently at man's disposal are insufficient to reveal the phenomenon, except for some Russian researchers who have discovered the nature of the bio-plasmatic body and its capacity to survive.

Marie Curie. October 1982

Does the perispirit change each time a person is reincarnated?

The spirit seeking perfection will not separate itself from its dwelling place or from the vehicle it needs in order to evolve.
Perispirital matter is extremely small and invisible but it nevertheless exists. It is structured from radium and deuterium to which nickel and manganese have been added. It is for this reason that oligo-elements will have a beneficial effect on its cells.

Does the perispirit disappear when perfection is reached?

Despite being minute and ethereal, the perispirit can not escape the evolutionary law of matter. Consequently, it will be subject to the supreme act of evolution, i.e. its permanent end.
This aspect of its future is the beginning of a harmonious encounter with God and the birth of the whole of the spirit.

Are certain spirits that visit us aware of this condition?

No spirit that approaches us is aware of this condition, otherwise it would be impossible for it to come towards us. This is because the semi-material perispirit is there to transport the spirit as much in the vibratory layers of matter as in the ethereal ones.

What is the aura?

Your double or your perispirit is inside your material envelope. When it shows itself it can sometimes be seen in light forms around the person. This, for the sake of simplicity we will call the aura. However, one must not see any form of extra body in this.

Does the semi-material envelope of the spirit take on determined forms and is it perceptible?

Yes, depending upon the wishes of the spirit, the perispirit takes on the desired form and expression. So, although the perispirit has no bodily handicap, a spirit may present itself crippled or wounded if that is what is required to identify it. It is exactly the same for clothing.

Is the perispirit simply the double of the visible body?

The spirit will delve into the universal fluid to constitute the semi-material contours of its double that we call the perispirit. The latter is not limited to the contours of the visible body. It is also the double of the organs. The double of a hand is not only the double of its surface area but also of its internal structure and of its cells.

Does this double matter explain the materialisation of certain parts of the body? (ectoplasm)

Most certainly. Otherwise the phenomenon could not take place.

Testimony by Gustave Gelay (taken from his book "Ectoplasm and Clairvoyance")

"In the most perfect cases, the materialised organ has all the biological properties and looks just like a living organ. I have seen perfectly reproduced fingers with fingernails I have seen hands complete with bones and joints. I have seen perfectly formed faces, living and human faces".[21]

---

[21] *The Kirlian brothers were the first to discover, observe and photograph the aura: the « Kirlian effect ». It is a pity that this was considered more as a photographic feat than a fundamental discovery. Many scientists from different countries nevertheless took an interest in it and they soon discovered that the coloured efflorescence shown in the photos gave precious information about the health, the psyche and the personality of an individual.*
Using these photos, doctors were able to detect problems even before they became apparent (depending on the colour, the form and the luminosity of the rays). It is said that in 1969, a potential cancer of the oesophagus in President Brejnev was cured several months before the first symptoms became apparent.
After many years of debate, scientists no longer doubt the reality of the Kirlian effect. Many universities work with electrographs; studying their techniques and applications (medical, technological and agricultural), for example at the Universities of South California and Chicago.
The Russians continue the research of the Soviets and in France the department of biology at the University of Orsay is studying the phenomenon

THE SPIRIT

Physical science will prove that the spirit is an existing reality within the Universe.

Robert Andrew

When the superficial "me" links up with the profound me, flesh will no longer be necessary and the spirit will reign, becoming pure.

The genesis of the spirit

The spirit:

Let us gradually look at the way the spirit progresses so as to understand its relationship with matter and how it turns into a human being.

All too often man has defined the spirit as the anti-thesis of matter. The spirit is responsible for matter. Without it, the physical world would be devoid of life and hence without the movement needed for creation.

Life-giving energy should be considered as being timeless, eternal and of a loving nature. This is what man should remember when he procreates because sexual intercourse is the distant equivalent to divine creation.

So the spirit is, above all, the result of love, the consequence of a God that can not be defined by religion.

As spirits are of the same origin, what they have in common is unity and this unity will become obvious when they enter into matter.

When it is still very basic and unintelligent, the spirit will instinctively formulate its destiny by creating what is suitably called matter.

The subconscious:

When the superficial "I" links up with the profound "me", then flesh will no longer be necessary and the spirit will reign. It will be pure spirit.
One must look at the history of the subconscious in order to define and understand it. A spiritist perspective reveals a side of this that psychoanalysis had never envisaged. To break through the mystery of the subconscious one must go back to its source.

Where does the subconscious begin?

The spirit is pushed by the energising force of divine love and is born into life. It then begins the first stage of the construction of its psyche in the subconscious which begins revealing itself. The spirit, pushed forward for the first time, is ignorant of its source and its origins.

The first repression of the spirit in its ethereal state is the repression of the Father, of God. This is also the first subconscious memory created by the spirit.

What happens to the spirit at this stage of creation?

Unknowingly, the spirit is setting out on a very long march toward what will become the utmost expression of its quality as a spirit – purity.

It is not possible to know about life and the world by remaining alone. The evolutionary instinct that has been programmed by the divine creative force will force the spirit to descend towards the vibrations of matter. At this stage, the spirit is just a life without meaning, with no contacts. Its descent toward the world of matter will thus be in relation to its basic nature. It will therefore be embodied on a lower sphere where the vibrations of gravity are such that it will develop in the most vulgar of forms.

What are the first contacts the spirit has with the outside world at this stage of evolution and incarnation?

functions of its body. At this stage the embodied spirit will be guided by hunger, thirst and the will to survive, defending itself against all the onslaughts of matter.

What is this first sphere of incarnation of the spirit like?

On this first planet everything will look monstrous. Nature will have vulgar and enormous forms. Giant trees with viscous bark, over 10 metres high and 6 metres in circumference will emerge from moss and lichen-covered earth. Light will be poor. The newly born perispirit will also vibrate in time with this coarse and vulgar world.

The first feelings will be those of anguish, fear, self defence and aggression.

How does the spirit live its afterlife following this first incarnation?

This first experience of life will soon be forgotten upon death. This is the second repression of a spirit that is beginning its existence. The image of this life is nevertheless indelibly recorded in the memory. Gradually the subconscious will accumulate images and feelings that have been naturally repressed over several lives and on several planets.
It would be impossible for the spirit to consciously master the entirety of these vital elements. For the individual to be balanced, each life should carry on from the previous one, forgetting the one that came before.

Is the subconscious simply repression experienced in successive lives?

After the first three or four lives, the now-formed subconscious is not simply limited to physical lives or incarnations. The subconscious is also the other life that is lived on the other side in between two lives on earth.

Do all spirits follow the same path?

All spirits experience these events through the natural channel of palingenesis. Each and every one of you carries the entire memory of these events.

Is psychoanalysis on Earth limited in how far it can go in its investigation?

Yes because psychology stops at what has been repressed in one life. Sometimes situations arise that belong to a former life and which determine or condition present situations. Sources of conflict, of imbalance, psychosis, madness or physical disability.

A perispirit remembers not only what happened in the present life but also in previous lives. The past must then be looked at through the windows offered by psychoanalysis. But this venture into the genesis of the spirit must be undertaken methodically and this method has not yet been really well defined on the Earth.

FROM LIFE TO DEATH

*I claim that the tomb that closes on the dead opens onto the firmament.
And that what we consider to be the end is only the beginning...*

Victor Hugo

A man who dies is a star that lies down to sleep and awakens in another hemisphere

Goethe

Is it not necessary to die to experience the pleasure of finally dying on arrival in port?

Paul Verlaine

Death means being reborn. This life is a dream and death is an awakening

J. Simon

Death

Death is a daily occurrence. Do not fear death for it is a stage of life that it would be stupid to ignore.

Man has disguised death as a form of torture and anguish. It is time that its rags were taken from it so that the flame of the spirit can sublimate the eternal character of life.

Death plunges souls full of hope into the depths of the Milky Way, showering a rain of stars into the eyes of believers who silently leave for a better future. Death is a gentle and peaceful experience that leads spirits into the voluptuous ether of eternity.

Death is a stream that carries our souvenirs and our future missions in its celestial limpidity.

What does the spirit feel at the moment of death?

At the moment of physical death, when the spirit leaves its home, it has the strange and still material feeling giving the impression of falling into a black hole without a bottom.

What is the meaning of this feeling?

This feeling means that the link with the material world still exists via the perispirit and that the metamorphosis is not complete.

Can you describe in detail the passage into the afterlife in its successive stages?

The circular, elliptical movement is the initial movement of terrestrial life. DNA reminds us of this movement because of its helical shape. When a human being dies, the shape and the initial principle of life in this circular movement return.
A heart attack always gives the impression of falling. This fall is felt by all spirits at the moment of death. It is followed by a circular downward movement that will cease more or less quickly depending on the person.

When does one encounter the tunnel described so often in NDEs?

The end of this circular movement means encountering a long a narrow tunnel lit by a yellowish light similar to that produced by electricity..

What is death? The breaking of this terrible knot, the adulterous hymen between Earth and soul to finally rid oneself of this terrible weight.
Death is not death, my friends, death simply means change.

Lamartine

Do all spirits pass through this tunnel?

Certain spirits pass through this tunnel. Others do not.

This tunnel leads towards something blue, like a blue sky. This sky is there before the eyes of the spirit who looks into it, safe in the knowledge that he will meet those he has loved and usually his guide.

If the spirit does not enter the tunnel, the circular movement continues with weird and wonderful images appearing that relate to life in the flesh.

In fact, few entities enter the tunnel easily and this state of events could alter thanks to the development of spiritism.

What is felt by those who do not enter the tunnel?

Fear, doubt and bitterness are the feelings that dominate a troubled spirit. The spirit sees what it refused to acknowledge on Earth. Its nightmare can last a long time and give rise to feelings of shame on Earth. As it no longer has a body at its disposal, the troubled spirit uses its perispirit and becomes a ghost.

The passage below is a mother speaking to her daughter (ouija board):

I know you are suffering. It all happened so quickly. You know, I soon realised I was dead. I was in the room looking at you and my body from above. Then I saw them trying to wake me up but I felt so happy. I did not wish to come back. I then became extremely lightweight and I left the room only to find myself in an enormous tunnel. I could hear your prayers. Then I heard music, like choir music and I moved towards my guardian angel, or "guide". I could see you all crying but I was unable to do anything about it.

It's wonderful here you know. I can live and feel free. I think about you all. I send you all my love.

Another account:
I am in the shade and I am aware that I am dead. I need help as I am afraid of what I will discover. It is all so different. Help me to forget my body. I hear voices and I know they are calling me. But I am so confused. I have the impression that too many people on Earth do not want me to leave. A little help from you should put everything right. Thank you.

> *Woe betide he who loves only the body and superficial appearances. Death will take everything from him. Try to love souls then you will meet them again.*
>
> Victor Hugo

Trouble

Many spirits leaving both the Earth and their body find themselves in a state of turmoil.

Faced with death, man suddenly panics and feels lost. Even if death is accepted as our earthly goal it still involves many different and often hidden feelings such as:
- fear
- anguish
- sadness
- refusal
- revolt
- incomprehension
- doubt
- suffering

All the feelings that have been experienced in life do not disappear with death. This means that even if the passage from the physical to the spiritual life involves a change of condition, it does not mean a change in the *state of spirit*.

The way in which the afterlife is presented by religions does not tell us much about the "life" of spirits. This is why the image we have of it is only the reflection of our education.

We have images of a Paradise, an idyllic place where there is only bliss and beatitude. We have obscure and uncertain pictures of Purgatory; obscure and eternal fire in Hell with God on one side and the Devil on the other with elected or fallen angels.

Spiritism and communication with the deceased has, from the 19th century until the present day, helped elucidate all the questions relating to the afterlife.
Indeed, is it not true that the disembodied are the best placed to talk about the afterlife, their survival and their condition?

This is what is original and special about *spiritism*: it is not the thoughts or the philosophy of a man. It represents the thoughts, the ideas, the certainties or the doubts of thousands of men and women via their posthumous testimonies.

Other parameters may affect this troubled state:

- the age of the deceased
- the cause of death (illness, accident, suicide)
- beliefs
- the last preoccupations
- the evolutionary stage
- how much they were attached to life

Spiritism has changed the entire way in which death is viewed. Henceforth, a future life is no longer a possibility but a reality. The state of the soul after death is no longer a system but is the result of observations. The spiritual world is presented to us in its practical reality and we discover spirits at various points on the spiritual ladder just as we meet people on Earth who are at different stages of their evolution.

Numerous entities on Earth know and have known the passage to the spiritual life in particularly dramatic conditions. The spectacle of death on Earth is often related to unjust violence and suffering. In fact, few deaths are peaceful. Here and there an accident or suicide takes place, war rears its ugly and brutal head, crime is rife. It is not surprising to find that turmoil and suffering exist in the afterlife.

The afterlife has its roots in the Earth. Even though it may be hard, unjust and painful to hear in the messages of all the troubled spirits, the basic problem stems from the way of life, from Man's responsibility on Earth.

After experiencing a brutal, savage or unjust death, a great deal of strength and certainty is needed for the spirit to get through the negative images surrounding it and which prevent it from seeing a healthy and pure light.

For many of these spirits, the brutality of their final moments on earth, the suddenness of their death if it was an accident plunge them into a psychological and physical suffering like the one they felt during the final moments before death

Hence, many of these troubled spirits manifest themselves during spiritist seances, talking about an accident, a crime, a drowning, a suicide or about fire, continuing to suffer, in a sort of congealed present, from the way in which they died.

One very common phenomenon with troubled spirits is for them to believe they are still alive. This illusion can sometimes continue for a number of "our" years (as time has no meaning outside matter). During this time the spirits continue to have all the feelings associated with life in the material world.
Their afterlife, of which they are not yet aware, is represented by their thoughts and is revealed in images via their own mental projections.

In the case of violent death, time stops at the moment of death. This can often be a brutal shock provoking surprise, anguish, fear and suffering. In this case time continues in an eternal present.

Other spirits are aware of their death yet remain distraught because they do not find what they thought they would find in the afterlife. The latter does not correspond to what they had imagined or been taught. Hence their trouble.
In the face of this double-sided reality of the afterlife, in its suffering and hatred, faced with the dangers it may represent for an already tottering humanity, the spiritists of our association have understood the extent of the fundamental action they can take. On the one hand, they can receive "bad" spirits and direct them toward their guide and also receive suffering spirits, guiding them toward an awareness of their condition and their afterlife.

Liberating the afterlife means liberating humanity from a part of its suffering. This means simultaneously enabling a certain number of entities to become aware of their spiritual condition and preventing the suffering of many people on Earth from spiritual disturbances stemming from the invisible.

Listen to the teachings by the voices from the afterlife.
They bring to us a new way of looking at things, a reality from beyond the grave that man needs to know in order to live better, to act better and to die better.

Why are many spirits from Earth in turmoil?

Each death is of great importance. It must be said and repeated that crime, war and suicide are sure to create a troubled spirit that continues to live its final moments.

Must we remind ourselves that the Earth is an inferior sphere and that consequently the majority of the spirits leaving it cannot experience peace and serenity when they reach the invisible world?

After living in the flesh, in what way does the spirit feel turmoil in a non-physical world?

When the spirit leaves the flesh it moves around in ethereal space with its double, the perispirit which is semi-material (see chapter on The Perispirit). Hence, for the spirit that has just given up its soul, the afterlife is not something totally immaterial. This semi-materiality of the afterlife shows that the spirit takes certain notions of time and space with it.

With regard to the various violent deaths that people have experienced during their lives, why do that certain spirits manage to leave the state of turmoil more easily than others?

This is due to the nature of the prayers that the spirits receive or whether they receive any at all. It depends on the nature of each individual. Certainly, when faced with the same type of death, two spirits that have evolved differently will not experience it in the same way. This depends on whether or not it is possible to enter into contact with their guide.

Do troubled spirits always suffer?

No. Many spirits are indeed in a state of turmoil but do not suffer. We will call this spacio-temporal turmoil. These spirits have neither left their century nor their dwelling place.

Can we conclude that ghosts and haunted houses are manifestations of a state of turmoil?

Absolutely. The majority of the spirits experiencing this state of turmoil stay at the place they died and are definitely the reason for ghostly manifestations.
Many of the legends, stories and tales concerning "white ladies" are in fact based on past drama as well as the tangible and visible manifestations of those who have died.

Do ghost vessels and trains exist? How can this be explained?

These phenomena really exist but only when the real vessel or train has come to a tragic end.
Such manifestations are indeed linked to accidental tragedies and as such they involve a large number of troubled spirits which have remained in a state of shock. They unconsciously manifest their presence in this way.

How can the turmoil of the afterlife be transformed and overcome?

Spirits have lived on the Earth for millions of years and after millions of years suffering, crime, war, hunger, torture and tears they have contributed to the turmoil that exists within incarnation. The result of this inferior nature of things is that there is a similarly inferior condition in the world of the spirits.

Planet Earth will have to change entirely. Its global spirituality needs to change for the spirits that are reincarnated on Earth so that the afterlife can also change.

How did certain spirits leave this state of turmoil before the spiritual revival?

All positive prayers, whatever their religious nature and all positive, sincere thoughts act as fluids that move towards those who have died and are beneficial to them.
This means that the men and women currently on Earth who are not spiritists but who nevertheless firmly believe in life after death can send positive thoughts to their loved ones who have died. These thoughts will reach these troubled souls and do them a great deal of good.

Are these spirits helped by superior spirits and by their guides?

This is very difficult as all the souls in a state of turmoil[22] are present, close to your bodies, to your world and to your lives. When these spirits die they

---

22 We have seen that « turmoil » is a common condition in the afterlife and can be long or short. It generally is associated with people who have died a tragic, painful and unexpected death. These spirits are close to our vibrations and are easily able to enter our physical spheres. This can explain phenomena such as haunting, ghosts and white ladies.
Some examples:
"it's hard, it's hot. I'm in pain, my bones are broken. I can feel the steel and the petrol. I am suffocating. I am in a steel coffin with enormous teeth that are hurting me. Everything is spinning. Make it stop."
"I am drowning I can't breathe. Help!! There is water all around me, darkness. Help me!!

These spirits who have all died an accidental and brutal death speak about their suffering in the present when they manifest themselves. Why is this? because their contact with the flesh was suddenly broken. But the vital energy linking the spirit to the body carries the memory of what has just been experienced. For the recently deceased spirit, this experience is not in the past. It continues to be the present but a present that no longer has the notion of time.
The spirits that appear in a spiritist seance will be freed thanks to fluidic action (prayers and thoughts) during or after the seance.

remain inside the very same place. They have simply changed rooms; you are in one room and they are in a room that is just next to yours.

We are the "sky". We are above these circumstances. All these entities are closer to you than to us. We are constantly calling them but they do not always hear.
The evil within the invisible is the direct expression of the state of the Earth's evolution.

Other examples and generally accepted religious ideas:
"I am aware of my condition and I refuse it. I am walking in the country, attached to my childhood. I am on a path, looking for snails. It is raining. I do not want to be disturbed. I am afraid, I am afraid of hell."
"I am spinning. I am searching for the Madonna. I am looking but I can not find God. I need a rosary, novenas are no good without a rosary".

Testimony of a spirit that has had no problem entering the afterlife:
"When you reach the end of the tunnel you do not know exactly what is going to happen. You can clearly see people coming to meet you and some of them you recognise –parents, friends. They are surrounded by a whitish halo. You move forward cautiously, wondering whether you are dreaming. And then suddenly you become aware, brutally aware of the fact that you are dead yet you are alive. You then understand everything. Time no longer exists. Former lives come rushing forward like a fountain of awareness. If you have love in your heart this is a great moment. Mistrust gives way to joy and trust especially when a friend holds out his arms laughing and saying: you see, it is simple and just.
So you walk in the clouds discovering the afterlife"
"If it is necessary to speak about life after death I will willingly do this. I always believed in the afterlife, thinking that my friends had not permanently gone. It is said that all artists belong to one big family and this is correct. It is not simply an image but very real and true. I was so depressed and desperate. I knew I was to leave my Theo.
I could no longer bear my heart but I had the strength to think and pray.
Death was so sweet, calm and peaceful, just like relaxation. I rose up from my body and I began to fly in space, light, happy and free. Free. Free at last and all the other actors, singers were listening to me, watching me and waiting for me. I went through the tunnel and arrived in a great light where I saw all those I, Edith Gassion, Edith Piaf, had loved. The telepathy of love sometimes has terrible consequences and my brother in a former life, Jean Cocteau, racked with sorrow, let himself die the very same day so he could be with me. Our spirits are united in the afterlife essentially by love and the desire to create. Listen well, you who are on the Earth. The singer will always sing, the sculptor will always sculpt. The artist transcends himself and because others are with him nothing is finished and in this place, God takes away our cares and worries.

Edith Piaf

THE OTHER SIDE

There are several dwelling places in the house of my Father.

Jesus

From beyond the grave, the door opens onto Eternity

THE AFTERLIFE

From the very beginning man has always believed in the immortality of the soul. This is why the oldest philosophers have taught that there is a double aspect to our being: the body and the spirit.

The world of the afterlife is immense and unlimited. Since the Asians with Zoroastre, the Greeks with Homer, Pythagorus and Plato, since the Hebrews and in the time of Buddha, the Druids and the dolmens of Gaul, since Jesus Christ and the gospels, Mahomet with the Koran to the Sewedenborgians, the theosophists, scientists and spiritists of the 19th and 20th centuries, numerous hypotheses have been put forward as to the condition of the soul after death and in future life.

Paradise, hell, purgatory, limbo, celestial planes and the mysteries of space have all been described.

Whether or not it is clearly defined, the belief in a future life dominates all nations and religions because man feels the need to know. He is seeking to explain why life and the Universe exist.
Religious doctrines are insufficient and obscure. They have been the cause of so much abuse, pushing man towards materialism, atheism or dissatisfaction. Each religion represents a God, a Master who does not give the same laws to each of his children. They impose faith when in fact Man is in need of knowledge.

Believing and *knowing* are two very different things. We know that the afterlife exists and it is this very afterlife which is presented and described to you below by the spirits themselves.

A General Description of the Afterlife

What is the afterlife?

The afterlife is a universe of consciences that embrace one another, bump into one another
and sometimes tear each other apart in the lower astral spheres.
The afterlife is complex, multiple to be precise as it contains all forms of human consciences.
In fact, the afterlife is not particularly different from your world as it is not a transformation of the latter. It is another dimension of it, different in its forms but not different in its character and nature.

Does the conscience therefore remain the same even after death?

In your world there are human beings that suffer, others who ignore each other, others who live in relative happiness whilst thoughtless and flippant others believe they have approached happiness. There is also sacrifice and torture in your world. Some people fight for justice whilst others live on love alone.

There is all this in your world. And there is also all this in the world of the spirits. Hence, the afterlife is not fundamentally different from your world. It is not a transformation of the latter. It is another dimension of it, different in its forms but not different in its character, movement and space.

Where is the afterlife located?

The afterlife is not a place or a geographic location that needs to be situated in relation to the Earth. The afterlife is the new condition of a spirit living outside the flesh, beyond matter and its heavy vibrations. The afterlife is close to you, it is beside you. It is your parallel and is constantly next to you.

What does the astral world look like?

This world has the appearance of a brilliant and colourful vapour. There are groups everywhere, gathered together by affinity to act for the good of the Universe. The afterlife is a world of many, unlimited encounters. In fact, only thought is needed to see and to touch.

Does paradise exist?

This notion should not be spread around. Paradise does not exist as such. What does exist is the notion of work and of effort and a certain joy and pleasure can be derived from this work, even if it is often short-lived and subtle.

Does bliss exist in the afterlife?

Bliss is often spoken about. No-one should believe that this bliss is complete and whole in the afterlife. We remain in the same worlds even if the forms differ. The spirit often manifests itself at its best on the Earth.
The spirit is *science*, it is *art*, it is *love*. Everything is there. The spirit will be noble, beautiful, fair and just. It will only live to the full within the three forms expressed above.
Why is this? Because these are the three key words that will help you find your origin. And you all know this has a name: God.

Do shapes and form exist in the afterlife?
Forms are extremely important and remain in the afterlife but they are split from matter. Curves and straight lines imagined by artists become the direct transposition of thought.

What kind of reception does a spirit get when it arrives in the afterlife? What are its first tasks?

Most of the time, a spirit is welcomed by several entities when it arrives in the world of the invisible. The first is its guide. A guide is usually someone the person knew in a former life, someone who is immediately recognisable.

The guide is often surrounded by the immediate family from the last life, the life he has just left in order to arrive in the afterlife.

Such a welcome is reassuring, the aim being to gradually lead the newcomer towards the spheres of the invisible.

Is the afterlife very different from life on Earth?

The afterlife is a spiritual world that continues to live with its character, its psychology, its evolutionary difference in the same way as the world of man. The spirits are former men and women and their behaviour does not change as if it were a sudden metamorphosis. This is why we keep our character, our ideas, opinions, hopes, joy, anguish and sorrow.
This is why the world of the spirits is a simple and natural world that has no need for angel's wings.

So what is the difference between the two worlds?

Freedom.
It is true that when freed from our earthly bodies we are much freer with regard to matter. However, it must be remembered that we are part of an evolution.
And as we belong to this evolution, we create our own encounters within the invisible world. We beckon other spirits towards us in our relative state of consciousness.

How is the afterlife perceived?

In the afterlife, spirits obviously no longer perceive their environment through their physical senses as on the Earth. Perception still exists however, and is the creative result of a natural energy, qualified as eternal and spiritual. It is in this way that the spirit "creates" its own environment in the afterlife.

Is this afterlife different depending on which spirit is concerned?

It will display different images and differing interpretations depending on the nature of the spirit or spirits that are there.

Does an afterlife without images and environment exist?

A considerable amount of strength, love and clairvoyance are required to break away from the instinctive process and experience the ether in a more subtle manner with no images involved.

Is the perispirit perceived in the same way by all the surrounding spirits in the afterlife?

No. This is not the case. A group of spirits that encounters a spirit that they have known at different periods will all have a subjective view depending upon what has been experienced in the past. This is not a simultaneous modification of the perispirital nature of the spirit observed. It is a subjective modification of the consciousness of the spirits observing it.

Are spirits located in a determined and well-defined region in space?

In fact, the afterlife is more like a condition than a place. What does the expression "to be in the heavens" mean? Everything is in the heavens. The Earth you live on is a star in the sky in the same way as the other planets. We know that there is neither an upside or downside in the Universe. The sky or heavens is a universal space. For you at the present time it is the Milky Way of which the Earth is a tiny village. The afterlife can not be thought of as a precise world. It is everywhere and nowhere, outside your concept of time and space that is based upon three dimensions. There is in fact a fourth dimension that we might call "hyperspace". The afterlife is a world of vibrations.

Is the afterlife divided up according to the planets?

In certain cases, yes because your planets are infinite in number. The word "your" refers to your galaxy.

The disembodied spirits coming from these different worlds can not always meet for obvious reasons. But these divisions are not exclusive and even less definitive as it is important for spirits to meet.

Are there any hierarchical structures in the afterlife?

Indeed, there is a precise and well defined hierarchy in the world of the spirits and this structure corresponds to a state of consciousness, to many states of consciousness.

Are there any dominant classes in the afterlife?

No. The only dominant in the Universe is God. If those who believe themselves to be strong on the Earth were to turn their eyes towards infinity but for a few seconds, they would be frightened when they saw just how small they really are.
Money and material possessions have never been moral or intellectual criteria.

Is there a determined number of categories or degrees of perfection among the spirits?

The spiritual afterlife can be divided into three main categories:

pure spirits that have arrived at the end of their evolutionary journey
spirits having awareness
spirits in a state of turmoil

The psychology of the spirit comes from the one that belonged to it when it was on Earth.

The spirit scale represents the whole scope of evolution: good or bad spirits, spirits that are more advanced than others, spirits of learning, from research and knowledge, spirits that welcome the souls of those who have recently died, playful and frisky spirits, jokers and unconscious spirits, artistic spirits, spirits that express their desires, their thoughts and their work via their disembodied conscience only. This manifests multiple images. Spirits express their desires and thoughts via a mental projection of images.

What do the pure spirits do?

Pure spirits, that is to say those that have arrived at the end of their evolutionary journey will not need to be reborn. They become part of the creative force again, nourished by the rays and the light of this divine energy force.

Why do all the disembodied not say the same things?

Those who die do not all change in the same abrupt manner. There are spirits that will come to you and speak in a profoundly human way. They still reflect the mentality that grew and developed on Earth even if they do not vibrate in their flesh.

These spirits will not explain what they are living but what they are thinking. This is why their language or message will appear different from one to another.

How can we distinguish between what has been experienced and what comes from the mind?

Spirtism means a long process of compulsion, selection and thought to be able to make the difference between the real and the imaginary. There is only one reality, not described but recorded in the spirit. There is only one, single reality.

Doesn't evolution take place more rapidly in the afterlife?

Evolution is a real phenomenon which is slow and difficult. Evolution is like a difficult and painful birth of the conscience. To reach this state, this consciousness, the path is littered with obstacles both for the embodied and the disembodied, both on the planet Earth and in the world of the spirits.

Why do certain spirits spend so much time in the afterlife?

In order to correctly understand our world, it is important to understand the Universe in its diversity and in its infinite nature, whilst never forgetting that other planets exist.
Man often limits his thinking to his own sphere, omitting the extraordinary interstellar parallel of other worlds. The afterlife is also the afterlife of an infinite number of spheres that are equal, inferior or superior to your own. Any absence of reincarnation on the Earth does not mean that there is no reincarnation on other asteroids.

There are certain souls that are not reincarnated as their past is laden with heavy fundamental incarnations. These entities prefer to complete their evolution in the invisible world.

Why are certain spirits happy or unhappy in the afterlife?

The state of the spirit depends on the extent to which it has attained purity and rid itself of its imperfections. Perfect happiness is likened to perfection, i.e. the total purification of the spirit.
Any imperfection is the cause of suffering and of a deprivation of pleasure in the same way that any quality acquired is a reason for pleasure and a reduction of suffering. The result is that, in its spiritual life, the spirit suffers the consequences of all the imperfections that it did not rid itself of during its physical life.

Does the spirit continue to evolve in the afterlife?

According to the law of progress, any soul has the opportunity to acquire the goodness it is lacking through effort and will-power.

Is the spirit aware of its former lives in the afterlife?

On the day that you leave your body, your earthly life will suddenly return to you in its tiniest details not via images perceived but relived very quickly. The day you leave your body, these images will not only penetrate your psyche but also all the lives you have lived. Time will gradually allow you to understand them.

Does all the love and affection that human beings give to one another on Earth continue in the afterlife? Are families reunited?

Entire families are reunited in the afterlife due to the natural attraction of their members to each other. Many spirits contact each other via a thought process and get together, thereby creating a feeling of security. This makes it easier for them to cope with the afterlife.

In close-knit families where many of the members have died within a short period, the need to get together is very intense. But this is often made difficult by the existence of spirits in turmoil.

Are they reincarnated together?

Following the initial contacts between brothers, sisters, parents and children, the most difficult thing is to then learn to exist separately because the laws of reincarnation very often force spirits to take totally different paths.

In this respect, guides are a precious advantage. They are excellent instructors, bringing whole families together to prepare them and give them the strength to return. Those who remain in the afterlife will receive regular information about the new state of a reincarnated family relation. Things will continue in this way until we have sufficiently evolved to understand that, in fact, separation is a very small reality within eternity and within the happiness that awaits us all.

Do children that have died young and who were bad in their previous life remain as children in the afterlife?

They will remain as children in the world of the spirits. They will be surrounded by other spirits but their soul will remain child-like and they will soon be back in the natural cycle of their incarnation by returning to life.

Do spirits need time to cross space? Can they go where they want?

Not all spirits can go where they want. Their overall objective is evolution once the conscience of the spirit has come into existence.

This existence will increase the thirst for knowledge. Each spirit will then be able to move around easily in an ethereal and light manner in a world that no longer depends on matter.

Movement is comparable to the speed of thought. Consequently, time has no meaning.

*Death is the end of a dark prison for noble souls
but others who have placed all their concerns in the mire will feel uneasy.*

Petrarque. The Triumph of Death

The afterlife of evil spirits

Evil spirits and spiritism: "The Deliverance of Worlds" by Olivier Fauvel

The book by the spiritist Olivier Fauvel is an account of our meetings with evil spirits over the past thirty years.
It also talks about what spiritists have done, not to instantly turn them into good spirits (as this would be contrary to the law of progression) but to make them aware of just how low they are. They have helped them meet their guides so they will become aware that they can indeed progress. Awareness is the first step on the road to evolution.

Evil, both in the visible and invisible worlds shows how far the planet has advanced on its evolutionary curve. If evil exists it is also there to be fought against.

During our interviews or conferences many people are surprised and even disturbed at this manifestation of evil within our Association.

Given that the souls of the dead are merely the souls of people that have lived, it would be very naive to think that the passage from the condition life to death would suddenly purify all spirits.

Certain theories put forward by spiritualist thinkers claim that they only get in contact with highly evolved spirits (via individual meditation). They refer to the law of affinity saying that one gets what one deserves......

This is a precept based somewhat on the pride of a "chosen few" who believe that they have progressed sufficiently to receive only the greatest spirits.

Others accept the idea and the reality of communication with the spirits but only as a consolation or as education (good spirits, guides, close family).

Evil certainly bothers, disrupts and unsettles people. But if those referred to have a similar attitude to evil, i.e. to avoid it or close one's eyes to it, it is little wonder that the planet Earth is stagnating in the grip of evil.

Evil also needs to be interpreted for what it is It would be too easy for us to constantly appeal to "God and his saints" to make mankind improve.
Being born into the theatre of life makes us all actors and participants. Evil is part of our lives and something to be fought against.

The path of spiritism is a path toward deliverance. This deliverance involves the fight for the freedom of mankind, of the spirit and is an important part of our thoughts and actions.

(Below are the answers to questions put to the spirits).

To what extent do evil spirits influence humanity?

It must be understood that particularly aggressive and negative disembodied forces, (the spirits of evil), also enter into contact with people or groups that are equally evil, hard and negative. Birds of a feather flock together...

This is also a reality of the spiritist ideal. Being a Medium does not mean being superior and there are not only "good" mediums (in the moral sense of the word). There are not only "good" human beings. A negative energy will be produced by the meeting of evil spirits and evil humans and this energy force will be directed towards others in order to encourage them to perform evil.

If these evil spirits do not appear in groups in which they can flatter the elementary human instincts, they can, via their invisible presence have an influence on certain people, bringing a wealth of negative thoughts, negative fluid and negative intentions.

Who is influenced by this negativity?

The victims of this negativity are those who have a similar propensity towards evil. But unfortunately the influence does not stop there.
Like predators, evil spirits are on the lookout for their prey, exploiting certain human weaknesses and vulnerabilities. Intent on harming humanity, they will spread their hatred by using human agents who will gradually become obsessed then possessed, pushing them to commit crime, even causing disasters.

This work will be made all the easier if they encounter the "sorcerer's apprentices" of spiritism. So many young people gather around a table with a glass and the letters of the alphabet to have fun by calling upon the spirits of the dead.

They have no idea of the risks they are running because troubled or low level spirits that are close to our vibrations are attracted by the flickering of candlelight. And they spread their trouble or their hatred to those that are there to receive it.

Faced with these two types of communication, people must know how to react and especially to how to act.

Can films such as Poltergeist, The Exorcist and Malediction involving adults and children have psychological repercussions on the actors to the extent that they may die?

A certain taste for the morbid does not always go hand in hand with the artistic values of the cinema. It is for this reason that I will answer "yes" to the question.

Both the children and the adults taking part in these morbid films are bound to suffer an intense psychological shock. I am not saying that this can be a cause of death but that this shock can certainly be the cause of a psychological disorder especially as most of the stories have their origins in true events that have not yet been solved.

Let us take the house in Amityville as an example. We know that this house exists and that evil entities continue to visit and live in it. It is therefore bad to "reawaken" this disembodied evil. It brings these very same spirits onto a film set and even if nothing is said, it has happened that certain actors have often been "possessed" during filming.

This is why such ridiculous and morbid films should cease to be made as they can cause disorder and even more so for the viewing public.

With regard to the cinema, we would like a good film producer to transmit the spiritist truth in his message in an authentic manner so that it may be passed on to others from the afterlife to those on Earth.

Liberation and Repentance.

Since Allan Kardec and the history of spiritism, the manifestations of the spirits have all been studied, analysed and codified. In fact, all the evolutionary stages have been found in the afterlife in the same way as they are on Earth.

Overall, the Christian type of spiritist message implies the manifestation of evil, suffering and well-being in the afterlife. This is why many evil spirits have revealed themselves to our Group either freely and spontaneously or guided, pushed towards us by guides and by the protective spirits around us.

Thanks to the practice of spiritism, the spirits have taught us to neutralise this evil. This means, on the one hand, that there should be less evil the planet and, on the other, that these evil and hateful spirits should become aware that they have survived, that there is an afterlife and that they have a protecting guide.

As the majority of these spirits have manifested themselves by means of incorporation, the role of spiritists is to use dialogue to offer certainty, love and forgiveness for their sins. These seances are often extremely tiring not only for the mediums but also for the spirits as they can last for several days before obtaining the desired effect.
What is sure is that all spirits are received, whatever their evolutionary level and only leave the seance after having been given the energy and information necessary to progress.

Do evil spirits do any sort of penitence after being made aware of their crimes?

Following their repentance, their guides ask them to do penitence by praying to God to help them do only good from now on. This period of time can span between 2 weeks and 6 months depending on the entities themselves.

Do all incarnated or disembodied spirits that repent receive forgiveness?

Repentance is the first step on the road to progress but it is not sufficient. There must be atonement and compensation.

Repentance, atonement and improvement are all necessary to receive forgiveness for a wrong-doing.

Repentance eases the pain of atonement as it confers experience, preparing the way for rehabilitation. But compensation alone can cancel out the effect by destroying the cause.

How can evil be overcome?

All wrong-doings and all evil acts are debts that must be paid for one day. If the debt is not paid in this life then it will be paid for in the next because there is inter-dependence between all the lives that one spirit lives.

To put an end to suffering, God requires that there should be a serious and real improvement with a movement toward good. In this way the spirit has freedom of choice over its own destiny.

What does atonement[23] and compensation consist of?

Atonement means physical and moral suffering. It is the result of a wrong-doing and will take place either in this life, after death or in a new embodied existence.

---

23 *To atone: to repair by suffering an imposed or accepted atonement. Suffering the consequences often with a feeling of guilt.*
The word atonement should be thought of in terms of cause and effect. Atonement is carried out during bodily life thanks to ordeals that the spirit has imposed on itself and during the spiritual life thanks to moral suffering attached to the inferiority of the spirit.

Compensation means doing good to those to whom one has done wrong. Those who do not repair their wrong-doings in this life will find themselves in contact with the very same people in the next life.

After having contact with their guide, will these spirits choose to have a mission in reincarnation?

These spirits are not capable of choosing a mission in a new life. Moreover, their ethereal envelope is impregnated with all their past actions related to their inferiority. Before any project begins, good spirits will surround the inferior spirit by directing all their fluid towards the double so that it will be protected by total amnesia in its future life.
For cruel types, it is indeed necessary to forget as their cruelty could suddenly reappear when they come back to Earth. The spirit will then be reincarnated close to those it has harmed, not as punishment but so as to compensate for the harm done.

It is a good thing to spread this message as this is the true meaning of Christianity. It is not the notion of eternal damnation.

The story of a deliverance in 1987, one year after.

1). What was your intention when you came towards us?

I came towards you one year ago and was incorporated, guided by a feeling of hatred, domination and destruction. I came in the hope that you would grant me all my requests, hoping that I would be able to act as I wanted with you, that you would obey my every whim and help me to do evil and to continue doing evil in the astral world.

2). What was your existence like in the afterlife?

I lived in my universe and continued to live as I lived on Earth. Nothing had changed as far as I was concerned. When I fell asleep in death I could see no difference. I saw my body, my coffin and I was aware that I could continue to act and to think as before.

3). Were you alone?

I could hear voices calling me to reason, to forgiveness but I would have nothing to do with them. I then encountered spirits I had known. I went towards them and took delight in their fear at seeing me again. I thought to myself " maybe I'm dead, but they are still afraid of me and that is good". The pleasure of doing evil and of perpetuating hatred encouraged me to carry on frightening them.

4). Did you attempt to frighten embodied people?

I quickly realised that it was possible to frighten people, to continue visiting them, to create knocking in their homes, to appear in hideous forms and to cry at night to make them shake with fear. I hated people.....all the people I had known.

5). Can you describe the lower astral?

We can hear laughter, crying, moaning. We can not see ourselves very well as our bodies are misshapen and we are constantly under the impression that we are going to fall asleep. We feel very sleepy. Sometimes we feel glimmers around us but we push them away violently. We can hear the cries of pain and of refusal, moaning. We are in a thick fog.

6). Why did you come to visit us?

I came to visit you in the same way as many spirits that have been bad on the Earth, always ready to take pleasure in it. I arrived sure of myself. You listened to me. After several minutes you interrupted me and asked me to remember who I was. You spoke to me of love, of light, you prayed for me and you asked God to forgive me for my sins.

7). What did you feel, and think at that moment?

Like all spirits in that situation, I felt as if I was suffocating. I wanted to run away, far away from you but I couldn't. Each time I tried to leave the body of you medium there was an invisible hand over me, keeping me in place. I was stuck between your prayers and the fluid of your guiding and protective spirits. I was unable to leave.

8). What happened then?

Gradually your prayers and fluids made me feel lighter and lighter. I then began doubting myself. When a negative spirits begins doubting itself, those who wish to lead it towards the light have triumphed. The spirit can say anything it wants, its insults are directed towards itself.

9). What happened when you asked God for forgiveness?

I felt a strong burning sensation when I finally pronounced the word. I saw an unbearably bright light then I turned, turned and turned again to finally see a calm and peaceful face opposite me. It was the face of my guide, a smiling, forgiving face that made me understand that life goes on. This face helped me to see that, beyond my wrong-doings and my crimes, I was not a demon and that I could and I should live. This was the start of something new for me.

10). Did you see any of your victims again?

I met my guide thanks to your thoughts and your words. All those that I hated were delivered from the fear that I continued to inspire in them at the same time as I was.

I was frightened as I observed them. They were transformed. It was then I who began to be afraid of them but they looked at me innocently. It is so wonderful to discover that love exists, that we can continue to exist and that we can repair and compensate for our bad deeds of the past.

11). Do you intend to reincarnate?

I must be reincarnated but I am no longer afraid of anything. I can now say that, despite my inferiority, I am happy to return to the Earth. I am pleased to live because it would have been a sure death to continue to perpetrate evil. I woke up to life only one year ago. Thank you indeed.[24]

---

[24] *As we have seen, the afterlife is more a condition, or state, than a place. As spirits are nothing more than people's souls, we remain within humanity when we communicate with them.*

This also means that the afterlife is populated by spirits that are all different from one another, either in their level of culture or in their level of goodness (or the opposite). Therefore it is not surprising to find the same good and bad points that are to be found in humanity on the Earth. Death is basically the reflection of life. Hence, it is important to talk about the psychology of the afterlife as too many people believe that death transforms those who experience it.

There is a variety of different types of psychological condition in the afterlife:
-spirits in a state of turmoil
-evil or negative spirits
-good spirits
-superior or guiding spirits
-pure spirits
(see The Book of Spirits by Allan Kardec for more details)

All these spirits live in different states in the afterlife depending upon their level of consciousness. « Live » is indeed the appropriate term, the important difference being that this life takes place outside the requirements of matter. Matter too often slows down the aspirations of the mind and clear thought. As spirits are freed from matter, they can judge things in a much more absolute manner. The mere fact of observing that they have survived and that they are eternal is in itself sufficient to widen their horizons. They begin to understand their errors and their relative interests. They change their ideas, ridding themselves of human prejudices.

The activities of the spirits in the afterlife

What are the activities of the spirits of those who were not known for anything particular on Earth?

It is true that on Earth, certain people are more remarkable than others. Here, I am only speaking of those who are genuinely considered as remarkable and not referring to the social definition of superior.

To coin a phrase: what happens to the humble and the obscure?
Several things must be taken into account here. First of all, the idea of reincarnation that turns the spirit into a complete being when it becomes a spirit again. Any given spirit may well have had some lives that were more remarkable than others. The main aim of spirits is to learn and to learn from superior beings. Another activity is to help those who wish to be helped. The rest will be helped by man (via spiritism and communication with them).

Helping disembodied spirits

Death is rarely experienced calmly. When it arrives it surprises many men, women and children. There is pain, crime, violence or natural disasters.
A misunderstanding and incomprehension remains for those who have experienced a violent and untimely death. Sometimes they are painfully or violently disturbed. So many spirits need to be looked after, reassured, loved. And there are many well-intentioned spirits that are responsible for looking after them.

How do you help suffering and disturbed spirits?

We welcome them and reassure them. Guides are forever sending salutary fluids to wipe away fear and anguish. Some children scream out for their parents, others go round in circles, still asleep, others appear paralysed with their eyes wide open unable to move.[25]

Helping living and incarnated spirits.

Every night our spirit feels the need to leave the body to return to its true spiritual nature. This nocturnal journey that is part of physiological sleep lasts for about 2 hours.
Depending on how advanced the embodied spirit is, leaving the body in this way means that it is able to meet up with certain disembodied spirits. In certain cases this can be really important for people who are having problems coping with life on Earth.

How can you help those living beings who leave their bodies during the night?

This will depend on the circumstances. For example, some of us help the black South African slaves who flee their bodies during the night. An orchestra of 40 musicians helps to perform this therapy. We play the music of freedom with all our strength and the happy spirits sing and dance all around us. This is very important and gives them the strength to carry on.

Writers

Writers continue their work in the afterlife. The non-material world however, supposes that they find other forms of literary expression and this they find in telepathy.
The novels produced in the invisible world are experienced by those who enjoy them. The characters come alive and become real......simply imagining them makes them appear.

---

25 This testimony was obtained after an earthquake in Armenia. The spirit we communicated with had looked after children who had died in this quake. This explains the distress of these children in the message.

In what way do artists evolve in the afterlife? Do writers really write?

The Universe is a total awareness in constant activity. The spirit lives everywhere and its action is never-ending.
An imagined book, poetry, a song or music played, a sculptured form or love imparted are all recorded for all time in the collective consciousness of the divine world.

How can a novel be read?

The novel continues to exist but in a very different way than on Earth. Inspiration begins to take shape and all the narrated stories materialise before the delighted eyes of the astral spirits. It is also a form of therapy. An imaginary thought show. Music is added to the spoken word, to the descriptions and the invented characters.

Do artists get together in the afterlife?

There are numerous gatherings in the afterlife. Many creative people, (such as the spirit of Mozart), who have completed a cycle of reincarnation, like to confirm their musical style in the afterlife. They attract other spirits with similar artistic tendencies toward them. In art forms, colour and sound blend into one another in harmony and love.

It is music that enables us to enter into contact with the afterlife.

Robert Schumann

Music

Does music have virtues in the afterlife?

Music in the afterlife comes directly from the heart and from the mind. It is not only enjoyable and a pleasure. Music here is a therapy. It provides a balance for all the souls feeling heartache, anguish, sadness and torpor.

How do you go about provoking this awakening?

Often, we direct our musical thoughts towards thousands of entities in order to awaken them, to reassure them and to transport them.
Using chants, choir music and the sound of instruments we can direct souls towards their guide even if they were totally unaware that they existed beforehand.
By using our creative force, we can help any spirits leave a state of turmoil, bringing them joy and happiness.

Do you need to create instruments?

The freedom to create means that we can think and hear a note even before it has been produced. We can create music without instruments which means that we can produce without hindrance.

Many mediums have said that they can hear music. Is this music different from that heard on Earth?

Mediums in spiritist groups often speak of the wonderful music they can hear coming from the afterlife. They often speak of crystal clear music. These mediums hear clearly. They are receiving our messages in as much as music is a limitless message. Music in the afterlife comes directly from the heart and from the mind.

Psychologists

Their work deals with the essential problem of recently disembodied spirits, i.e. the memory of previous lives. The memory of all those previous lives should not be something brutal, otherwise this may well be the cause of a further trouble or disturbance. The weight of time and of past experiences must be allowed to develop gradually via a dialogue that the guiding spirits conduct with those who discover their true nature.

Social action

It is possible for the deceased to undertake action for the good of society from the other side.
This is the remarkable effect of the will of the spirits to support human nature. Spirits work with the means at their disposal, which are basically fluid in nature. However, they do not provide miracles or immediate transformation in various areas. On the other hand they do bring hope and strength.

REINCARNATION

*Living, dying, being born again and constantly progressing.
This is the law of life.*

Allan Kardec

The reasons for the diversity of human lives can be explained by peoples' previous existences

1st Book of Principles. Origène.

There has never been a more beautiful, more righteous, more consoling, more moral or more plausible belief than reincarnation. Single-handedly it accounts for all intellectual and physical inequality, all social inequality and the unjust nature of all destinies.

Maurice Maaterlinck

The present is the fruit of the past and the seeds of the future

Liebniz

Pythagoras was the first to introduce the doctrine of the renaissance of the soul. There were two doctrines: one reserved for the initiated and a second for the population. The latter has been responsible for the error of metempsychosis.

For the initiated, the ascension was gradual and steady with no regression towards lower forms. The poorly educated population, however, was taught that evil souls were reborn into the bodies of animals.

The "Father of History" also believed that souls could evolve and progress on the other stars in the heavens. At this time the following secret principles were taught:

the unity of God
the plurality of worlds and the rotation of the Earth (later confirmed by Copernicus and Galileo)
the multiplicity of successive existences

Plato adopted Pythagoras' idea of palingenesis. He based this upon two principles that he put forward in Phedon:

1).It is logical to state that life follows-on from death because death is the natural follow-on from life. As nothing is born from nothing, if all these human beings that die were never to return to life on Earth, then everything would, in the end, be absorbed into death.

2).The great philosopher then bases his thinking on reminiscence as he believed that to learn was to re-remember.

Going even further, Plato claims that the soul gradually rids itself of its imperfections, finally becoming saintly and here reincarnation ceases.

Reincarnation:

Belief in evolution of the species through palangenesis (reincarnation) goes back as far as man. It is to be found in the origins of Brahmanism and is the foundation of Buddhism. It is in accordance with the ideas and beliefs of the greatest geniuses of Antiquity, with the teachings of Socrates, Plato, Origene and the Druids.

The word palangenesis comes from two Greek words: "palin" meaning *again* and "genesis" meaning *birth*. This term puts forward the notion of the progressive evolution of an increasingly aware and active psyche.

Hence, the spiritist notion of successive lives excludes any idea of regression which in itself excludes metempsychosis (reincarnation as animals).

Allan Kardec shed new light on the idea of reincarnation when he introduced the spiritist philosophy. In the 19th century and for the first time, it was the souls of the disembodied that taught the philosophy which brought answers to all the great metaphysical questions of the time.

The deceased speak and they can cast away the veil of the mystery about death. They provide answers on the meaning of life. The idea of reincarnation is essential to the philosophy of the spirits which is based on the understanding of life, of death and of existence.

Is reincarnation an interpretation of the resurrection?

"In truth, in truth I say to you. You will need to be born again into the flesh".

These were the words of Jesus Christ, spoken 2000 years ago and he was, of course, referring to the natural law of reincarnation[26]. The first Christians took this information into account along with so many others that still exist in the gospels.

So, the Catholic and Christian church accepted the law of reincarnation from the very beginning. It was even included in the texts until the 16th century when a Papal council decided that it would be taken out of the texts of the Catholic church.

Why did the church abolish the law?

Reincarnation provided man with too much freedom on the Earth and society could no longer accept such freedom. This was indeed becoming more of a social necessity than a religious one because there was a tendency for human hierarchy, based on divine reasoning, to impose itself.

What were the consequences of this?

In the 6th century A.D. there was a fundamental separation of the two dominant religious ideas: one was situated in the West and the other in the East.

This separation was no good for either of the religious currents as the law of karma developed and this law does not reflect the one that the spirits wish to transmit to you. The spirit constantly advances. Do not fear punishment on the Earth or elsewhere in any way. You should, however, be more fearful of the responsibility of your acts.

What is your opinion of the Eastern concept of reincarnation, the Karma?

The Karma[27] is a negative concept of reincarnation. Why is this so?

---

26 Reincarnation was accepted by Christianity until the year 537 A.D. It was only following the council of Constantinople that the belief was abolished.
27 The Karma: the idea of the Karma is linked to that of reincarnation. It expresses the sequence of cause and effect, the good or bad repercussions of our individual,

The basis of this concept is that man progresses by suffering (injustice, famine, accidents, illness etc). We believe that suffering slows down the evolution of the spirit and that turning it into a means of evolution would amount to giving it credit. According to the karma, no suffering should be relieved as it is simply a means of paying for one's "crimes".

Message from Allan Kardec (October 1978):

Friends of the Earth, you could have been told by others that you were simply conforming to your karma on the earth. Friends, I have come to tell

---

collective thoughts and our acts in this life as well as throughout all our successive lives. This notion of the Karma has been the object of misleading comments and interpretations, both theosophical and spiritist. Much suffering has been accepted because of the notion of a divine "punitive choice".

Divinity has thus been endowed with a certain power to see that justice has been done which amounts to no more than "Talion's Law": an eye for an eye and a tooth for a tooth. That is to say, legalised vengeance.

Certain reincarnationist books have asked: "why have people been born as dwarfs or handicapped? It is because they have been evil in a previous life and are paying retribution for that in the present life".

Here is a typical example of an incorrect interpretation of the karma.

In Sanskrit, "Karma" means "action".

With regard to this, Alexandra David Neel, the first woman to enter Lhassa, the capital of Tibet in the last century was able to clarify the thinking of the Tibetan elders: "the incessant activity of the body, of speech and of the mind creates the destiny of each individual within his existence from reincarnation to reincarnation by a succession of lives and deaths".

Doctor Gustave Gelay in his study on reincarnation quoted a hypothetical crime that a savagely beaten horse was said to have committed in a previous life. He corrected the fundamental error of systematically believing that the suffering of any life form in due to their acts in a previous existence.

Pain is not necessarily a punishment rooted in the past but is more often due to the generally low level of evolutionary progress, to the inferiority of beings and of worlds.

The theory claiming that all individual situations are due to previous actions cuts out the inter-dependence of human beings in their evolution. It has led other writers to claim that reincarnation provides an explanation for social inequality. This is quite untrue. It may account for natural inequalities which is quite a different matter. Social inequality, on the other hand, can be explained by the structure of society. As Allan Kardec said, we must not confuse spiritual hierarchy with social hierarchy. Herod was a king..........Jesus was a carpenter.

you that in no way are you are being subject to any bad luck nor has any spell been put upon you.

You could have been told that you were here to pay for your previous wrong-doings both in this life and those that have gone before. I have come to tell you just the opposite because the message that you may have been given to this effect is totally unacceptable in my eyes and contradicts the spiritist movement in its most intrinsic definition.

I have come to say that when the spirit truly manifests itself, it comes with constructive messages. Although it may take time to put them into practise, they are thought out and based upon a charitable notion that should embrace the entire Universe.

What is the spiritist view of reincarnation?

Reincarnation is a positive law of existence, of existences. It means that all existences are added together, all experience is gathered with the aim of developing the intellect and a moral code.

The spiritist concept of reincarnation has a tendency to make man free. The eastern concept holds that man is completely predestined. He is subject to events rather than acting upon them. There are no punitive laws, only the consequences of our actions.

Why is the idea of reincarnation a logical formula?

From a moral point of view, it is based upon the idea of justice. As the human being is the result of his evolution through a series of successive lives, his intelligence, character, faculties and his good or bad instincts are of his own doing. He will suffer the positive or negative consequences of this.

Do we choose where we are reincarnated?

A distinction must be made between spirits in turmoil and those which are aware.

A deliberate return and a deliberate birth remains the fundamental decision of the spirit which decides to reincarnate in order to continue its evolution. The spirit decides. Reincarnation does not take place purely by chance.

Because of its past, the spirit will have to select where its progress will be the most efficient. The spirit will come back into a family in which it will find the support necessary for its evolution.
Reincarnation takes place in two ways: either deliberate or instinctive.

What is the difference between the two?

Deliberate reincarnation comes from the spirit that wishes to return to the flesh and that has the choice of being able to do so.

Instinctive reincarnation is the response of a spirit that does not think, that has no control over its return to the physical world. This means that it does not choose and is in a state of turmoil.

How does the reincarnation of non-conscious or troubled spirits take place?

It is a heavy process. The spirit "falls back" into the flesh in an instinctive manner.

Do all reincarnated spirits have the same mission?

All spirits that deliberately reincarnate choose a way of life, a mission or wish to accomplish something.
The problem with many spirits is that they often reincarnate whilst disregarding the invisible promise, disregarding the mission that they are unable to complete.

What happens if man does not follow the path he had set out for himself?

For these men and women, life becomes boring, banal, sometimes frightening, sad or tragic if taken to the extreme.

How long does a spirit spend in the afterlife before reincarnating?

There is no fixed time limit between two incarnations. It can vary between a few years and several centuries.

Do our previous lives have any influence on us considering that we do not remember them?

Via the marks that are apparent in your character, your previous lives affect your tendencies, your affinities, aspirations and particular tastes. Your previous lives gradually created the nature of your feelings as well as that of your intellect.

Do the skills acquired in previous lives remain with us?

Yes, they do, but may remain dormant from one life to another if the spirit wishes to acquire new skills[28]

---

28 In theory, one of the consequences of reincarnation is that previous lives are forgotten. However, this principle is not at all absolute as many people throughout history have talked about their memories from a former life. Pythagoras remembered three of his former lives. Other people have feelings of deja vu rather than precise memories. Lamartine in his "Travels to the East" claims to have had some very clear recollections of a distant past. On a planet such as the Earth it is often necessary to forget. Indeed, if man had retained the memory of his actions he would also have retained those of others. The consequences of this on social interaction would be tremendous. Sometimes, human beings reincarnate together in order to forgive each other for their wrong-doings in the past. Forgiveness would be that much more difficult if the memory of these wrong-doings existed. Hatred and resentment would constantly be present. What is more, the memory of a former life is not necessary to prove that we have lived it. It is true that we forget most of the days and the years that

How can we know if we are making the right choice of lifestyle once we have returned?

The spirit must advance. For this to happen it retains the ways in which it intends to do this within its consciousness. Beyond their present state of awareness, this is what your spirits perceive in dreams, in the division of the spirit during sleep. What you have acquired through your previous lives will guide you towards the right choice of life.

How does the spirit decide where it will return to?

First of all, the spirit is in contact with its guide, with its past and with all its past lives. All this is important when making a choice about the future. After having taken an overall view of what it has experienced, the spirit will choose a mission, a country, a family and its sex. This choice will be completely under the protection of the guide and the entities surrounding the spirit in the invisible world.

---

we are living in the present life and yet no-one would claim that they have not lived them.
However, many people remember having lived. Poets have written about it, children are well aware of it until they lose the memory because they are surrounded by non-believers. Professor Ian Stevenson, a Canadian psychiatrist, listened to the stories of 2600 such children. He is the principal authority in the scientific world when it comes to the subject of reincarnation. For the last 30 years he has been collecting information, observing and listening. He has written nine books since beginning his research in 1966 in which he explains his certainty that reincarnation is a reality. "Yes, reincarnation is a reality" he claims (The Journal of Nervous and Mental Disorders, 1977). He believes that this philosophical reality will be proven true in the next 10 years.
His most recent works: "Children who Remember their Former Lives" and "Reincarnation and Biology: the Crossing of the Paths".
Birth marks as well as other physiological traits linked to the memory of former lives are at the very heart of this meticulous research.
"I have discovered that certain cases are inexplicable, neither genetically nor by the influence of the surrounding environment and not even by a combination of these two factors". Ian Stevenson.

Is the spirit happy to return?

The spirit that is to be reincarnated will be gradually led towards the doors that open onto the world of matter before re-entering the physical world. In general the spirit is happy and serene with regard to this return but as the operation of the return to the flesh begins to materialise, an apprehension begins to appear.

What does this apprehension mean?

Transported by its perispirital matter, the spirit returns to the flesh. All the data concerning the physical world are recorded by this perispirital vector as it approaches this world. And if it is a return to the planet Earth, the spirit that hopes to advance and progress is no doubt hit by the apprehensions which form the essential burden of the planet. Fear and apprehension arise out of this.

Can the guide calm this apprehension?

The guide is always there, present and close to the spirit. He speaks and reassures but soon the physical vibrations are so strong that the spirit can no longer hear the guide. This is the moment of conception. This is the essential moment when the perispirital micron enters the body of the future mother-to-be by means of the sperm.

Is the spirit aware of what is happening at this moment?

The spirit is in a state of total unconsciousness for several days. Then the speck awakens and begins vibrating gently. A little numb in its new consciousness, the spirit must now forget all that it has just experienced in the invisible world as it must devote itself to the essential task of creating its entire organism. The vibrations of the parents also play a role in this.

Must the spirit necessarily experience life in both of the sexes?

In order for the spirit to develop completely, it has to experience life in both of the sexes.
But the number of times this takes place is of no consequence as there is no dominant polarity on a spiritual level as far as evolution is concerned. There may nevertheless be a dominant polarity throughout your evolution on Earth or in the afterlife.
In fact, this polarity is only temporary and is simply necessary to become aware of different states of consciousness and of different types of feelings.
The day the spirit reaches its highest point, when it attains its goal there is no polarity, no dominance and no sexuality. There is simply the spirit.

Does the fact of having experienced more lives as a woman or a man have any influence on behaviour?

Reincarnation is closely liked to sexuality. You have your past lives behind you and at this stage of your evolution there is a sexual dominant, either masculine or feminine. Some people also experience new forms of sexuality. We hold no judgement on these different forms of sexuality. We simply have trust, knowledge, help and love. The form itself does not matter as long as it is governed by love.

At which moment in the development of the embryon does the formation of the sex take place?

This happens in the second month. The decision is made by the spirit depending on its ethereal existence in the afterlife.

Is instinctive reincarnation more difficult?

Turmoil should be compared to gravity. The spirit that is reincarnated in a state of turmoil will have a hard time as the return to the flesh carries a number of risks with it.

The biggest risk of such unconscious and instinctive returns to the flesh is that of premature death. Another risk is that the embryo may develop badly.

How does the turmoil of the spirit affect the embryo's development?

The embryo can develop badly because the spirit is reincarnated carrying its apprehensions and its nightmares. For many spirits, turmoil is a real nightmare. A nightmare is not only a feeling, it is also an image. Moreover, memories of former lives and particularly the most recent life may be the cause of certain turmoil.

How can the apprehension of a returning spirit in turmoil be reduced?

There are two essential elements affecting this situation: the father and the mother. If a spirit in turmoil is reincarnated into a couple that we will describe as being "well-balanced", this spirit can react to the call of its future parents and feel a sense of security. This will enable the spirit to develop decently, providing it with a proper earthly envelope.

After several lives on inferior planets, the spirit transfers itself to a planet such as the Earth. Why do certain spirits manage to create a decent body for themselves whilst others do not?

With regard to the first life on Earth, the reason why reincarnations are good for some but bad for others is that, between the inferior planet and the planet Earth, the spiritual and afterlife encounters have not been numerous enough, if they have existed at all.

What risks are run by spirits coming from an inferior planet when they incarnate?

Every spirit that reincarnates brings with it the memory of its previous life. Hence, the perispirit that has already existed in a simple and basic form on an inferior planet will acquire its earthly shape for the first time in your history, on the planet Earth.
The more or less vivid and defined memory of its previous form on an inferior planet will be one of the most difficult handicaps both for the spirit and for the flesh. The spirit may thus construct something awkward, clumsy, apprehensive and horrible.

How is trans-sexuality understood where reincarnation is concerned?

Trans-sexuality is the result of an emotional disturbance at the moment of reincarnation, the moment of conception. Trans-sexuality is the result of a change of sex which means that the man that has become a woman or vice-versa can not accept the sexuality which is to be conferred on him/her.
Is it possible to alter trans-sexuality? Is it possible to apply a therapy to this particularly disturbing emotional condition? Clearly it is not.
The only therapy possible is an individual and social family therapy, a therapy of love and acceptance. It is up to the trans-sexual to accept his condition. I am absolutely sure that this is what the trans-sexual believes. I am not sure, however, that this is what society, the family or friends believe.

Is birth control part of the law of evolution?

Evolution implies, or should imply, the gradual transformation of your civilisations. Evolution implies harmony in the world and its basic, underlying factor is balance in all its forms. Nature is not prevented from expressing itself in this way, remaining free to the extent that the spirit can always decide to reincarnate.
Birth control means a demographic evolution of your planet. So the answer to the question is "yes".

What is the origin of blindness when it appears at birth?

There is not only one reason for the phenomenon of blindness. Reincarnation itself can explain a certain number of cases. An individual suffering from blindness may have had an extremely traumatic experience in his/her previous life. Burned or slashed eyes have been affected perispiritally and do not develop completely at the moment when the spirit returns to the flesh and the embryo develops.
A very sudden transfer from an inferior planet to the planet Earth can also be responsible for blindness.

Why is there a higher incidence of Down's syndrome in children born to women over forty years old?

This is more of a cultural phenomenon than anything else. It is the very idea itself that is frightening. In fact, this fear dwells in the subconscious of women aged forty and over. The relation between subconscious nature and the blood structure of these future mothers is extremely important. The blood itself is constantly subject to stress, anguish, repression and in this case, to cultural and social pressure. All this will alter the blood structure.
Increasingly, the realm of psychology must become aware of the importance of the relation between people's emotional and physical conditions.

How can the births of a baby fish and a baby bird at Nancy's maternity hospital about ten years ago be explained?

These are not isolated cases. This happens regularly but the truth is withheld and hidden. We are faced with cases of phobia here.
In this case, following an extremely traumatic shock related to the image of a fish or a bird, the woman's subconscious will modify the structure of the foetus she is carrying. There is a telepathic interaction between the spirit and the pregnant woman. This could be avoided if such interaction was accepted. If the medical profession would admit that, at the foetal level, there is not only a psyche that has reflex movements but also a spirit that reacts in total empathy with the anguish, turmoil or joy of its mother. The truth must be told. And now that you are aware of this, do not hesitate to spread the word.

How do you explain the illness of premature ageing?

This illness can be attributed to turmoil in reincarnation. The spirit suddenly becomes aware of what has happened previously and its present state of consciousness receives all the subconscious weight of its former old age. The latter has a direct effect on the cells of the body and this produces an incredibly fast acceleration of the ageing process, destroying neurones. There is only one solution to this which is to use hypnotism to return to the lives that the spirit has previously lived.

How do birth marks appear?

The enigma of birth marks is of course linked to your previous lives, previous shocks to the skin, at war, in a fight, a murder or an accident. However, the mother too can be subject to outside events beyond her control and record them in her subconscious, conveying them telepathically to the embryo inside her. These messages can come out on the skin of the newly born child.
The mother is in constant contact with the child she is carrying and this means that there are two reasons for these marks to appear on the skin. One is palingenesis and the other is the telepathic relationship between mother and child.

What is your opinion of the "Better Baby Institute"[29]?

My answer to this is somewhat brutal when I say that I believe in reincarnation and therefore I believe that it is not possible to go against nature. People must not think that evolution can suddenly be transformed by some sort of acceleration process. The spirit reincarnates itself at its own rhythm on this planet and nothing can alter this rhythm. Man is often

---

29 *John Watson created this Institute in 1975. Following studies on behaviourism he tried to show that geniuses are not born but created, and the sooner the better. So parents leave their babies with him so that they can receive intensive training.*
«Give me a dozen children in good health and I will turn them into any specialist I choose ». The results are quick: the first words are uttered within 4 months. At the age of 3 the children can speak two languages and are learning the violin. To be continued....

devoid of love and morals. He is often devoid of security and the affection of a family.
Here, it seems that the wish is to go against nature in order to suddenly create instant geniuses. This is not possible and shall not be the case.

Can you give us an explanation for the empty egg?

The desire to bear life and to carry life naturally depends upon the spirit. But, what is the spirit if it is not the feelings of a mother and a father who long for this incarnation to take place but who are not able to make it happen.
The spirit therefore reflects: the spirit is creative. In this instance, for the individual desire of the mother (which is sometimes linked to the desire of the father), the spirit becomes a creator of the image, of matter but it can not, for some reason, obtain the end result of its desire, i.e. to capture an entity from the other side that would have liked to be reincarnated.
Therefore, shapeless matter materialises within the body (creation by the power of thought and desire). This gives rise to an accumulation of fatty and nervous fibres. Here we are in the presence of shapelessly created matter due to a physically impossible desire.

What is your opinion on test-tube babies?

The subject of test-tube babies is not a problem for the spirits. I will explain why.
A sterile woman who knows for sure that she will never bear children is certain to have psycho-emotional problems that will affect her everyday life. The test-tube baby is in fact carried in the womb of the future mother for a little less than nine months. Hence, with this technique, telepathic love will continue to exist.

Do you have an opinion concerning surrogate mothers?

A woman has every right to help another woman become a mother, to help her to love the spirit she has called upon with all her strength in the hope that she will have a baby.
The spirit often knows the place and the atmosphere of this context that will eventually turn into a human being.

It does not matter where the baby gestates, the most important thing is the love that is given to it. If the mother is indeed sterile we have to accept the circumstances that help her to become a mother.

Whether it is the body of another woman that is borrowed for the occasion or whether the incarnation takes place outside the body, the spirit is in favour of life.

We are against the termination of pregnancy and against all human experiments that alter the evolutionary process. However, we agree with man when he uses all the means at his disposal to enable life to flourish.

How do you explain multiple births after women have been treated with infertility drugs?

The physical and surgical treatment of sterile women has no direct effect upon multiple births. These cases are often reported by the media because they are remarkable.

It is nevertheless true that several spirits can decide to reincarnate within the same family unit following this treatment. In certain cases there is a connexion therefore, but this is of a purely spiritual nature.

Think for a moment about the character, the state of mind, the feelings and the desire of the woman who, up until now, thought that she would never be able to have a child. This is a perpetual desire compared to other women and turns itself into fluids that are perceived by the spirits on the other side.

This sterile woman has had previous lives with various, intimate relationships: brothers, sisters, parents, children ands friends all belonging to these very same lives. These spirits get together and all decide to return at the same time.

Hence, I suggest to the sterile woman that she implores with all the strength of her desire the reincarnation of multiple spirits in that her desire is stronger than that of another, non-sterile woman.

Some thoughts about child prodigies.

If life is merely matter and genetics holds the answer to everything, what is the explanation for cases where there are no logical answers either via education not via genetic heritage?
Who are these people that we call child prodigies?

Beethoven was the son of an alcoholic and a servant. Despite being partially deaf from the age of six he had a remarkable talent for playing music.

Michael Angelo at the age of eight was told by his Master Ghirlandaio that he knew everything there was to know about his profession.

At the age of ten, Haendel was composing motets. Mozart composed his first sonata at the age of four.

Pascal reinvented geometry at the age of twelve. Inaudi calculated the speed of a computer.

CONCLUSION

Reincarnation is an absolute necessity, a law of nature. Only reincarnation can teach man where he comes from, where he is going and why he is on the Earth. Only reincarnation can justify all the anomalies and injustice found on Earth.

The principle of reincarnation is a consequence of the law of progress that can explain the difference between social life today and that which prevailed in barbarian times.

If the soul was created at the same time as the body, those being born today would be as ignorant and primitive as those who were born more than 1000 years ago.

In fact, there has been a slow but sure evolution of man, even if it is (falsely) claimed that the superiority of present day man is due to hereditary influences and social conditions. Heredity is powerless when it comes to explaining the natural and contrary tendencies, skills and characters of children born into the same family.

Where did these highly intelligent people that were born in the century of Pericles come from?

Who educated the geniuses whose names will remain forever engraved in the memory of mankind?

Where did they acquire all that beauty and all the truth that they spread around them?
Most of them were simple citizens of Greece, some of them were sons of slaves. It was certainly not in the place they grew up that they acquired all the knowledge that was to turn them into educators of humanity.

There seems to be no other way to solve the enigma except by saying that they were "superior" spirits who came to fulfil a mission at a certain moment in time. They were reborn into a society that was sufficiently advanced to be able to understand them.

If it was accepted that these qualities were the result of a former condition of collective progress, or that the character of those who have recently been born is the result of all the influences they have been subjected to, then the problems would still remain because inequality, whatever the reason, would be an injustice.

Why are some individuals born into civilised societies whereas others are born into barbaric or poverty-stricken societies?

Are not the people born in this century luckier than those born in the stone age?

If God granted a similar understanding of both good and evil and if man is of the same origin, it follows that the means available to evolve and progress are a universal right that everyone can benefit from. But if our Lord had granted any form of superiority outside of that resulting from individual effort, then the conditions would then be unequal and our divine ideal would be destroyed.

How can we explain the death of a child who is still unaware of life if he has only had one existence?

The Church places him "in limbo" ....a mixed situation that has never been defined.

EVOLUTION

*Love life with others.......do not love it without others.
Love life with awareness
Do not love it with ignorance
Love life with the duty of justice......do not love it in opulence*

Jesus

The Evolution of the Spirit

How would you define evolution?

Evolution is a slow and difficult process. It is a laborious and painful delivery of the divine consciousness. The road to this state of consciousness is long and laden with obstacles both in life on Earth, in the afterlife and in the world of the spirits.

Why is life in the flesh so important for evolution?

Your spirits are not sufficiently advanced for you to live serenely, in love and harmony in the invisible world. Materiality is needed in order to understand love and harmony. You live with one another on Earth and you can also identify each other. You are learning to understand and love each other. This is God's meaning of incarnation.

What helps advancement to take place?

Knowledge and morality........that is to say, love.

Should everyone study the various fields of knowledge?

Man is reincarnated and essentially returns to learn and to love.
Let us take the case of a man who is currently living on the Earth and who has completed his mission within a particular field. Let us take the example of medicine.
This man may naturally have the desire to learn about philosophy, electronics, poetry or literature. Should he return and choose a different field of knowledge, he may well be the worst of all philosophers or poets despite his perfect knowledge of medicine. He will then accept this difference (not as a regression) as it will contribute to his own evolution.

Why does evil exist?

It must be understood that we are born in a shapeless and unconscious glaze and that the sculpture of our spirits gradually takes place throughout our lives. Knowledge is certainly an advantage as it teaches the need to fight and to combat all forms of injustice. From the family unit to the very corners of the Universe, the unhappiness of certain human lives is merely prompting us to become someone else in the quest for future happiness.

Have we all been bad spirits in the course of our evolution or is this something that can be avoided?

It is not possible to avoid one's own nature. Spiritual natures that are currently human nature living on the earth for example, have been thrown into the divine, creative movement. This has given the following result: a simple and ignorant spirit living in a basic state and totally unaware of everything. During the course of successive reincarnations all spirits have been in contact with evil and have committed evil. There is no escaping this divine and natural law.

Where do the sorrows of mankind come from?

The sorrows of humanity come from the imperfections of man. They harm to one another because of their vices. As long as man remains depraved he will continue to be unhappy because a struggle based on self-interest can only generate poverty and misery.

Is it God that decides to punish souls that have taken pleasure in evil?

It is the soul itself that carries its own punishment around with it wherever it goes. Hell can be anywhere that souls are suffering. As the justice of God is infinite, He does not take evil into account. In order to stop suffering, God needs to see a real improvement and a sincere return towards good. The spirit can always decide on its own destiny. It can prolong its suffering by getting deeper into evil or shorten it by doing good.

This is the law of divine justice: "each according to his deeds on earth and in heaven".

What are feelings?

Feeling is the manifestation of sensitivity in many different forms. We suffer because of injustice and also when faced with people dying of hunger. We sympathise with the pain of others. We cry, we sing and we shout. This is good. This is the proof that we exist. There are people who do not sing or cry. They are the living dead.

Are certain people devoid of feelings?

It is not normal to have no feelings. But abnormal people do exist. However, the law of reincarnation and of universal evolution constantly teaches us that we have a tendency towards good.
He who does not love does not exist. Love can not be learned as it is inherent in your nature.

Feelings are often expressed following a shock, whether this shock has provoked hatred, suffering or joy.
The suffering that a person can feel when they lose someone is real. In the same way, the joy felt in the presence of art or at the birth of a child is not an illusion. There is also the hatred that we express in the face of terrible injustice.
There are people who remain cold and indifferent in the face of these things. And the more humanity suffers from indifference, the more people will suffer, the more injustice and wars there will be.

An awareness which is based upon reason and true feelings will mark the arrival of a new era.

Is it possible to evaluate the number of lives needed to reach God?

(Account related by the spirit of Plato)

I had to live exactly 387 lives on the Earth and other planets in order to reach and be as one with the force of creation. This figure is merely a figure and I have only quoted it to show that man must understand the exact meaning of palingenesis.

Man can not suppose that a state of grace will suddenly appear. He must not think of perfection without understanding that it requires a labour of love. Thought and feeling must be the subject of a long development.
I know the joy of a job well done, accomplished with good measure over time and including suffering. It is essential that things should be deserved if any life is to progress.

Is there a more direct route to the Father?

The truth of a Father is an absolute truth. There is no detour possible. In fact, it is very dangerous to witness the development of certain theories in your societies nowadays. These ideas suggest to young people that perfection can be attained with no effort and without awareness via an individual meditation. But this individual meditation can only lead to anguish, torpor and even suicide.

Are all spirits equal or is there a hierarchy amongst them?

As creation is constant, spirits do not all have the same strong and weak points. Some, of course, are more advanced than others. There are different orders of spirits with respect to this evolution and to this genesis of the spirit just as there are people who are more or less advanced on Earth.

Do we evolved more as quickly as an embodied or disembodied entity?

This depends on the nature of the spirit. In the afterlife, spirits live out a relative period of evolution which may be the equivalent of 3, 4 or 5 reincarnations on this planet. In the afterlife, certain entities are ready to receive a true and real education from their guide.

However, nature wants the spirit to return to matter. It is necessary to have many different physical experiences. These can be of a spiritual, moral and intellectual nature.

The spirit evolves in both the visible and invisible worlds.

The Evolution of Worlds

How advanced is the planet Earth?

The planet Earth should be considered as an inferior planet in the sense that there are still wars, frontiers, racism and injustice with all the consequences that this brings. It is at level 2 of a 10 level scale compared to other (inferior and superior) planets.

When did the Earth pass from level one to level two?

We are of course giving imaginary figures when we speak of the level and scale of planets. We do this so that man can appreciate the difference between worlds.
Concerning planet Earth it is possible to say that it passed from level one to two around the year 1945.
We give this date because we consider that the development of science and of philosophical thinking, the end of so-called world wars and the freeing of colonised lands was the beginning of considerable change in the lives of all those concerned. This answer of course is as relative as it is global.

What criteria are used to grade a planet?

This is based upon the intellectual and moral advancement of the people on the planet as a whole.

In the beginning, were all planets on an inferior level? And if not why not?

Most planets have gone through the natural process of evolution. This is a long, slow and difficult process. Many of these planets receive life forms as they are created in infinite space. Gradually, these planets change and alter depending on the individual and collective advancement of their inhabitants.
However, we can not say this about all the planets. Some of them have been visited by superior, extra-terrestrial life forms that have decided to develop new civilisations on these very same planets. The appearance of life forms is therefore artificial and can not be considered as a natural evolution.

Has the planet Earth evolved since 1945?

Can it be considered as having passed level 2?

Planet Earth, like all planets, is in constant evolution. It is now at the beginning of a metamorphosis. This can be seen in the individual and general advancement both on a moral and an intellectual level.
After more than 50 years the Earth may be considered as a planet having progressed by a half level, that is to say two and a half, between two and three. This means that the very crust of the earth will alter and that a new type of vibration will emerge. This vibration is dependent on individual and collective spirituality. The great change in intelligence will lead to great changes in matter.

THE MANIFESTATION OF SPIRITS IN THE PHYSICAL WORLD

I do not say that this is possible. I say that this exists.

William Crookes

The white lady in a veil or mourning passes through the cold and icy space in the ether and through the air. And the earthly surroundings kneel before the living spirit so dear to the eternal.

Have spirits always revealed themselves?

Since prehistoric times, spirits have always known how to reveal themselves to those who are naive and rough yet sensitive enough to the light and to the appearance of their (already existing) guide.
Spirits have never stopped revealing themselves in this world, no matter which period of history was concerned. They have always been there, badly defined and depicted in writings and images.
Spirits have constantly appeared to man who, in turn, has refused to believe this and has given various interpretations for it.

Do spirits regularly reveal themselves in the physical world?

Men and women receive sparks, signs and gestures every day that suggest the presence of spirits in the physical world. This is also true for other planets.

We enter into the daily lives and homes of everyone. We strike the walls of these houses. We move objects, we stimulate the conscience of people while they sleep. We bring forth our light, even our luminosity.
Our living ghosts reveal themselves in numerous places and yet man remains silent, not daring to say that we exist.

The numerous manifestations of Mary, the mother of Jesus, are often spoken about. Are they all credible?

There is nothing preventing Mary from manifesting herself[30] but is not acceptable for man to pervert the truth.
Many spirits are seen by children, fortunate children who are visited by their protecting guides. Men and women have often turned the innocent words and remarks of these children into religious terms, provoking turmoil and inventing miracles.

Was it Mary who appeared at Lourdes?

During the last century a young girl called Bernadette claimed to have seen the Virgin Mary during a period of intense prayer.
We are in complete disagreement with this apparition, at least with regard to the identity of the person.
Mary is a very common name and was even more so at the time when Bernadette was born. This manifestation was indeed that of a spirit named Mary but was nothing other than Bernadette's protecting spirit.

Account given by Bernadette Soubirous and received on the 14/04/1986 by automatic writing.

"I saw a spirit appear in Lourdes. It was that of my guide, Mary a woman I had known in a previous life. This is all, absolutely all I heard and saw. The spirit appeared several times in the cave and also at the house. Priests came to ask me questions every day. They asked me whether I had heard the "Immaculate Conception"[31] mentioned. I replied that I had not. They questioned me for months and in the end they managed to persuade me that I had seen Mary, the mother of Jesus.
My parents were simple people. We were afraid of the authorities and especially the religious authorities. If the priests said that I had seen Mary,

---

30 Over a period of 10 centuries, Mary is said to have appeared 21,000 times.
31 It must be remembered that the dogma of the Immaculate Conception was proclaimed in 1854 by Pope Pius IX who imposed this belief on all his followers. In 1858 when Bernadette saw the spirit of Mary, much pressure was put on her to give credit to the very personal declaration of Pope Pius IX.

then surely that must have been the case and I ended up believing it myself. Everyone looked at me in astonishment and people came from far and wide to see me. I found this very amusing.

All my life I continued believing this. I was occasionally visited by my guide. I saw her crying as she was disturbed by lies and wrongdoings. This entire story is due to my relations with the Church. I am very pleased if today people are cured by going to the cave in Lourdes but I am convinced that this is due to the power of their own thought".

What is your opinion on people who are healed at Lourdes?

Cases of healing have indeed been reported by doctors at the very place where Bernadette said she had seen Mary of Nazareth. Thanks to this, the town of Lourdes has become the subject of much discussion and contradictory debates over a period of years which in itself provided a lot of publicity for the town. Today Lourdes has become important and is witness to many pilgrimages and much business.

The phenomenon of healing is purely suggestive. We indeed believe that suggestion and the collective unconsciousness are in operation here.[32]

Who are the Korrigans, sprites and elves?

As Allan Kardec said in "The Book of the Spirits", spirits can reveal themselves to man in many different forms. Korrigans, sprites and elves are generally manifestations of the invisible world.

Are they bad spirits or practical-joker spirits?

No, they are not of an inferior order. They are more the manifestation of the consciousness of superior spirits. They reveal themselves in particular places, heavily loaded with telluric energy and their presence is turned into

---

32 It may be said that much spontaneous healing, wrongly called miracles, is the result of psychosomatic processes. Places such as Lourdes receive all the sincerity and prayer of those who have been visiting the place for decades. These thoughts and prayers are not lost. They will be added to the faith, the prayers and desire to be healed of everyone concerned. In the case of Lourdes, the church has been careful, only recognising 49 cases out of 2,200 as being « miraculous ».

thought – protective thought, thought that can protect humanity and avoid certain disasters or even natural cataclysms.

MEDIUMSHIP

Your sons and your daughters will be prophets

Jesus

We can assume that mediumship has always existed as spirits have always manifested themselves since man has been on the Earth. However, it happened mostly in an empirical manner. It was only when Allan Kardec and other remarkable men such as Gabriel Delanne, Leon Denis, Camille Flammarion, Leon Chevreuil, William Crookes, Gustave Gelay and others came on the scene that a coherent movement appeared.

After the prophetesses of Delph, the visionaries of history, the sleep-walkers of Messmer, the era of mediumship really began with Allan Kardec ("The Book of Mediums").

Nowadays numerous adverts and publicity can be seen for "mediums, fortune-tellers, disciples of Allan Kardec".
This is an outrage in the face of spiritist philosophy and to Kardec himself. It is what he wanted to avoid at all costs.

When he was alive, he refused to publish a practical manual briefly indicating the way in which people could get in touch with the spirits. This was because he believed that it would do more harm than good. There are many problems connected with spiritism and Kardec believed that it was not possible to deal with them all in one simple book.
Moreover, spiritism is based on a philosophy. Mediumship must thus therefore include a moral, ethical and behavioural code.

Kardec had understood all this, which is why he believed that mediumship would not develop without the parallel development of spiritism.

This is not to say that there are no mediums outside the practise of spiritism. Spirits manifest themselves where they can even if the conditions are not ideal. But, according to their degree of advancement, their moral code and their freedom, I can assert that they do not appear "at the request of the client". They do not answer dishonest compromises concerning speculation or lies.

You will find certain books on the market nowadays entitled "How to become a medium in 10 easy lessons". Some companies sell games on the supernatural or the occult with ouija boards and instructions. This type of irresponsible action can give rise to psychological disorders which must not then be attributed to spiritism.

If some people have fun with spiritism (at their own risk) others take it much more seriously, practising it in a group. It is in this context that the answers obtained from the invisible world should be considered.

What is mediumship?

Is it easy to appear in the physical world?

The spirit manifests itself as best it can and it is true that mediumship enables it to appear in various ways. It would be very naive to believe for a single moment that it is easy to do this.
An enormous effort needs to be made because we are no longer of a physical nature and for this we need to use your energy, i.e. all your fluids added together.

Does mediumship mean a perispirital texture?

First of all, mediumship means a choice. This choice is made in the afterlife by a spirit before returning to Earth and is made in conjunction with the protecting guide as well as other spirits.

Do all mediums on Earth choose to do this?

Certainly not. Historically speaking, if some mediums have displayed certain advantages very early on in the development of their mediumship, it is because they have prepared their future mission on Earth before coming. It can be said that these mediums have chosen this mission before returning to Earth but it is not the case for them all.

In these cases, does mediumship have to develop itself?

Mediumship must follow the laws of progress, of passing time, the laws of patience and hard work. Obviously, in these instances the development of mediumship will take much longer. It will also be harder and more difficult.

To what extent can the subconscious of the future medium influence the development of this skill?

The subconscious can reveal itself in many ways. The importance of this should be underlined with regard to mediumship.
The medium needs to rid him/herself of all anguish, worry and anything that may prevent him/her from receiving the thoughts of the spirit.
The medium must therefore be able to express very openly and freely what he/she feels. The messages produced at the beginning of his/her development should not be analysed in a negative manner but should be the stage for encouraging the medium to develop further. The subconscious must be allowed to rid itself of its psycho-emotional load in order to leave space for the disembodied spirit. This will take more or less time depending upon the condition of the subject, and can vary between one and four years.

When spirits use a medium can they call on all the various forms of mediumship or are they more sensitive to one form of it than another?

Depending upon who is concerned, the spirits have varied reactions to the way in which they can reveal themselves to the physical world. It is not easy for the disembodied to penetrate the vibratory field of the Earth. To do this they use their perispirital envelope and reveal themselves via a medium.

The perispirit is made up of a set of memory cells which are particularly sensitive. This sensitivity must match that of the perispirit of the human go-between, i.e. the medium.

It would appear that the ouija board is the easiest way for the spirit to reveal itself for the first time. Writing is used as it is a very practical means of communicating whereas incorporation requires a basic affinity between the medium and the spirit.

But this affinity does not exist when very inferior spirits reveal themselves does it?

In all cases of inferior spirit manifestation, all organised spiritist groups are protected by superior spirits from the afterlife. When inferior spirits are received by a medium outside such an organised structure, there is a risk that the medium may die.

Can a medium only communicate with one spirit?

By definition, a medium is the receptacle for spirits and hence there are no mediums worthy of the name who can only receive one entity.

Are there cases where a medium can receive two entities and two messages at the same time?

This could only happen in two ways – by the hearing of voices (clairaudience) and by automatic writing. It is possible for an ambidextrous person. It happened in the musical dictations received by Rosemary Brown in England.
This lady received a melody from Liszt and an accompaniment from Beethoven. She wrote the melody from Frantz Liszt with her right hand and Beethoven's accompaniment with her left.
It is also possible in clairaudience when two spirits reveal themselves to the same medium, one in the left ear and one in the right, one by the left encephalon and one by the right.

How are messages transmitted to us during magnetic sleep?

Magnetic sleep: sleep caused by magnetic induction on a medium who will transmit what he/she hears, sees or perceives via speech as the medium is then outside his/her physical body.
This is the thought process of the spirit. It is a telepathic process. When the medium sees us in the afterlife and when he/she looks at us we voluntarily take on a human appearance. This is to reassure the medium so that

he/she will not be distracted from the message that we wish to send you. Consequently, we use telepathy directly toward the medium who then turns this into speech.

Can mediumship or other skills be used for the service of evil?

It is possible to use psycho-kinetics, telepathy, clairvoyance or mediumship to further evil. All psychic forces belong to the spirit of man and can therefore be used in a particularly evil manner.

Could you define clairvoyance?

Clairvoyance is a particular condition of man that enables him to perceive a set of psychic impressions that are particular to the embodied or disembodied subject. Thanks to the life within him/her, the subject will emit an undulating formula that is spiritually received by the clairvoyant.

What actually happens in reality?

Clairvoyance is a particular condition in which the perispirit partly leaves the body.
At the moment this takes place, the subject is just outside the body but nevertheless remains very close to it.

What use are supports such as cards and photographs?

Clairvoyance can be direct and with no such support, but very often the support enables concentration and reverence to take place, bringing about a state of clairvoyance.

What is mediumnic clairvoyance?

As suggested in the term, this implies the presence of a deceased human being, a disembodied subject and the messages received will come from the other side.

Is clairvoyance a permanent and constant condition?

Because the real state of clairvoyance means the perispirit leaving the body, it can never be a permanent state. No human being could bear this condition for long.
Certain people claim they have a permanent state of clairvoyance for business reasons. This is a complete lie and the only reason the so-called clairvoyants do this is to earn money.

What is your opinion on trans-communication?

It is extremely difficult for the deceased to print the force of their thoughts on a magnetic tape, to send them via micro-waves that will then turn them into a picture inside a tube.
We are not talking about receiving messages, speeches or thoughts. We are talking about occasional manifestations that come in answer to a call, to a meditation. In many cases, the answer sought by those who go into the experience does not materialise. This type of communication is nevertheless possible.

How far has work on trans-communication advanced?

The spirit can manifest itself in this way[33] because the spirit is freedom itself. All these spirits that are free do whatever they please can act here or there as they wish.

---

33 *The first so called trans-communicationist manifestations took place at the beginning of the 20th century in a continuity of the Kardec and spiritist era (see F.Brune d R.Chauvin for a history of these manifestations in «Listening to the Afterlife»).*
Father François Brune, priest and theologian, examined many stories from across the world and discovered that the dead could communicate with the living, a notion that

But the spirit does not seek to reveal its existence via a TV screen in answer to rational expectations.

What should be remembered that spirits will take every opportunity to prove their survival, whether this manifestation is televised, telephoned, in the form of an ectoplasm or spiritist. The essential thing is to get together and to communicate.

---

the Church had rejected for a long time but which it now accepted. In November 1996 the Reverend Concetti made a statement that was widely reported in the Italian press. Here is an extract: «According to modern Catholic teachings, God has enabled those who have left us and who live in another dimension to send us messages to guide us at certain moments of our lives. The Church has decided to no longer forbid these dialogues with the deceased as long as they are undertaken in either a scientific or religious frame of mind. The messages may come via words and sounds but also via dreams or visions, images or concepts which penetrate our spirit».

In his book «Listening to the Afterlife», Father Brune says this: «I personally regret the cleavage that arose too long ago between the Church and the spiritist movement, particularly that led by Allan Kardec».

ART and MEDIUMSHIP

Mediumship as art

Many deceased artists wish to perpetuate their creativity in the physical world. Their problem is to represent the new feelings that they have in the afterlife.
Whether it be in painting, sculpture, poetry or music, the deceased artist wishes to send his message, to transmit his impressions and what he feels most deeply.

How does the transmission of art take place for a spirit?

If the spirit decides to paint a clown, he will first of all think of a clown. This clown will appear to him in full dress, fully made-up and with a tragic or comic expression. At this precise creative moment, the spirit will move around the room where the medium is waiting for him, taking his image of a clown with him.

The spirit will act upon his double in order to reach the medium and to guide his/her hand. The artistic spirit will use telepathy to create a vibration on the ethereal body of the medium. This vibration will be transferred to his/her physical body.

The medium instinctively knows what to do. He/she will automatically choose the shapes and colours necessary and will receive from the spirit the feelings that it wants to be put into the character on the canvas or paper.

Poetry

Art can also be expressed by poetry and music via mediums who are sensitive enough to perceive it.
Poetry is received by semi-automatic writing, also known as intuitive writing. Here, the spirit does not act on the hand in order to make it write. It neither holds nor guides it. The spirit identifies with the spirit of the

medium and acts upon it. Under this telepathic impulse the medium writes what the spirit sends to him/her. The latter is acting as an interpreter in this case, understanding the thoughts of the spirit and seizing them in order to faithfully transmit the message. No thoughts come from the medium who is simply used as a passage.

Medical Mediumship

What is a healing medium?

These are mediums who, in the same way as artists, receive the presence of doctors from the afterlife only.

Hence, they will be guided intuitively or automatically. The energy from the spirit of the doctor will be transferred to the physical intermediary (the medium) and then on to the patient. The spirit is not incorporated into the body of the healing medium for medical action. The spirit remains next to the medium whose double (the perispirit) is externalised. This externalisation simultaneously frees up the vital fluid used by the doctor's spirit. This can act upon the body and by the body of the medium by the creation of an automatism.

Message from Jean Rostand (1980):

"The healing spirit transforms matter, changing it by the use of the fluid of the spirit. This is quite an extraordinary process. The bio-chemical structure of the human being is represented by a set of apparently instinctive movements, but without the force of the spirit which comes from a loving urge, the whole thing collapses.
By transmitting your love to the patient, you will reactivate the biological process he/she needs to live".

THE EMANCIPATION OF THE SPIRIT

Your young people will have visions.
Your old people will have dreams

Jesus

Consciousness

What is consciousness?

It is the ability of humans to memorise the physical and psychological world by means of the intellect and feelings.
It is in this way that we become aware of our existence in the world, of our relationships with others and of the need to live with the elements around us.
The embodied consciousness uses codes to reveal its presence, the main one being language.

Are there other aspects to consciousness?

Sometimes human beings carry memories within them, over and above the memory of their present life. Some individuals reveal the existence of other lives and other experiences when in a state of awakening or under hypnotic sleep.
Others, despite the existence of language, spontaneously enter into telepathic communication with other embodied consciences. If consciousness does not stop at the simple recognition of the world it is in, then its new dimension needs to be found. This is the eternal dimension which is why we call it *the spirit*.

> *Sleep is the most noble river of life and dreams are its alluvium.*
> Pierre Billon

> *Dreams are the key to getting outside ourselves.*
>
> Georges Rodenbach

> *Dreams are what we read when we sleep.*
>
> Jean Cocteau

Sleep and Dreams

Sleep is like a minor version of death on a daily basis. It enables us to capture spiritual energy so we can cope more easily with our physical lives.

There is no life without a spirit. Man therefore needs to feed on the cosmic fluid to keep his physical life well balanced.

A person whose spirit and perispirit can never get outside their earthly envelope will gradually die due to the lack of fluid. Or worse still, be plunged into a long coma.

So, every night the human spirit goes off on a trip into the afterlife to meet its guide and other people who have died.

Although the memory of these journeys is blocked out by the barriers of the subconscious, the knowledge and the spirituality acquired from them have an influence on the behaviour of the individual.

Charles Rydsberg (1987)

Is the embodied spirit content to remain without its bodily envelope?

The spirit is essentially spiritual in nature. It is therefore necessary for it to regularly refresh itself outside matter and this is why all of you leave your bodies for a short time during the night in order to return to what you really are.

Why do we leave our bodies every night?

This is simply because, by nature, you are basically spirits. Your physical being is temporary. Just as your physical bodies need to rest and to sleep, your spiritual nature also needs to return to its source, to go back to its element.

Does this explain dreams?

Dreams can be explained in many ways. One of them is indeed the meeting with spirits in the afterlife and this will be remembered via images.

Are dreams sometimes an open door onto the other side?

Man is in constant contact with the cosmos, thanks mainly to the phenomenon of sleep.
A more useful form of psycho-analysis would involve the spirit, its genesis as well as its spiritual and divine ontology. In this way, it would be more beneficial for those who are in mental suffering.
Nightmares would no longer be restricted to the spirit's reaction to what has just been experienced. The nightmare could also be related to the repressed memory of a previous life on an inferior planet.

Man will learn to decipher his dreams. The faces he meets that he thinks he recognises and which upon awakening have no meaning. They will become the faces of his guide, his parents, friends and all those who have belonged to previous lives.

For how long do we leave our body at night?

This varies according to the individual and depending on the number of meetings that are to take place during this period.

The period does not necessarily have to be continuous, but on average it does not generally exceed two hours.

Is it dangerous for this to happen outside natural sleep?

Any leaving of the body is monitored by the guide if it is natural. Any artificially induced condition, performed in pure curiosity does present a risk.
We estimate that about 50.000 induced possessions took place following the reading of books such as that by Lobsang Rampa.

The invisible world is in constant contact with the visible world. Hence, man is responsible for what he does.

Is it possible to live in the dream state of traumatic events and suffer the psychological consequences?

The spirit does not always move around in ethereal spheres when it is in its physiological sleep. It does not always meet the spirits and the deceased.

The spirit can visit other living human beings who are in turmoil and consequently experience a trauma.

Despite the memories having disappeared upon waking, is it possible for behaviour to change after meeting one's guide?

Yes indeed. Everything is retained and contained in your respective subconscious, meaning that you are not guided by destiny but by yourselves thanks to the advice that is given to you every night while you are asleep.

How can we explain premonitory dreams?

This undoubtedly corresponds to some information that has been received. This information can have come from any one of three different sources: it can be telepathic, clairvoyant, or from an astral meeting with one or more spirit.

Does every living person meet their guide while they are asleep?

This depends on how far each person has evolved. Spirits that have reincarnated instinctively will not have met their guide before returning to life. Following reincarnation, their nocturnal outings will be very similar to

their palingenesis. They will leave their bodies by physical and perispirital necessity but no more.
Having said this, leaving one's body during the night does enable many humans to meet their guide.

Can you give us a definition of a dream? What part does imagination play in dreams?

Can you give any universal symbols regarding dreams?

Message from Sigmund Freud received by trans-mediumship on January 8th 1988:

I have written a lot about dreams and for a long time I thought that dreams were a revelation of the depths of the human subconscious.
These depths of the subconscious reveal a number of questions that man has during sleep, within his cerebral activities.
I said that the majority of these impulses were of a sexual nature and today I would like to add that I did not reveal everything………I would also admit that I was sometimes mistaken.

I firmly believe that man needs to find a balance. Through dreams and the expression of the psyche, Mother Nature has enabled him to reach this balance via dreamed, transformed or nightmarish impulses.

I continue to believe that during sleep, man expresses a number of repressed elements that he is incapable of expressing when in a conscious state. I can confirm this as I have studied it, but I would also like to state that the images created in dreams are not sufficient to interpret these dreams.
I also know, as I discovered this and because I am now dead and in the afterlife, that images received are also those of previous lives. They are the images of meetings with other spirits, the images of advice given by guides, the images of previous lives that belong to each individual.

I also know that turmoil is not simply something of the moment and that, beyond the question of time, it can be a response to traumas experienced in the past. I know that in dreams, as in hypnosis, a trauma can be relived to help the sub-conscious bear the weight of these traumas because the sub-conscious has a natural tendency to keep them.

So dreams have several sides to them but I limited my work to one aspect only during my time on Earth.

Dreams are the urges of the soul and these do not always match those of the body in which the soul lives. The urge may also be the result of memories of former lives, of the afterlife, on the Earth or other planets.

Dreams have one major function: they act as a balance and are present in all physical or non-physical consciousness. I mean that the disembodied spirit also has dreams. The disembodied spirit does not always have the strength to carry the past around with it. Hence, it is often forced to cut out the past so as to better appreciate the new world immediately following disembodiment.

Symbols are related to your civilisations and to your individuality and family lives as well as to your genetics. I can not define all that in detail here.

These universal symbols concern geometry, materials, colours and emotions.[34]

---

34 *Dreams from a psychical point of view.*
Dreams open doors onto the unknown. A new world opens up beyond our dreams and every night our spirits can explore the different dimensions of the universe.
Has the answer to a problem never appeared to you in the morning that you were unable to find the day before?
The expression « let's sleep on it » takes on all its meaning as throughout history people have revealed this has been the case.
It is often in a semi-conscious state that artists and geniuses have their inspiration. All poets have experienced this. Alfred de Musset was in a nervous, almost trance-like state when he composed the « Immortal Nights ».
La Fontaine dreamed up his fable "The Two Pigeons".
Puccini claimed to have often had creative instructions to follow during his dreams.
Rodin said that he had often had the vision of his works in his dreams before creating them.
Niels Bohr, a theorist on the new science of the atom, found the basic hypotheses to his atomic designs in his dreams.
Einstein, like many others, was a medium unknown to himself. His friend Antonia Valentin noticed how he looked like a visionary whilst at the same time being attached to earthly matters. Einstein himself sometimes remarked on the purely psychic processes of some of his findings.
"Albert, how did you arrive at this discovery?" asked his son in law one day. "Thanks to a vision" he replied.
This vision of the Universe was described by Jacques Madavle: "suddenly the clear, gigantic map of the Universe folded out before me in a blinding vision".

Thought and will are organising and creative forces.

Ernest Bozzano

Telepathy

The word telepathy appeared for the first time in 1882, used by Frederic Myers, founder of *The Society for Psychical Research* in London.
Many people such as J.B Rhine, Zener, R. Warcollier and Doctor E. Osty have carefully investigated this faculty.

An inventor is often the person who receives a flash, the light or a sudden revelation from the world of the spirits. He/she is a sort of medium and the invention is very often the result of a dream or a premonition. An invention is the result of much research at the end of which an answer appears like an inspiration. Many inventors have been inspired by the afterlife.

Posthumous account by Leonardo de Vinci, (1982):
When I went by the name of Leonardo on this earth I used to sleep and dream a lot. I used to receive images, diagrams and the geometry and mathematics necessary to create my invention. I partake of my invention because I am a spirit in constant research, a curious spirit but I am only a participant like so many other living or deceased participants.
Inventors are mediums that are instinctively led by invisible powers. It was not I who imagined the plane or the helicopter. I did not invent all these shapes and forces alone. I received, heard and took what was necessary at the right moment."

Message from Albert Einstein (1982):
Everyone on this Earth has a relationship with the spirit. The mere thought of relative time itself came to me when I was spiritually out of my body. Philosophers, men of science, poets, painters or simple men are all inspired by this relationship with the spirit.
The idea that dreams are nothing more than repressed desires is now outdated. Admittedly there are dreams which allow wishes or apprehension to be expressed. Dreams can also be about inescapable truths, philosophical sentences, memories, plans, expectations even telepathic visions or about intimate irrational experiences.
When we enter into the calm of sleep it would appear that, far from resting, our intelligence perceives and receives information. Premonitory dreams that come true are just one example of this. Sometimes a strange worry or a hallucination suddenly awakens people at the very moment when someone close to them dies. This is telepathy that can be verified.

Even today, despite all the research that has been carried out, this phenomenon has never been rationally explained. For many people it remains a figment of the imagination and a total illusion.

Today the general term of telepathy covers anything that concerns thought transmission or feeling transmission without the use of the sensory organs. For the disembodied, telepathy is the universal language.

As they have no articulated language, animals are very sensitive to telepathy just as vegetables or minerals can receive our thoughts, whether they are positive or negative.

Telepathy was common in primitive man but slowly disappeared as other forms of communication came into use.

This intrinsic skill should be worked on. It reappears from time to time when great tension, emotional shock or misfortune occurs. It is easier to establish between people who are psychically or emotionally connected such as twins, in children or with people who do not have all their senses (blind, dumb, deaf) as if this absence increased their telepathic powers.

What prevents telepathy from being expressed?

Telepathy should be rediscovered and taught. It is true that your modern day world does not easily lend itself to such an exercise. Discordant, modern day noises prevent the existence of simple, true and natural phenomena in connection with your spirits.

Will telepathy ever be recognised?

This law, and it is a law, will eventually be recognised by the same scientific world which took so long to admit the physical unity of matter. Whatever its form and its individual quality, the psychic wave can travel the length and breadth of the inhabited spheres of the Universe.
The psychic wave is the wave of supreme communication and remains the first quality of the spirit, and of all spirits whoever and wherever they are. The psychic wave that crosses a single material is capable of spreading through all your respective cerebral forces.

This is why by placing their hands on a table, the receptive person can, via his cosmic force and meditation, transmit the character of the person who designed and built it (psychometrics).

Thought chains or fluidic chains

What is fluid?

It is the vehicle for thought like the air is the vehicle for sound. As thought creates fluidic images, it reflects in the perispirital envelope like a mirror.

Fluid is therefore essentially the result of thought. If thought is good and positive then the fluids are good and vice versa.

What is a vibration?

All thought emits a fluid which leaves the physical body, freeing itself from physical ties. It is after this that we can speak of vibrations. Thought becomes a vibration which is like a wave. And starting from your thought and spiritual reflection, this wave, like a curved line, will extend into space.

What is exhalation?

When the vibration reaches its destination it will become an exhalation. This means that thought is *a fluid* when it belongs to the body, becoming *a vibration* when it leaves the body, becoming *an exhalation* when it reaches another body or an inert element of matter.

What is a fluidic chain?

This is a concentration of the action of thought in the sense that several people take part in the chain[35].

Dowsing

What is your opinion of dowsing?

The Earth lives with a rate of condensation crossed by fluids that can be picked up by a dowser using his pendulum. Because of this, the dowser can often get close to the fourth dimension. This will enable him to detect a vegetable or animal spiritual presence more quickly than others, who remain in a state of ignorance.

The current picked up by the dowser can also enable an early medical diagnosis to be made.

The problem of dowsing is that it can be overdone. It can be used and misused by unscrupulous people who claim that the pendulum can be used for fortune telling. This is not true.

Dowsing is a science that needs to be developed and this is why it still remains only partially defined.

---

35 Go ahead and have positive thoughts, with your friends and family. Create fluidic chains:
-The condition: that there are at least 3 people
-Aims: multiple (death, illness, depression or more generally peace in the world)
-How to practise: hold hands and form a circle. Concentrate and constantly think about the wish (by repeating phrases in your head or by imagining the person or the desired situation) for 3 to 5 minutes. After this time one person from the group will break the chain (by breaking off the hand grip or saying stop).
Music can be used as a background to this activity.
If your chain is for someone who has died recently, think very hard about their spirit being propelled into the afterlife, about meeting their guide. Help them become aware of their new condition of being disembodied.

What are the laws governing dowsing?

Matter is governed by the laws of atomic energy. It can be split into electrons and now down to quarks.

The basis, called D7 base, is a subdivision of matter into 7 parts:
neutrons
protons
electrons
deuterium, a heavy hydrogen isotope
tritium, a radioactive isotope
the spiritual programming of God in the perispirital particle which actives everything and charges the atom
the seventh part of the atom is the intelligent potential of the spirit that fits into it. This clarification about atomic physics is necessary to understand the phenomenon of dowsing.

How can this phenomenon be explained?

The use of a pendulum, made of either pure or alloyed metal, in fact amounts to "remembering" matter. So, as you are 100% matter at the present time, using the pendulum is equivalent to subconscious telepathy with atomic structure. This transactional telepathy between the spirit and matter via the use of a pendulum will help the dowser to locate living matter and inert matter. This is how the pendulum can detect an organic illness in its perispirital manifestation. It will also detect the presence of a given material such as gold, silver or lead as they radiate naturally. So dowsing is really atomic clairvoyance with a material support.

Why use a pendulum?

The pendulum is a measuring instrument that will respond in either a negative or a positive manner, e.g. the use of an architectural plan in a particular place. This is just one of its applications.

Is there an agreement between person and pendulum?

This depends solely on the person. The only rule is that the same one must be kept throughout one's lifetime. The dowsing agreement must remain free.

Does faith or belief play any part in this?

Because matter is the product of the spirit, the dowser must believe in God and in eternity. If his relationship with nature is devoid of spirituality then I solemnly declare that his work is of no value.

What are the most appropriate materials in divination?

Copper, gold and granite are the best materials to use in divination.

Where do so-called "wave shapes" come from?

The major elements giving rise to wave shapes, thus provoking the movement of the pendulum, are such things as the roundness of the planet, the different altitudes of the Earth, the depths of the oceans and the gravitational force of the Earth's core. This means that all credible dowsers must be as one with the Earth, with the ground and the living or inert materials surrounding his field of action.

If the shapes are the result of intelligent, creative thought, whether it is a building or a rock, the wave shape it emits will possess the same quality as its creator.

Hence, nothing should be feared in the realm of nature. Human construction, however, may be the source of great fear if it has been undertaken without taking the geometrical relation between matter and the spirit into account.

Can certain shapes be harmful?

Post war architects were very keen on cubes, rectangles and acute angles so they designed dwellings that were unsuited to the natural circulation of the energy in the ground and the cosmos.
It is no wonder that we are witnessing an increase in stress and depression and often cellular anarchy in human beings.

Psychometrics

What is psychometrics?

The sense of touch was one of the first senses to reveal a great deal to the human being. The sense of touch provides much information about the nature of a material and consequently about the vibration naturally emanating from it.

Some people can guess the colour of a material just by touching it. Psychometrics brings together the tactile sensation and the information contained in the basic atoms of an object. A telepathic relationship between the spirit of man and the living molecules of an object can take place.

What is the difference between this and standard clairvoyance?

In the case of a clairvoyant, the perispirit exteriorises itself slightly, thereby giving rise to a state of perception outside the senses.
In the case of a psychometric subject, the internalised and somewhat innervated perispirit makes the subject more sensitive to the vibrations of matter. The psychometric subject is extremely sensitive to tactile elements.

Is psychometrics a form of mediumship?

Any faculty which does not involve the realm of the spirits and the afterlife can not be considered as being a "medium" in the strict sense of the word.

In what way is psychometrics useful or how might it be?

Particle physics will go increasingly further in this area. Man will soon be able to scientifically demonstrate that electrons have a memory. When this is the case, it will no longer be possible to say that matter is a dangerous acid and psychometrics will then enter the realm of natural science.

If all the museums on the Earth would agree to lend historical objects, people with psychometric powers could then put together the detailed and accurate truth of the past.

Black Magic

What is the difference between black magic and white magic?

So called "black" magic does not involve any particular acts or knowledge. It is simple and easy to initiate oneself into this type of evil spell, into this constant desire to kill or destroy others.

Black magic is a death wish, engraved in inferior consciences. It is an instinct that displays hatred and which unfortunately works sometimes.

Does it involve the presence and the force of evil spirits?

It is quite certain that there is a sort of fluidic solidarity of evil. According to the law of attraction, evil thoughts obviously give rise to the presence of evil.

It must be understood and accepted that particularly aggressive and negative disembodied forces – evil spirits – do enter into harmony with entities that are equally as evil and negative.

What are the feelings that unite the actors of this practice?

This practise can be explained by a number of well known words: hatred, jealousy, pride, desire and domination.

In order to think, man must cross through the ambivalence of his moral code and tend towards either good or evil. With words he can be aggressive and insulting but by using the source of the word, the existential cause of all words pronounced, he has the gift of thought. This can destroy or create in one and the same movement.

Because the Earth is not very advanced, negative logic has the edge over positive logic with many of your thoughts transmitting evil, discordance, opposition and destruction.

The expression "return shock" is often used in relation to black magic. Is this true?

Most certainly. The world is based upon the laws of physics and one of these laws states that "all action creates a reaction".
Faced with these particularly base acts of thought, the best line of action would be positive thinking and indeed, love itself. A positive reaction of love will protect you from evil thoughts whilst at the same time sending back this positive thought to its sender. Thus, by natural equation, love becomes superior to hatred.

The astral journey

The existence of the astral journey or the leaving of the body which is present in almost all cultures comes from the desire to go beyond the limits of matter.

How does one leave one's body?

The natural way of leaving one's body can be experienced during a coma, fainting, anaesthetics, falls, traumas, accidents, illnesses, hypnosis, mediumship or Near Death Experiences.
When we dream, our conscience is no longer inside our physical body, it is on the other side.
Undertaken in a conscious manner, it means leaving the physical body and moving around with the perispirit. Techniques do exist to reach this passage, this journey. They are however, risky and we would advise against using them.
An artificially created "leaving of the body" does present a high risk of being "possessed". The spirit has estimated that about 50,000 cases of possession have been recorded after people have read books such as the one by Lobsang Rampa.
The invisible world is in permanent contact with the visible world and the latter naively believes that the afterlife is devoid of any evil.
To our mind, the afterlife should be approached seriously, with an awareness and a structure. I personally decry those who do the opposite and harshly criticise those who encourage young and often confused people to experiment, sometimes pushing them toward madness or even death.
Some teenagers have committed suicide or become murderers after playing with "ouija" boards. This is not a game, but it has been sold as such since 1996 and more than 25 million copies have been bought in Europe and the USA.

An increasing number of internet sites sell them at prices ranging from 17 to 120 euros including full instructions. Even the medallion of Allan Kardec can be found on sale at 24 euros (even though it looks nothing like him). The buyer is advised to place it on a table as it will make communication easier.
All of this is obviously scandalous business practice in which some people have much to gain but many others much to lose.

Does the fact that NDE (near death experiences) are increasingly common mean that the spirits wish to appeal to the human conscience?

The accounts by Raymond Moody[36] or Elizabeth Kubler Ross do not mean that the invisible world or the afterlife has chosen to alert humanity to the existence of life after death.

It is much more interesting and comforting to say that these experiences will become increasingly common because humanity is advancing and evolving. This means that the human spirit will remember the astral journey after clinical surgery, following a short anaesthetic or a short coma. Human beings are thus moving towards their spiritual and perispiritual nature. This also means that an increasing number of children and teenagers will spontaneously remember their previous lives.

The accounts recorded by Dr Moody reveal an overall evolution of humanity. If other doctors were to undertake similar research in Europe or elsewhere, they would observe the same phenomenon.

Alchemy

Was alchemy a reality and did Nicolas Flamel succeed in the transmutation of metal?

It was indeed a reality and the alchemists of the Middle Ages did manage to transform metals. They succeeded in transforming lead into gold. This truth must be told.

To obtain this transformation, alchemists needed the philosopher's stone...and they had it.

---

36 *Since Doctor Moody's book in 1977 many doctors around the world have conducted similar research and have obtained identical results. Nowadays several million people are said to have experienced this phenomenon. We therefore find many similarities and interesting consequences. There is one factor common to all those who have experienced it: life does not stop with death. Their journey has brought them this certainty thanks to both the feelings and the people they met. Beyond all the theories and hypotheses put forward by science, each and every one of these people now has an indelible memory deep inside that makes them look at life in a different manner.*

Do not seek it, you will not find it!!

The philosopher's stone does not exist as a simple material. Above all, it is about the strength of the spirit, of thought and the distribution of fluid on matter.

Using this fluidic source, gold can be obtained from lead in the same way as thermo-nuclear fusion is obtained.

Let us suppose a society of alchemists in which lead would become gold. If this was the case, gold would no longer be a noble and precious material because it would be abundant.

The most important truth for Nicolas Flamel is above all the transformation of man, the transformation of his mentality within evolution. We can pass from a raw material called lead to a noble material called gold.
In fact, the spirit that is simple and ignorant in its creation must strive to evolve through work and a labour of love, in order to become a pure spirit. Alchemy is above all a philosophy.

> *When the facts turn into a legend it is time to publish the legend.*
> John Ford

Levitation

How can levitation be explained?

Matter can not exist without the spirit. It is the result of a process of projection whose source is the spirit.

The genesis of matter is the history of the spirit and of its creative force. This is why the process of levitation on living or inert matter revolves around the ability of the spirit to modify the molecular structure of a body in order to make it lighter.
The disembodied spirit that moves or lifts an object exerts a psychokinetic force on matter.

Man can do the same if he exercises his spirit (a prisoner of matter) to concentrate on surrounding materials and little by little to command them.

It is very difficult to achieve levitation on Earth as it depends on the surroundings. However, it has become quite banal and almost logical on superior planets.

Do flying carpets exist?

Absolutely. This remains an oriental practise and is part of the phenomenon of levitation in space. The object itself is nothing magical.
However, it must be underlined that this phenomenon is very rare as it requires a very high degree of mental control.

Occult practices

To what extent do yogis manage to eliminate the pain, burns and physical effects that arise during their experiments?

This faculty does not belong to the term "yogi".
It is, in fact, the force of the spirit and the power of mind over matter concerning the physical body.
There is no manifestation of magic or of a super-natural force.
It is the result of a high level of meditation and of a strong belief. What happens is the result of a set of exercises designed to arrive at this end. This power of mind over matter is not geographical, nor is it eastern or western. It is something that you have in your nature. That is all.

Do lucky numbers exist?

Man has always thought that numbers are a form of magic. The discovery of numbers, of mathematics and arithmetic, mainly thanks to Pythagorus, a superior spirit, has been monopolised by a naive form of mystic human.

In fact, numbers themselves are of little importance. It is useful for the geometry of human beings but its use stops there in as much as it is only a means and not a spiritual goal.

What are Zombies?

Zombies actually exist. It is possible to reanimate a body in a vegetative manner and to use it for daily tasks.
This is practised in Africa and Central America. The spirit of the deceased person is taken out of the body which maintains its consistence and movement via the thoughts transmitted by those who command it. This practise is impossible in Europe as it requires an atmosphere that would be impossible to create on your continent. It also involves the consumption of certain drugs.

How long can a Zombie be used?

A Zombie[37] can be used for a maximum of 6 months and its use depends on the remote thoughts that guide it. Zombies looks like a moving corpse and as a rule are not seen by the general public. This surprising and frightening phenomenon is not morally acceptable.

What do you think of hibernation or induced hypothermia? Has this been performed on Walt Disney

Planet Earth exists in a context of heavy gravity and a strong condensation of matter which is the result of its gradual evolution. Planet Earth is far from being perfect. Trying to freeze people in order to bring them back to life in the future is pure fiction and can be very dangerous.

---

37 Doctor Yves St Gerard published the book « The Zombie Phenomenon » in 1992. In it he distinguishes two aspects of the phenomenon: one is drugs and the other is hypnosis that is used to make the person dependent.
Definition of the living dead: a ritual where a witch forces the soul of a person to go back into the dead body. The Voodoo tradition is said to use herbal preparations to do this.

In fact, the more refined perispirital matter undergoes a deterioration that is damaging for the spirit and often prevents the spirit itself from freeing itself into the afterlife.

Walt Disney was lucky. He was a spiritist and belonged to a group that soon realised the mistake that had been made. His body is still in the container but his spirit is free[38].

---

38 Cryogenisation: a term first used by the American professor of physics Robert Ettinger in 1964. He published these theses in his book « Is man immortal? »
Three years later James Bedford died of lung cancer at the age of 74 and was the first man to be placed in a DEWAR container full of liquid nitrogen. All we have to do is unfreeze him several hundred years into the future.
Nowadays cryogenisation is a real business and hundreds of people have now been placed in DEWAR containers.
Cryogenisation:
1. Nourish the brain with oxygen and nutritive elements
2. Rapidly bring the temperature of the body to 0°. During this time a « heart lung » machine continues to feed and circulate the blood.
3. Medicine is injected into the patient to prevent coagulation and the development of bacteria.
4. The body is put into storage.

ANCIENT CIVILISATIONS

Granite of the Celts that is mute in the mist, seeming to magnify the history of all those people.

The Druids

For how long did the druid practises go on? And where?

Druid practises began with the migration of Eastern populations towards Western Europe about 12,000 earth years ago.
Druid practises ended roughly 150 years after the passage of the Nazarene prophet. The practise went from the Isle of Man and Scotland to lower Egypt and mainly developed on the Atlantic side of Europe and within the Nile Valley.

Are there still druids with their powers alive today? Does Allan Kardec, who was formerly a druid, reveal himself to them?

Allan Kardec's answer:

Current Druid practises are of no value compared to what we practised thousands of years ago.
It is true that there are people on the Earth today who work in the druid tradition but they have too much of a taste for secrecy and mystery. I am totally opposed to this.
I will no longer be a Druid as I became a spiritist.
In the time of the Gauls, druidism was very important for the intellectual and spiritual advancement of man. Today, however, contact with the invisible must be less elitist and be open to everyone. This is why I do not reveal myself to present day druids.

What is the meaning of the menhirs or standing stones from the druids past?

Thanks to dowsing, the druids were able to discover the most sensitive spots on the land.
This discovery meant that the druid candidate could then undertake a particularly difficult task.

After determining the area and the spots where telluric forces crossed, the stone had then to be raised and planted in the ground using only the power of thought.

Hence, each stone that has been placed represents the labour of a student of the university of the druids

What was druidism exactly?

Above all, the druids taught how to penetrate infinity and the Universe in its immensity using the physical and existing elements available to man.
The druid formula was to discover the Father in everything that was visible and tangible, whether in rocks, in the oceans, the wind, the sky and the stars, in flames and the heat of a fire, the soft taste of spring water or the healing powers of plants.

Throughout their history and the progression of their knowledge, the druids always included the divine element in all of their research

Which sciences of the past did the druids learn?

Druid society was structured and organised according to the laws of the intrinsic knowledge of nature. This is why the druids studied the sciences related to nature: physics, maths, geometry, as well as what man has grossly named the paranormal (dowsing, alchemy, levitation, telepathic thought, psychokinesis and the sciences of the spirit). The study of tellurism was at the top of this pyramid of knowledge but today has been transformed or forgotten.

What means of navigation did the druids have?

Even if druids used to live apart from the rest of the population in villages, they had frequent contact with them as they were the wise advisors of the people. They used to teach the idea of a raft made of tree trunks. They also used to travel around thanks to large birds that have since disappeared.

These birds, called Kormarus, had a wing span of 10 metres and took people from island to island. They were a true friend to man and were in telepathic contact with the druids.
Prehistoric animals were not all starving monsters. Most of them lived in harmony with man.

Due to the absence of any form of technology, nature manifested itself telepathically between the animal and the human kingdoms.

When was Allan Kardec a druid?

His druid life goes back 10,000 years.

Can you give us the definition and the role of a mantra?

Embodied or disembodied, we all live in a world of vibrations. Our lives all came from vibration.
The vibration of love is a creative vibration and can be defined as the mantra "God". This is why tones are very important in the behaviour of souls, whatever their condition.

Mantras are a way to capture the force of the cosmos by rhythmically reciting a certain number of syllables that will have an effect on ethereal matter. Hence, someone reciting the mantra "Aum" or "Mahé" will find him/herself partially disembodied and able to practise levitation, clairvoyance or psychokinesis.

What were mantras used for?

Many different mantras were used depending on the subject. Some were used by all druids who wanted to levitate bodies and stones.
The peculiar tone or sonority of the mantra had the effect of transforming the molecular structure of matter which then gave rise to a short term anti-matter formula providing lightness and energy through the inversion given to the cycle of neutrons and protons.

What is the difference between the tumulus and the dolmen?

A tumulus is a Celtic cemetery. A dolmen is a tomb or a burial monument where only druids and their families were buried.
The tumulus was part of a particular rite as the druids gathered there at every summer solstice to recite a mantra that was aimed at liberating souls.

Were the great megaliths levitated by one or several druids?

The megalith of Locmariaquer was levitated by 300 druids at once. This was via the power of thought based around the mantra.

The great menhir aged 10,000 years was pulled from the base of Mount Snowdon in Wales, levitated into space then transported and planted in Locmariaquer.
This menhir was the symbol of the union between the Bretons and the Welsh as well as having the strongest telluric energy charge in the whole of Wales
Despite partial destruction by an earthquake, some of the menhir measuring 2.50 metres still exists in the ground.

Everyone came to this place to recover strength and health. Many also entered into contact with the invisible world.

How and why did Druid society disappear?

Throughout the country we had to fight to maintain our values. On several occasion we had to confront the German and Viking invaders.
Many druids died in battle. The barbaric invaders pushed the menhirs over and turned them into torture tables on which they set fire to our leaders.

We defended ourselves poorly as druids were non-violent. Many of us died, taken by surprise as we did not believe that men could attack each other.

The Romans finished off the work of the barbarians and the new religion buried us completely by teaching lies about our ideals.

Irwin de Kermario, Druid.

Civilisations follow on from each other. They are born then die, letting others take their place. But they never disappear completely.

Philippe Beaussant

Atlantis

Is there a connection between Atlantis and the Bermuda Triangle?

The people of Atlantis were present in various parts of the Earth as they originally came from another planet.

The people of Atlantis were present in a place called "Bermuda" and it is here that they left a trace of their magnetic force.

Do the reported disappearances have anything to do with this magnetic force?

Bermuda leads to the world of Atlantis. Some people who fly over Bermuda or who go there by boat find themselves on another planet and meet those who lived there thousands of years ago. These people are much more advanced than you.

Did the people of Atlantis have any contact with the inhabitants of the Earth?

Yes they did. They had physical contact with them and have left traces of this in the flesh as they printed a part of their being onto your genetics.

The vocal chord, linked to certain foreign languages is of Atlantis origin.

How do things or people disappear in the Bermuda Triangle?

There are different points on the planet where man can go to reach other spheres, if this is included in his mission.
How can someone in flesh and blood be projected into your three-dimensional space so as to reach another sphere?

In fact, it is not, strictly speaking a projection but more like magnetic knots with suction which will capture the body of a spirit.

I insist on the word *body* as the psychological nature of the person who experiences this must be emphasised. The person going there decided long ago, that is to say before reincarnation.

Enigmas

Did the continent Mu really exist?

The Pacific continent of Mu really existed. However, it was not the home of a particularly advanced society. This continent, like the rest of your globe, was subjected to the effects of an enormous earthquake and it subsided. The inhabitants of Mu all drowned. Overall they were a rather primitive people, part of the human race.

What is the meaning of the signs found next to the drawings on the walls of the caves at Lascaux?

The idea of artistically representing what has been seen is connected to the ontology of your earthly nature. This is why prehistoric man always painted what he experienced in his primitive world on planet Earth. But there was already extra-terrestrial life present on this planet. Many space vessels landed on your planet and none of them was a threat to man.

The signs you speak of are the drawings or writings from another planet, observed by prehistoric man and drawn on the walls of these caves. In this case it was at Lascaux but there are others all over the Earth.

What happened in Jericho?

Centuries ago, the solidly built walls of the town collapsed due to particularly high sound vibrations emitted by musical instruments.
There was no spiritual or paranormal phenomenon in this case, simply a fundamental demonstration of the laws of physics. The walls of Jericho[39] crumbled due to the powerful sounds emitted and whose origins were the wishes of man.

---

39 *The trumpets of Jericho: according to the book of Joshua, the walls of the fortress town collapsed at the sound of the trumpets of Osiah, son of Noun. The Hebrews then took over the town*

Can the voice produce the same effects?

Destruction can happen due to a sound vibration. This vibration can be emitted by an instrument or simply by the human vocal chords. When this voice represents a group of people that create such a strong physical wave with a very high-pitched sound, any material form that gets in its way can be destroyed in a matter of minutes.

Certain people have spoken of the "killer scream" that can be heard in certain Asian and African civilisations. This exists. It is nothing to do with knowledge but simply the result of observations made down the ages.

Stonehenge[40]

My name is Tixeve. Three thousand years ago I belonged to the planet Mektra. This planet was scientifically and technically advanced as we were able to travel through inter-galactic space.

We arrived on the Earth by chance as we needed to land for a while. We encountered several human beings who were surprised and frightened to see us.
They constantly pointed to the sun and bowed down before us as they believed we had come from the sun.
We decided to demonstrate the power of the mind and the spirit by erecting this site at Stonehenge. It is true that the stone comes from west Wales and was transported by the power of thought, by the combined forces of the school of the druids and the extra-terrestrial world.

---

40 The megaliths that form a circle on the site of Stonehenge remain a mystery of neolithic architecture. Archaeologists have all put forward ideas that would explain how these enormous stone blocks were transported and erected.
Stonehenge is thought to have been built over a long period – between 2750 and 1900 B.C. The granite that the blocks are made of can only be found in Wales.
In the opinion of many scientists, the complex architecture of the site suggests an astronomic observatory. How were these enormous blocks of stone brought from Mount Prescelly to Salisbury plain?
The archaeological hypothesis is the following: the 600km were covered both overland and by sea. The blocks were taken to the coast by rolling them on tree trunks, pulled by rope by at least 100 men. They were then put on rafts and floated down to the Bristol Channel where they were pulled up the River Avon to dry land.

These stones were erected in a circle. They still radiate a strong energy force that is good for the health and the spirits. These stones were to be the trace and the proof of our passage on the Earth, the souvenir of our encounter with the human race on planet Earth.

Unfortunately, humans interpreted the construction wrongly. As they believed that we had come from the sun, they decided to make this place sacred and dedicate it to this star.

Where did the statues on Easter island[41] come from?

Art exists all across the Universe. In former times on planet Earth, there were many meetings with civilisations from outer space which were rich on many levels.

Today, the stones are upright and the sharp faces gaze out to the distant horizons of the island.

---

41 Easter Island: a small ,triangular shaped island of 165km² with a volcano at each end. This small land mass, lost in the eastern Pacific Ocean, is lined with a large number of statues all facing the sun, as well as drawings and artistic objects.

The island was discovered on April 5th 1722 by the Dutch navigator Jacob Roggenveen. It was the Christian day of Easter. Hence the name of the island. The 500 "moai" statues are between 3 and 10 metres tall and weigh up to 80 tons. They were cut out of volcanic rock, the oldest dating back to the 10th century.

According to the Pascuans, the present day inhabitants of the island, these statues represented powerful and initiated ancestors with strong mental powers ("mana"). This could refer to the influence of highly evolved extra-terrestrial life that came to initiate the island's inhabitants in the past. The "moai" could thus be a representation of these visitors. But this is only a supposition.

If there is a message it is not esoteric nor is it cabalistic. It is rather a message of universal brotherhood. It is the souvenir of another time when other worlds could reach the Earth without risk.

Another visit by the inhabitants from another planet would certainly not be considered as a visit from the gods. Even if ignorance has given way to thought and logic, we can not say that fear has given way to a sense of welcome, hospitality and brotherhood. Fear has turned into defence and defence has turned into aggression.

Like the pyramids of Egypt and the stones of Stonehenge, Easter Island is existing proof of what took place in times gone by.

All thought leaves a trace. All life leaves its mark. Just as the memory of certain people is celebrated on Earth, we welcome the day that we can celebrate the passage of our brothers in space on the Earth.

These stones have been erected according to the plans and indications of extra-terrestrial beings that came to Earth for a very short time to show the primitive humans who lived there at the time how to build and erect these shapes.
Technically speaking, the shape is of a spiritual nature. The stones were erected by the mantra and by this mantra alone.

How did the inhabitants of the island react?

In the eyes of the inhabitants, the extra-terrestrials were powerful, God-like figures that had come down from the heavens. Fear and surprise were the only feelings that these primitive people had. To their mind, beings that had come down from the heavens could only be gods that had to be worshiped and adored.

PHILOSOPHY

Philosophy is nothing more than the love of wisdom

Cicero

Land of the future

The key to developing the planet lies in your hearts, your consciences and your acts. A planet where there is no more war, where no children die of hunger, where poverty will disappear along with the scorn of sectarian fools who believe that their money will buy them a place in heaven.
All there should be is the face of a mother looking at her child in the clear morning of a new day.
The face of a man gazing at stars that will no longer be an inaccessible secret, the face of a celestial old person calmly waiting for death to descend on him. An Earth where everyone can gaze upon the spirit as they wish, where you and the afterlife, reunited in one and the same flash of love and generosity, will be reflected in the eyes of the creator.

When does the happy new day begin? Whenever you like!!!

Philosophising means learning to die.

Cicero.

PHILOSOPHY

What is the difference between spiritism and spirituality?

Spirituality often means finding oneself in God or satisfying personal needs through prayer. Spiritism, on the other hand, involves the presence of the spirit in the world and man amongst his brothers. It is not the salvation of the soul but an invitation to partake in the happiness of humanity.

Is asceticism necessary for evolution to take place in life?

On this planet, certain people have more and more while others have less and less, remaining in ignorance and poverty. Asceticism will never really be a solution to this terrible contradiction. Inside the physical body there is a spirit that must grow into an adult. The body and the spirit have one function only; to act and to act all the time. A meditating silence may be useful to do this but it is not action. It may just be an introduction to action but in these times of uncertainty, one must act.

Is yoga good for man and can it help to open people spiritually?

Yoga is certainly beneficial for the body at first. It can place the individual in a mentally receptive condition regarding spirituality. The oriental origins and the sometimes unfortunate American version of yoga bring me to the conclusion that the spiritual openness in which many different forms of thinking are all mixed together does not necessarily imply an opening towards spiritism.
Having said that, yoga is certainly beneficial for the people who wish to practise it. For the moment, however, westerners are not very good at assimilating this wish. The only risk here is that the technique of yoga may lead certain people to let go of the physical world around them.

What is the key to evolution and development?

Thought and feeling are the two major forces behind evolution and development. Man should not believe in sudden grace. Nor should he believe in perfection without understanding that labour and love are required to attain perfection. Thought and feeling must be the subject of slow but sure progress.

Are there any faster paths to advancement?

The truth of a Father is the absolute truth and supposes no short cuts. Indeed, it is dangerous to witness the development of certain theories in your present day society that suggest to the young and innocent generation that perfection can be attained without knowledge or effort, via an individual meditation that can often lead to turmoil and even suicide.

What do you think of mystical faith?

The problem with the history of spirituality is the blindness involved, i.e. the immediate desire to be with God whilst forgetting man. It is indeed enviable and easy to get wrapped up in a mystical faith in order to reach the Eternal Father whilst at the same time believing that we will live better at a later date in some shape or form. The fact that thousands of children die of hunger every day is perhaps one of God's conditions, a karmic law.
You have been incarnated. This is your condition. It does not allow for ecstasy, it requires action.

India and the Orient are often given as spiritual models. What do you think of this?

A priori, there are no spiritual models on the Earth. There is a movement towards the spirit which includes the heart and the mind and which must find a way to go beyond religiousness. A spirituality exists which takes on the form of the coming of man on the Earth.

India and the Orient have often tried to progress too quickly. Advancement can only take place inside a single being. These two worlds or countries have been able to capture the vibrations of the spirit but have forgotten their brothers. They have not been capable of using the energy from these vibrations in a positive manner.

What is the state of materialism?

Materialism is dying, however hard it tries to survive. It has betrayed the younger generation. It has stifled artists and misled medicine. It has deprived man of his true needs and has prolonged its existence by the use of force. No longer will it vanquish man.

Can you give a definition of true spirituality?

True spirituality means opening up, it means seeing and considering others, it means paying attention to the real world. It is the path to justice and sharing, the path of labour and will power.

Could you define happiness?

Justice, truth and freedom are three ingredients that go together to form happiness. It is no good imagining, projecting or supposing that happiness can exist without these three ingredients. They are the essential conditions for the birth, growth and transmission of happiness on the Earth.

Does perfect happiness exist?

Perfect happiness goes hand in hand with perfection.

RELIGION

It is always the right time to bring in the religion of love

Louis Aragon

Spiritism, the third revelation of God, is not a new religion

Let us first define the meaning of the word **revelation**. Reveal, from the Latin word *revelare,* whose root is *velum* -veil- literally means to **come out from under one's veil.** In a figurative sense it means to discover or talk about something secret or unknown.

Taken in this way, all the sciences that teach about the mysteries of nature are revelations.

The essential character of all revelations is the truth. Revealing a secret means making a fact known. If it is distorted it is no longer a fact and therefore is not a revelation.

Where would humanity be without the revelations of the geniuses that appear from time to time? Who are these men of genius? Where do they come from?

Many people believe that they brought inborn abilities with them when they were born.

So where did all their knowledge come from? How did it arise?

Will the materialists say that they were endowed with more and better grey matter than the rest?
Will the spiritualists say that God gave them a soul that had better favour than the rest of mankind?

The only rational explanation to this lies in the pre-existence of the soul and in the plurality of lives.

Men of genius have a longer past with regard to their reincarnation. Their knowledge is the fruit of labour in former lives and not the result of a privilege.

All peoples have had their men of genius who came at various moments in time bringing knowledge, a skill, a certainty and an impulse.

This is the role of a genius. They come to teach men the truth about certain things. These spirits are missionaries or messiahs.

If God makes revelations to demonstrate scientific truth, he could also use revelations for moral truths that are essential for man to advance.
This is true of philosophers whose ideas have been valid for centuries.

In a religious sense, we speak of a revelation for spiritual things and this knowledge is given to man by God or by his messengers.
A revelation is always made to special people that have been called prophets or messiahs - meaning spokesmen or missionaries.

All religions have had their share of enlighteners that were suited to the period and milieu in which they were living. Despite the errors of their doctrines due to man's misinterpretations or to the way in which they were harnessed, these prophets moved spirits and sowed the seeds of progress.

The day will come when all beliefs, however different they are, will come together as one. For this to happen, reason must win out over prejudice.

Religions are built on truths but they have all become instruments of domination because of the errors and the pride of man.

The words of truth that Moses, Mahomet, Buddha or Jesus received were sent via different means:

by pure and simple inspiration
by the word
by seeing the teaching spirits
by dreams etc

It is thus correct to say that most enlighteners have been inspired, (which is not to say that all mediums are enlighteners, far from it and they are even less of a direct messenger from Heaven).

Moses and Jesus are two great enlighteners who changed the face of the western world and this itself is proof of their divine mission. A purely human action would not have had the same power behind it.

Moses revealed to man the existence of a single God. Jesus added to this the revelation about the existence of a future life.
Spiritism adds the existence of an invisible world to the rather vague notion of a future life. It is thus quite right that spiritism should be considered as the third of the great revelations."

Allan Kardec

Religions should solemnly state that any warfare waged in their name constitutes true blasphemy.

Albert Jacques

RELIGION

Why do religions exist?

The phenomenon of religion comes in answer to the presence of God and to the call of God, Father of the infinite Universe and father of all life here and throughout the Universe.

The call of the divine is printed in your physical cells and in your carnal nature because you are the children of God.

How did religions begin?

Religions grew out of the fear of death. The anguish in religion goes back to the fundamental question of man. Religions also have their origin in the natural environment.

Think about primitive man in his cave. Think of the storms, the moon, the earthquakes and all the natural cataclysms that primitive man could not rationally or scientifically understand. This gave rise to a belief in divinity and religion naturally followed.

Is man more or less aware of his spiritual future?

The answer to this lies in the spiritual element that is in each and every one of us. Since man arrived on the Earth, he has had the feeling that a spiritual future exists. Even prehistoric man seemed to have felt this, given the cult he created around death.
The spiritual nature of man which is the result of divine thought and love is able to remember the meaning of this life in the light of its eternity. There is no period in human history that does not, at some point, refer to the metaphysical thought of the spirit that is embodied in matter.

Did this metaphysical thought give rise to the first religions?

The spirits multiplied, gradually occupying the lands. They developed and organised themselves into races depending on the climate, finally becoming nations.

Metaphysical turmoil never went away. Man constantly wondered about death for thousands of years. So, beliefs came into existence as an initial answer to this metaphysical turmoil. Superstitions arose, along with representations of anguish and turmoil. At that time man needed the support of an image, of a belief. He needed more than just a philosophy, he needed myths and religion.
This need gave rise to the first beliefs based on the elements of the Universe, on storms, fire and water. He needed to invent a supreme power for each of these elements, a God for everything.

Antiquity is a perfect example of this with the appearance of polytheist religions. They were appropriate for the period as they provided answers to the great questions of the time.

Did the great thinkers of Antiquity alter these beliefs?

Throughout his evolution, man has always asked himself another question that was nothing to do with the future or the anguish of mortals. It arose from the anguish of daily life, of defending life itself.
This is when the first thinkers and philosophers appeared. These embodied spirits arrived on the Earth to guide their human brothers, to reflect on their everyday life and to organise their world.
Science began to truly appear within the effervescence of religions.
In this area, the Greeks contributed enormously to human thought and knowledge. They made discoveries concerning the perpetual movement of life within the perpetual movement of matter and about the perpetual movement of the divine spirit within the physical movement of the spheres in the Universe.
It was at this time that the idea of the unity of matter inherent in universal plasma began to gradually appear.

The unity of this matter was meant to provide man with a further element to help discover another unit; the creator of matter, the Father of the Universe, the single God.

Will religions continue to exist?

There is no future in the old and disguised forms of divinity. The future must not be shrouded
in lies, domination and torture.
The future of life is to be found in progress and the phenomenon of religion will make way for the eternal truth of the all powerful Father.

What of the secrets of Fatima?

Religious secrets have often been invented to place man in a state of doubt or even fear. There are no secrets of Fatima. There are no secrets for God or for his prophets. This modern legend will be replaced by others in the future because the time is near when certain religions will come to an end. But to continue existing they will highlight certain mysteries to keep man in a state of fear.

Do religions exist on other planets?

There are other planets similar to the Earth in the infinity of the Universe and forms of religions exist on them. They are connected to history, to the civilisations on these planets, with their climate and geography. Religion is not therefore something that is peculiar to the planet Earth.

Is spiritism compatible with all forms of religion?

As has been said, spiritism is not for those who have faith and for whom this faith is sufficient.
Consequently, let those who come toward us be sufficiently honest to admit that there is something missing within them.

Is there any connection between spiritism and Catholicism?

Our history and that of Catholicism has nothing particular in common. The spiritist remains particularly Christian in his beliefs but not towards a superior God that he should fear. The spiritist remains Christian in his deep faith in man. It is in this direction that you should turn.

What is Christianity?

Christianity means fraternity in the knowledge that a Father exists for everyone.

> *Prayer is not about asking.*
> *It is an inspiration of the soul.*
>
> Mahatma Gandhi

What is prayer?

Prayer is not an expectation but an act of a responsible person who gives love.

Prayer is not a recital but a verb which carries its function to those who are in need of it.

Prayer does not mean begging God in apparent pain with a contorted face.

Prayer means joy and happiness, an inherent function of the spirit, a telepathy of the soul.

What do you think of churches?

Catholics, Protestants, orthodox, Brahman, Hindous, Muslims, Anglicans, Quakers and many others will all arrive with a flag in their hand and arms at the ready. Here are the Casts, the derision, the religions and the churches. A church does not mean a structure, it means a gathering.

Many societies and buildings have been built in order to define the Father, to enclose God. God is the property of no-one, nor is he a doctrine.

> *Jesus announced the coming of the kingdom but it was the church that came instead.*
>
> Alfred Loisy

Why did the Church come into being?

At the outset, the church was designed to carry the Christian message through time but time became confused with materiality, which is different. The law of reincarnation was indeed banned from the Church because of this basic confusion. This explains the attitude of the church to reincarnation. The difference between the church and spiritism is that hell is a dogma whereas reincarnation is a natural law.

What should the role of the church be?

The church should condemn crime, war and the meaningless shedding of blood. It should also condemn poverty and injustice.

What do you think of the moral and social codes within the Catholic church?

The Catholic church forbids divorce, abortion, contraception, homosexuality, test tube babies, surrogate mothers and sex before marriage[42].

The church is making a serious mistake by imposing such a moral code on people. It is creating yet another gap between reality and inappropriate concepts. Moral codes do not belong to the history of the church but to the history of man.

---

42 *The marriage of priests, canons, and monks was forbidden by the Coucil of Latran II in 1139. According to this council, it was forbidden to listen to mass given by married priests or with concubines. These unions were declared nul and void by the Church and those who had taken such vows were given penitence.*

In the name of a faith, is it possible to forbid a human being to live a physical life in sexual harmony?

This is an outdated, ridiculous principle adopted by the fathers of the church which totally goes against Evangelical principles. He who refuses his body refuses his spirit. He does not love the Father, he wishes to be his equal and this is a sin of pride

What is the difference between Catholicism and Christianity?

Christianity as defined by Jesus defends the principles of freedom whereas Catholicism is based on obedience.

Is there a future for the Christian church?

The future belongs neither to institutions nor to buildings made of stone. The future belongs to creative ideas and to love. Churches have already had their lifetime. They are empty and sad.
Churches continue to repeat the eternal litany that was heard in the temple of Jerusalem in the mouths of doddering old men who recited the words of the Torah without even knowing what it meant. Old men follow on from old men……..and Churches are overcome by their pride.
It will still take several decades but the awareness of man has been set in motion. The spirit will emerge victorious and the end of the church is in sight

Can mass or religious ceremonies have any influence on the afterlife?

Any human gathering creates a fluid and as such will affect the spirits. Did you know that ceremonies for the dead pronounced in a sad or fearful way make the turmoil and the sadness of the deceased longer and harder to bear?

By draping the deceased in black, by chanting sinister funeral laments you prolong the suffering of those who have departed, maintaining them in a state of turmoil.

If the gathering is for prayer or for hope then you will set your spirits free on the other side. You will encourage them to discover their freedom.

So, any gathering depends on who is taking part in it and whether they are religious or not.

Can an atheist advance in life without God?

He who cares about man will find his maker. He who cares about humanity will find Divinity in humanity. And he who cares about his fellow man will find his Father.

Does Heaven exist?

It is much easier to believe in heaven and the forgiveness of God than in the happiness that is earned through work and effort. There is no getting away from this is the afterlife as we are constantly subjected to the truth.

What does it mean to be a Christian?

Many people say "I am a Christian". They think they are following the word of Jesus of Nazareth, not in his acts but in his rites.
Being a Christian means loving your fellow man. So there is no need for temples or approximate interpretations. Nature in itself is a temple.

Should we adore God?

Being a Christian means living according to the verb "to love". Loving does not mean adoring. He who adores Jesus or His Father is not a Christian.

What do you think of the way in which the manifestation of Mary of Nazareth has been interpreted?

It is said that the spectre of this woman appears here and there, more often when things are going badly or to warn that they will get even worse.
Mary is not the spectre of bad omens. She is not a bringer of doubt or fear. Mother amongst mothers, spirit amongst spirits, she sometimes manifests herself to man with no religious formula attached, with no connotation of the immaculate conception, but simply that of a spirit that would like everyone to find peace and happiness.

> *In truth I say to you. No man who is born again will not see the kingdom of God.*
>
> Jesus

Why has the Church fought the idea of reincarnation that was taught by Jesus?

Reincarnation was accepted until the 6th century A.D. It was abolished by the council of Constantinople in 537 A.D.
This happened because there is a contradiction in the writings.
Accepting the law of reincarnation means accepting the law of evolution. This is not compatible with an eternity of suffering in hell. Hence, following this decision made by human beings, a fundamental truth was permanently erased from religious teaching.

Is spiritism compatible with attending mass and with the Holy Sacraments?

Spiritism remains a science because of the various phenomena that go with it, especially that of mediumship which is necessary to transmit the messages we wish to send to you. It is also a philosophy in the sense that the messages will define a state of eternity. This is called the state of evolution and is subject to a constant metamorphosis of human beings through successive life experiences.

This is the only claim that spiritism can make. It fights against no-one and is not incompatible with anything or anyone. It is a fact that certain political or religious groups attempt to go against philosophical and scientific spiritism. This is why the spiritist movement needs to be coherent with regard to what it states so that it is clear and precise regarding the main currents of religious thinking in the world.

Is spiritism compatible with mass and the Church?
In fact this question is not relevant. It would be more appropriate to ask if religions and churches are compatible with evolution.

No human being is condemned. But there is a state of grace either. Your freedom and responsibility as men lie in the love of God. God does not love his sons and daughters who pray to him on their knees. He prefers them to be standing.

Spiritism will help you find faith and belief with no dogma or principles. It would be better if only one religion existed on Earth so that all the existing religions could melt into one single religion of love.

Is spiritism part of the great plan of God?

The power of eternal life is present on all planets throughout the endless Universe. The Father constantly creates. He creates spirits, injecting brutal and ignorant consciousness which is incarnated in the alluvium of matter and in the weight of this uniform magma. In its initial torpor, the spirit gently and slowly designs its future conscience in the world.
God knows that the created spirit needs light. God is aware that the created spirit needs to remember where it came from, but it is too weak, too ignorant and too unaware to be able to remember. So, God sends you signs via spirits that have been created before you.

God called upon Moses who showed people the way, showed ideas and steps to climb and called upon man.

God called upon Jesus who showed the way, showed ideas and morality. He called upon justice and celebrated sharing, .inviting you to love.

Whilst others endlessly take turns with each other on the path of reincarnation.

Spirits of science, of philosophy, from all the art forms come, enter into the flesh, speak, struggle and write. Sometimes they are followed and understood.

But man persists in the error of his ways. Man makes no progress on the other side. Thousands of spirits get together and reflect upon the passing centuries, upon the weaknesses, the abnegation, the injustice and treachery.

Something more than a man was needed. So the druids of the past called with all their strength upon Allan Kardec who heard, listened and accepted.

And as the chosen one he arrived in France during the last century. He was not alone. He was accompanied by others to complete his mission that was to reveal what resurrection means.

After Moses and Jesus, God gave man this wonderful opportunity to love beyond the flesh. He thus established the link between the Earth and the afterlife. For the moment, man has taken little advantage of this link and the first spiritists were covered in ridicule because they attempted to spread the idea.

The Creed.

I believe in God.
I believe in Jesus of Nazareth his prophet and representative.
I believe in the universal communion of both good and bad spirits.
I believe in the union of men to build temples of love and reason.
I believe in the apparitions of the deceased.
I believe that we all come from the Father with the sole aim of returning to Him.
I believe in paying for our sins through work and thought
I believe in eternal and natural life through the metamorphosis of my open and sincere heart.
I believe this because I know it and do not wish to impose it. And I say:
Love one another in the certainty that God makes no distinction for his children.

Father Lenhard

Can it be said that Moses or Jesus were mediums?

Moses was a great medium and this is why he was put in contact with superior spirits that dictated the initial, essential and natural commandments to him. Moses was not alone. He was a guide to an entire nation and people gathered enthusiastically behind this man down the paths of truth through joy, pain and suffering.
But despite the dissention that soon arose, Moses continued his work as a guide and medium in the face of many trials and the tribulations, spreading the word.

Jesus was later sent on a mission to the Earth to speak, preach and guide others. His acts were incorrectly named as miracles. He was both a superior spirit and a great medium.

Yes, Mahommet was a medium. Buddha was a medium. Moses was a medium as well as Jesus Christ and many others.

Will there be other prophets to complete the revelation?

It will not be one, single man that can save this planet but a collection of strong will, efforts and courage expressed by an increasing number of people who seek peace and happiness on the Earth.
These people already exist........some have come and gone such as Mahatma Gandhi, Martin Luther King, John Fitzgerald Kennedy, Anouar El-Sadate and many others. All these people came to complete a mission.

The true wealth of a man on this Earth is measured by the good that he does around him

Mahomet

Mahomet

History (570-632: 62 years)

Mahomet was born in Mecca in the province of Hedjaz.

His father, Abdallah, died before he was born and his mother, Amina, died when he was still a young child.
Tradition tells of the extraordinary signs that accompanied the conception and the birth of the prophet. His name was apparently given to him following one of his grandfather's dreams.

Mahomet was employed by a rich merchant woman called Khadija to manage her businesses. She was very impressed by Mahomet's honesty and integrity and asked him of he wished to marry her. Mahomet was then 25 years of age.

Following the death of Khadija, Mahomet had several wives, the most famous of whom was the young Aicha.

Mahomet was 40 when he experienced his first revelation. This was during a solitary retreat in a cave where he had a vision of the "Archangel Gabriel". A long period followed between this revelation and those that were to follow, up until the death of the prophet.

After the death of Mahomet the revelations were all brought together to form the Koran but were not in chronological order. So, they were organised into chapters that were thought to correspond to the different periods in his life.

We know that the first short, clear revelations warned men that they would be judged by God for their acts. Gradually the authority of Mahomet exerted an increasing influence over the Muslim community that he had founded in Medina. The revelations became longer and dealt with solutions to the everyday problems that the prophet and his disciples came up against.

The revelations made by God (Allah) to Mahomet during years of prophesy at Mecca and Medina are all in the Koran.

These revelations are said to have been learned by heart or noted down on various supports: palm leaves or animal skins. The contents are basically a set of ethical recommendations or commandments, rules concerning religious life, culture, subjects such as marriage, divorce and inheritance.
His basic message is that there is only one God, creator of all things. God has never ceased to call upon humanity via the voice of the prophets that he placed upon the Earth. But these prophets have always been rejected.
The major themes of the Koran lie in the continuity of the sacred Jewish and Christian texts but are developed in a different way.

The posthumous message of Mahomet (15/01/1986)

My message has served the cause of death more than peace. Still today on Earth, it has become an excuse for crime, war and torture, be it in Damas, Cairo or Beirut. I see nothing but hatred, jealousy and treachery. No-one has really tried to spread my message.

I was sent from High Above to light the way for primitive and uneducated people. Mesopotamia is being crucified in modern day Iran. The traitors have distorted my message to justify their crimes. The supreme forces opened the way for me and others like me but none of us can feel happy today, no matter where we were sent.

Like many other prophets, I am in pain on the other side, in the afterlife, when I see and hear people killing and committing crime in my name.
Everything in the initial message has been forgotten, transformed or disguised. I came on Earth to give men an example, an ideal to follow and I had the impression they had understood my words.
But what has become of this message?
Fanaticism has taken hold of my wishes and thoughts. The name of Allah has struck at the very door of the Western world to instil fear into the hearts of people and to destroy lives by lying in my very name.

I fear the growth of Muslim fundamentalism. Islam has been betrayed and its message has been turned into a war-cry. My message was one of Love but has been turned into a message of war. I spoke of food for all, of respect for one another, of social balance, of a mixing of ethnic groups and peace. My message said: "woman, you have your just place because you hear, you listen, you console and you open your loving arms to the new born child. You are not the shadow of man, you are his equal."

I said this. They did not transcribe it. They have dared to tell lies.

Women of Islam, you do not need to hide behind your senseless veils. Your proud faces may shine forth in the sun.

The turbans of the inquisitors worry my disembodied conscience. Whips are being used again, ignorance is looked up to.

Islam, recover your soul and discover your God. These ghostly old men are destroying the hopes of your people.

Buddha

A short history

Buddhism has its origins in the life of a man called Siddhartha Gautama.
He lived about 500 B.C. in the Sakyas family in the north east of India, not far from present day Nepal.
His mother died shortly after he was born and so he was brought up by his aunt. His father had splendid palaces built so that Siddartha would not be subjected to any form of suffering. This wonderful life meant that he was very far from the reality of the outside world.

One day he managed to get out in the company of one of his servants. This was the day he was to meet several people who were to change his life. The first was with an old man. Siddartha had never been confronted with old age. He then met a man who was ill and in great pain. Siddartha had never encountered sickness. He then saw a dead body that was being transported to the funeral pyre. Each time he asked his servant whether he would experience these things himself one day. "Yes" replied the servant "sickness, old age and death are part of the lives of all human beings".
Siddartha learned all these things in the same day.

On the way back to the palace they came across a smiling ascetic. Siddartha was fascinated by the peaceful look on his face. How could a human being appear so happy in the face of all this misery and suffering? He was filled with a desire to follow in the footsteps of this man and to overcome the suffering he had witnessed.

Upon returning to the palace he told his father about all he had seen. His father was furious and tried everything to dissuade Siddartha from leaving. But all was in vain as he took no notice of his father's speeches and left to live in the forest. He swapped his expensive clothes for those of a beggar and joined a group of ascetic yogis. He was 29 years of age.

For five long years he lived with them in very poor conditions, often coming close to death.
As he had not found an answer to suffering he took up a meditation posture under a tree in the town of Bodh Gaya in India He swore he would not move until he had found the solution to suffering.

His quest lasted 49 days. On the 49th day the former prince had an inspiration……an awakening. From this moment on he became known as Buddha, meaning "the inspired one" in Sanskrit.
He gave his first teaching to the yogis (four noble truths) and then spent the rest of his life teaching people how to eliminate suffering.

The Four Noble Truths

1). Buddha teaches that suffering is universal. Everyone will experience birth, old age, illness and death. Buddha is not saying that life is only made up of suffering but rather that it is full of the potential for suffering.

2). People must try to find why suffering exists. The cause lies in our desires, in our love of our "self".
What does this mean?
Our desires increase as we gradually satisfy them. As we can not satisfy all our desires, we feel suffering. Satisfying a desire brings only a short lived pleasure, a temporary joy.

3). When we are aware of the problem (suffering) and its cause (desires, self-love) we can then seek a way to eliminate the cause. Buddha explains that we need to get rid of desire and self-love.

4). This ultimate truth is a path with eight branches. It shows how a person should discipline him/herself (morally) and how he/she can do away with desire and self-love.

The posthumous testimony of Buddha (1986)

I believe that what I became after several centuries is the fruit of real experience inside the cycle of palingenesis.
I was formerly the prince and the master. I had many slaves. I tasted the delights of the flesh and materialism, of power over others and the wonder of diamonds. I thought I was great but I was small. I thought I was strong yet I was weak. My knowledge was limited to what my body could see and touch.

One night I had a dream and I saw the people of my town, the people of my country. What I saw was horrible and unbearable: children were screaming and dying of hunger, their mothers had no milk left to feed them. Men were crouched under the weight of great carts and were whipped to make them go faster, sowing rice like robots. This nightmare was too much to bear.

Another night I suddenly awoke after a dream that told me "Go, leave this imaginary power, these imaginary riches. Go and call upon the forces of good in the cosmos. You must no longer support all this injustice around you".

The message was powerful. It came from my guide. I decided to answer the call of this dream which in fact was not a dream at all.
It was then that everything changed in my mind. And I left the artificial world to enter the real one.

What has been said, written, thought, supposed or invented by people, everything that those castes of the Eastern world have claimed in my name now that I am dead has caused me great sorrow.

Each man should indeed be able to distinguish true good from artificial good. But should he lose all dignity, should he become even more vile and forget his human envelope?
Should he continue to be a slave and become even more of a slave in my name?

They have betrayed me. They invented me and embellished me with images. I am not the prophet of renunciation. I am the prophet of true awareness and still today I continue to assert that people should abandon what is futile in favour of what is useful so as to serve the well-being of everyone. This concerns all people because man can not find happiness alone.

It is for this reason that I say: "People of India, wake from your torpor and see me as I beckon you. Seek simplicity of the soul in a basic and healthy life that is good for the body and the spirits around you.

People of India, hear me, listen to me: do not break your backs. I am here to call for justice. Riches and status symbols must disappear in favour of the development of the heart and spirit.
I pray with you for peace on the Earth and together we will wish for the end of appearances and the beginning of reality."

A prophet is someone who remembers the future.

Frederic Rossif

MOSES

A short history (XIIIth century B.C.)

Moses was reportedly born at Goshen in ancient Egypt. At the time of his birth the Hebrews who lived in Egypt were in slavery to the Pharaohs.
Shortly before Moses was born, the Pharaoh ordered that all baby boys born to the Hebrews should be put to death. In order to save her son from this massacre, Moses mother placed him in a wicker basket and let him drift down the waters of the river Nile. The baby was found by Pharaoh's daughter who raised him as her own child.

Later, when he had grown into a man aware of his origins, he visited one of the worksites where Hebrews were at work and killed an Egyptian who was persecuting one of them. Moses then left Egypt for the region of Madian. Upon his return he proclaimed that he was a messenger of God.
Moses' political objective was to free his brothers from the miserable life they had. He also wanted to conclude the covenant at Sinai and teach the Mosaic law.

First of all, Moses had the revelation of his mission at the Burning Bush: deliver the Hebrew people from slavery and guide them to the promised land of Canaan (the biblical name for Palestine Phoenicia).

Yahveh (God) then gave Moses the power to work miracles so that, firstly he would be accepted by the Hebrews as their leader and secondly so as to convince the Pharaoh. Moses went to Egypt with his brother Aaron and obtained the freedom of the Hebrews.

There were two distinct events during the march of the Hebrews in the desert:

- the passage of the Red Sea that opened to let them pass
- the covenant conceived on Mount Sinai that defined Mosaic law, the text on which Hebrew law was based

The law of Moses recommended strict monotheism and the adoration of a single, all-powerful God. Although it was enlightened by many wonderful events, the march through the desert brought to light the weaknesses of human nature.

However, the Hebrews managed to reach the land of Canaan. As for Moses, he died as they were reaching the Promised Land after having passed on the Tables of the Law to the elders so that they could teach them to the people.

What Moses said about his life and his mission.

(Message received on 15/01/1986)

The spirit of Moses is pleased to greet and visit you. Do not be surprised by our visits, they are natural and loving. Not many people are willing to listen to us.

I knew an undisciplined people who were unable to look after themselves. I led them far away from the Pharaoh, far from Egypt. I led them slowly and painfully but I did this because I knew there was something else waiting for us. I was pushed forward by something that was calling out to me "Come closer, this is where your freedom begins".

They all wanted riches. They all wanted power. I was lost. I knew not what to do or say. What could I say to the crowd?

So I kneeled and implored my Father with all my strength. In reply he said: "rise, my son, and observe. This is not the way in which I love you and wish to be loved".

And I arose and I looked and I saw his phrase and his wishes. I saw his feelings and I immediately saw what he wanted of me.

I was assigned the task of transmitting this message to my people. I had become my Father's medium for my brothers. They listened to me, they laughed, they laughed a lot, made fun of me and insulted me. But some of them did listen.

I became obliged to make them fear the word of God. But they only remembered this fear, this type of God.

Since that moment another man came to this Earth. He was born into the flesh and emphasised the meaning of the wishes of his Father. He transformed my words and writings.

Goodbye Torah of my past. I open my arms to you, Jesus of the family of David. Your present day Christians who have no form, rites or dogma, are concerned about the well-being of everyone and about respecting the word of the son of a carpenter. I proclaim his truth and I pray that the world will be forever Christian and that Jerusalem will be the city of universal peace.

Can you explain the passage of the Red Sea?

This is not a miracle. The phenomenon has taken place several times. A strong wind got up and a tidal wave was formed. The earth trembled and we crossed on dry land. The Egyptians became afraid and ran away but did not perish. Some of them told the tale…but it was later forgotten.

How did Moses receive his instructions?

Moses received his instructions by clairaudience in the mountains.

Did Moses or the Gospels forbid communicating with the dead?

Nowhere in the Gospels is it written that man should not communicate with the dead. It is only to be found in the law of Moses and at that time was well justified. He wanted his people to stop all the customs they had known with the Egyptians, especially as the custom in question had been the subject of much abuse.
At that time, communicating with the dead was a means of divination, used by charlatans to maintain superstitions. In fact, Moses had forbidden using the deceased to do business.

He was called Jesus and he came to stay with us.
He did so much good that he was considered mad.
His brothers put him to death because he was an
embarrassment. He had unveiled the hypocrisy of
those in high places.

Love one another

Jesus

Jesus

Jesus is an integral part of Christian education. 2000 years after his passage on the earth, he is still the subject of controversy and writings.

In the same way as for other spirits who were prophets on planet Earth, communication with the spirits has enabled many exchanges to take place concerning the mission of Jesus of the family of David, from Allan Kardec's era to the present day.

Considering he was a man who then became a spirit, questions have been put to him just as they would be to other representatives or witnesses of religious history.

"The life of Jesus according to spiritist principles."

It is in this way that we approach the questions so as to better understand the life of a man who, despite being a prophet and a superior being, was nevertheless a man.

Christ, who had a mission on the Earth, spoke and guided his brothers. This is what was wrongly interpreted as miracles.

Man had not understood that Jesus came to make people aware of the potential they had within themselves. Humility and abnegation and total love were needed to arrive at this point. And this man, Jesus Christ, always knew how to spread this truth and this love.

He brought people together. But dissention also arose. Hypocrisy emerged, pride won out over charity and clans and castes formed once again. Cowardice was soon to emerge….followed by treachery. The end result of all this was death.

Was Jesus a Man or a God?

Jesus is the son of the Father as you are all the sons of the Father. There is nothing mysterious in this. Simply the life of a man amongst men.

Was Jesus conceived by the Holy Spirit?

Jesus is not a miracle. He was the son of Mary and Joseph.

Where was Jesus born and in what conditions?

Jesus was born in Nazareth but not in a stable. He was born like many of the children of his time in poor countries, in the house of his parents that was made of stones and earth.

Why did Herod have so many children slaughtered?

There were many rumours in Palestine at the time that a king was to be born. Herod became afraid and had thousands of children of the age of Jesus put to death. This crime committed in the past is no worse than those you have recently committed on Earth.

Is the legend of the Three Wise Men correct?

This story is a beautiful image that expresses the idea that certain powers on the Earth accepted the existence of another power - that of the spirit. But it must be said that the details of the story are incorrect.

How would you define the mystery of the incarnation?

Like you, Jesus is the son of God. He returned to Earth under the Roman occupation. After completing the cycle, God became the flesh of Jesus with a goal but not a material reality. God remains the Father and man his son; *only the concept became flesh*. This is the mystery of the incarnation.

What preceded the life of Jesus on Earth?

The spirit of Jesus was born onto the Earth four times before being born as Jesus Christ. Mary, his mother followed him in his successive lives: as Daniel in the land of Egypt, as Ornus in Persia, as André on Aramaic soil and as David in Gaul.

Was Mary chosen on the other side as the person who had to be your mother?

I decided to return to Mary who had been my mother on four occasions. We both knew this, we decided it together. Today, I think about the human celebration of all mothers and I feel as if I were the son of all of them.

Are the teachings about the death and the assumption of the Virgin Mary correct?

My mother passed onto a spiritual life quite naturally

You say that Jesus had brothers and sisters. Was Mary aware that this would happen?

We were aware who would be embodied into our large family every time a child was born.

How many brothers and sisters did Jesus have?

He had eight brothers and sisters[43]

Can you describe the childhood of Jesus?

Jesus lived simply like all the others. I later taught him how to work wood because I thought he was handsome, just and almost noble.
He was a child who was completely devoted to his family but who soon sought friendship outside the family circle.
The scriptures speak of his rebellious side when he was 12 years old. In fact, he was undergoing a metamorphosis compared to his brothers of a similar age. He had sudden images where he remembered his spiritual past, his former lives and the meaning of his arrival on earth either during dreams or in a state of consciousness.
(Message from Joseph, the father of Jesus).

Did Jesus have a sex life? Did he marry?

Jesus was reincarnated on the Earth in the same way as any other spirit. There was nothing forbidden to him in his mission and as any other man he acted and had two sons.

---

43 In the 4 gospels we often find the expression "the brothers and sisters of Jesus". In Mark: is it not the carpenter? The son of Mary, the brother of Jacques, Joshua, Judus and Simon? Are his sisters not with us?
Thanks to the answers obtained via the spirits, we learn that Jesus had 5 brothers and 3 sisters:
Jacques (02/04/3 B.C.), Myriam (11/07/2B.C.), Joseph (16/03/1A.D.), Simon (14/04/2A.D.), Martha (15/09/3A.D.), Judus (24.06/5A.D.), Amas (09/01/7A.D.), Ruth (17/04/9A.D.).
The spirits gave us Jesus' date of birth: 25/12/7A.D.

Which is the more beautiful? To create life, to love a woman or to forbid this to oneself?

Truthfully, he who refuses the flesh refuses his spirit. He does not love the Father, he wishes to be his equal and this is a sin of pride[44]

> *If Jesus were to return to Earth, he would be surprised to see that people speak so much about him but that so few try to imitate him.*
>
> Jacques de Bourbon Busset.

Man has always confused you with God.

What can be done to make Man understand that this is not the case?

I always set myself apart from the Father and I even shouted at him for abandoning me on the cross. One does not call upon oneself, even in the face of death.

---

44 Jesus loved several women with his mind and body. He loved Mary-Madeleine then Christine with whom he lived and had 2 children. Christine followed him until the very end. She was thrown in prison and suffered a tragic death, eaten by lions like many Christians at that time.

In the eyes of spiritists (and others) Jesus was a prophet like others before him. He was a man born among men and a man of action. He had no dogmas or systems. Simply a solid personal ambition and a constant conviction because he knew he had a mission to accomplish. He stated that he was a missionary of God but at no time did he claim that he was God himself. He said he was in direct contact with God and with the son of the Father. Jesus was the human being with the highest awareness of God ever to walk on the Earth.

Jesus' God was not the deadly master who kills or damns us when it pleases him or saves us when he feels like it. The God of Jesus is our Father. He is not the unfair tyrant who has chosen Israel for his people, protecting them from everything. He is the God of humanity. Jesus wanted to establish God as the universal father.

As Jesus was born as a human being, as a spirit he is now free to manifest himself as he wishes.

A man amongst men, a spirit amongst spirits. Both his words and his existence have one single meaning, one single wish: the love of humanity and the truth about his humanity.

Every human being sometimes calls upon God sincerely but they are not God. I did the same. The kingdom of my Father was not your planet and to say this I had to set myself apart from it. I did this in the face of Pilate and the Sanhedrin who could not claim any blasphemy.

I am not, and will never be God. I have stated this and the apostles carried the message.
Religion lies to me as it lies to you[45]

> *There are no more miracles. We are witnessing the dawn of a new science.*
>
> Camille Flammarion

What is the meaning of the wedding at Cana?

Celebration means joy. This wedding ceremony was a time of gathering when two human beings celebrated their union. This wedding was beautiful.
I attended it myself. Long life to celebrations!!
A priest would say that I am being blasphemous but he would be mistaken again. Happiness is something that must be accepted. Changing water into wine is another image. All it means is changing from something tasteless to some thing with taste.

---

45 Jesus, the son of Mary and Joseph and a superior spirit, was reincarnated on planet Earth over 2000 years ago. He came to bring the news about the survival of the soul, a message of justice, sharing and love. God has not been reincarnated. The verb did not become flesh, but the spirit of a man was reincarnated amongst men. The idea of the Father was reincarnated, his message was reincarnated.
Is man so afraid to know that another man was courageous enough to love until the final moment of his life?
The answer is certainly "yes" because by making a God out of Jesus, man cleverly got around the problem.

When Jesus performed miracles what was the meaning of his question: "Do you have faith?"

And of his answer: "Let it be done according to your faith".

Are you aware you exist and that things are done according to this awareness. In this answer, the prophet Jesus is telling his brothers in a simple and natural manner, about the meaning of life, about recognising their condition and spiritual identity.

When Jesus answers in this way, he simply wishes to remind people that he is the son of the Father, the son of God.

The medical world should constantly be reminded of this notion of divinity in the love given by the Father as they can certainly make use of it for the good of society.

Did Jesus resuscitate Lazarus?

No. Catalepsy can display signs of putrefaction.

What is the meaning of the feeding of the 5000 with fish and bread?

Multiplying bread means multiplying what is vital to life. All it needed was for the crowd to be nourished with this idea for the people's hunger to be satisfied. This was the idea of the time. I am not saying that ideas nourish man but they do uplift him.

Multiplying bread in modern times should take on a material or physical meaning.
Famished man must indeed be nourished in his flesh. For this to happen, every man living on the Earth must want this food to be distributed.

I myself shared out the bread and distributed the fish, whilst advising all those present to do the same thing in their own home. This is an invitation bathed in love which, if remembered, will turn this planet into something wonderful.

Why was Jesus baptised by John the Baptist?

What was the connexion between this and the baptism of the Church concerning original sin?

The man, Jesus of Nazareth was sent to Earth on a divine mission as were other prophets and mediums.
It must be remembered that he was a man and that this man was part of his people, following their customs. What John the Baptist did was purely an initiation in the face of sin.

There is nothing beyond the image that I have just described to you. In the origins of man, only the very origin of a pulse of eternity is known as the spirit. Initially, this pulse of life is in a state of torpor and ignorance. It gradually builds itself up by embodying itself. Hence, there is no direct or indirect relationship between the act of baptism and that of any illusive sin. It is important to understand this.

Tell us about the Essenian sect.

Baptist was a friend of mine. He loved the pain within passion and invited me to partake of this pain with the people of the Essenian community.

I followed this passion for about two years but there needs to be a notion of measure in the relationship with the Father. So I left the group. With them I had leaned what I felt about the Father.

Was the healing that you performed only due to your power of hypnotism?

Hypnotism was part of my nature, part of my ethereal nature but was not sufficient to cure, not sufficient for my acts or for the help that I sometimes wanted to give others. Often it was not me, nor my spirit. It was a doctor from the other side that came to live in my body to heal others.[46]

---

46 Jesus was a medium, a great medium. Thanks to this he learned a great deal. We can say he was the medium of God as he was His go-between. This mediumship explains many of the so-called miracles. The main characteristic of a miracle, in a

I explained this to Peter, Mark, John, Luke and Mathew but they did not understand, would not understand. They spoke of miracles, saying: "It is you Master". And I replied: "It is the word of God, the power of the spirit".

Did Jesus say to Peter "You are Peter. You are like a rock and on this rock I will build my church"?

Jesus said nothing on this subject. He was more concerned that those around him should actively spread the message.
It was not a question of repeating words or gestures or of imitating Christ like so many priests on the Earth.
The aim was to discover one's duty, taking the life of Jesus as a model. Living with one's brothers as Jesus did and descending, as he did, into the arena. This is the duty of every human being.
Do not curl up in a corner or build a temple to honour some image or other. Carry the message in your acts.

---

theological sense, is something naturally exceptional that can not be explained by the laws of nature. As soon as something can be explained it is no longer a miracle. It is in this way that science has been able to make certain prodigious effects seem natural when their cause was in fact unknown. Later, knowledge about the spiritual principle and the action of fluids, about the invisible world surrounding us, about the faculties of the soul and the existence and properties of the perispirit provided a key to the understanding of psychic phenomena. All this has proved that they are not exceptions to the laws of nature.
Hypnotism, sleep walking, ecstasy, catalepsy, thought transmission, apparitions and transfigurations account for almost all the miracles in the gospels belonging to this type of phenomenon.
The vast majority of the acts performed by Jesus and called miracles can be attributed to hypnotism and natural phenomena.
Nevertheless, this does not mean that the love of Jesus was not superior to that of other people. Jesus gave a considerable amount of help to many men and women who were possessed. He knew he had to address the possessing spirit and how best to do this. Jesus healed and cured many people using hypnotism, to which he added his own words and his love.

What is the meaning of the words: "You will do this in memory of me"?

When the embodied spirit spoke in this way, it wished to emphasise what was most important around a table. The function of a table is to bring people together to exchange and to share.

We also know that there are symbols of life. On the Earth we know how important bread is.

Over and above the image, the real use of bread is more important…….it embodies the idea of sharing. You shall do as Jesus did, you shall share with your brothers on the Earth.

Does the Last Supper exist on Earth? This is a good question when we see the divisions that exist in the world. Less than half lives disgracefully and opulently whilst the rest suffers from a lack of everything.

Would it not be dignified for each and every one of you to share things between yourselves in memory of Jesus?

Can you speak about stigmatisation?

For a sensible and reasonable person this can only be the proof of the action of mind over matter.
Stigmatisation can be seen in the suffering of Jesus that is reborn in human flesh.

Posthumous account by Padre Pio:

The appearance of my life is nothing. The suffering and the blood from my wounds must not be remembered. The blood was the ardent proof of my faith but also of my blind passion to worship the cross. I was stigmatised by my love of Christ.
Our suffering must not be sublimated. Those who kill and torture must not be adored.

Can man survive without food for several years (as was the case of Theresa Neumann)?

Living without food for 45 years is something supernatural, yet supernatural phenomena do not exist and it is incorrect to say that Theresa Neumann was only nourished by the sacred host. There are lies and deception here in order to attract naïve people toward something marvellous.
It is possible for human beings to considerably reduce their intake of food but our role is not to try to contradict the basic rules of biology. As these laws are of a divine nature, no-one should attempt to prove their opposite. Theresa Neumann was stigmatised but the main elements of the story built around her are an insult to the truth..
In this case, as in others, spiritism has to agree with science. We can not agree with far fetched and nonsensical claims that would ridicule us.

Does Jesus intervene in certain cases of stigmatisation?

Certainly not. Jesus does not seek to make man suffer so that they will become believers of his word.

A question to Joseph, Jesus' father: "What were your feelings when Jesus was arrested and the events that followed?

We did not thank the Father. We did not praise the Lord when he was arrested to be tortured and murdered. And, from the kingdom of the spirits, we still cry when we look upon those who claim that redemption will come through this Christ.

There is no redeeming Christ in our tortured child but a brutally interrupted life. A life that could have given so much more to those around him. My son was murdered by man's shortcomings, by his blindness, his treachery like the son of one of your brothers who can still suffer today because he has unfortunately died too young.

Message from Joseph (the father of Jesus) 1985

"I loved Mary with all my body and soul. I loved this woman both for her beauty and for her spirit, the mother of our child who was conceived in the flesh and from our union.
Above all, Mary was sensitive. Today she would be called a medium.
One evening she received a message from a superior entity called Gabriel. Through clairvoyance and clairaudience this message said that a superior spirit intended to return to Earth. This spirit had already known Mary in another life.
He had a mission to fulfil which involved great sacrifice and unexpected difficulties for us. All that was said and written by men following this are pure lies and stupidity"

Message from Mathew:

Mathew revealed himself to spiritists in 1985, thus enabling us to fit the pieces of the puzzle together:

"When I met Jesus I was 26 years old. I met him when he was speaking to a small group of women.
He was the humblest of the humble. This son of a carpenter enthralled me with his words, his meaning and most of all his bright eyes and look. The power of the permanent magnetic fluid that flowed from the whole of his body was enormous.
The voice of Jesus carried far into the distance and large crowds could hear him great distances away. The truth is often transported on an echo to attentive ears.
This enchantment placed me on the path of Jesus, who gave me the most valuable of gifts, that of awareness.
He spoke in simple words, using many images. It was only a good while later that I understood how important these images were for us.
He talked to us about life, death and eternity. He surprised us because he did not judge us. I continued living with him and for him even though he told us not to adore him. But we were often guilty of adoring him. Jesus disliked this:
"It is not me you should be worshiping but the Father because of the message he has asked me to bring you".

Another account – October 1984:

"I am Mathew the evangelist, the companion of Jesus of Nazareth. I have probably spoken more than the others. We were fascinated and carried away like children in the presence of Jesus.
When he died our suffering made our fascination still stronger. We had to give a testimony so we gave one, but all too often like naïve children. Our memories were usually correct but we felt the need to embellish them, to transform them into something even more marvellous. Too often we added words or gestures that Jesus did not say or do. We did not think it was important. We had little education. The winner was the one who could say the most and captivate the audience the best. History has not forgotten how we exaggerated."

The fact that Mathew or other spirits from the past should manifest themselves does not mean that these spirits have been on the other since the prophet died. This means that, at the moment they manifested themselves, they were again on the other side after having been reincarnated several times since the time of Jesus.

As Jesus wrote nothing, his only historians are the apostles, who did not write either when they were alive. There are very few documents concerning the life of Jesus and his doctrine. The gospels are basically all that exists and they took several decades to put together.

All writing that took place following them, except for that of Paul, are only and can only be commentaries, appreciations and reflections of personal opinions. Paul writes 20 years after the death of Jesus. He was not in Jerusalem during the public mission of Jesus. He never met him when he was alive and at first he did not even appear interested in what Jesus of Nazareth did and said. For many years, witness accounts were only spoken and not written.

Short pieces of writing were gradually to follow these oral accounts about the life of Jesus. Historians think that the gospels were written in the years 65 to 80. Since this time, much ink has flowed over 2000 years and continues to flow, arousing passions between historians and theologians.

Was Jesus aware of the way in which he would die?

I, Joseph of Aramathea, wish to be a witness to that. I lived through the final instants and the days preceding the torment and torture in the company of and in the same way as Jesus.
These were difficult times: we constantly had to find a place to hide the man who was fast becoming the number one enemy of Rome. I remember the words of Jesus who was worried about the future of his spirit more than about the glory of a false resurrection.

Did he die prematurely with regard to his mission?

Jesus would have dearly loved to have more days, weeks and years to spread the message of love sent through him by his Father.

Is the Way of the Cross a historical fact?

I lived in ancient Jerusalem and I saw the prophet die. That day, I saw both a bitter crowd as well as embarrassment.
It is true that he walked through the entire town carrying his cross (a T shaped piece of wood) and it is true that he gave back his spirit on Mount Golgotha. There was no providential eclipse and the skies did not resound with thunder. Only silence prevailed like death in all its horror. All that remained was the awful image if this crime and the decay of the flesh. In this image there is no indication of any future glory. Simply of certain death for a tortured human being. Does this take God from your consciousness?

Message from Vincent de Paul (1985).

Jesus the human spirit, Jesus a man amongst men, Jesus your brother, Jesus our brother. Also a Jesus betrayed, a Jesus disguised, a Jesus transformed, a Jesus worshipped and a Jesus whose true message of love, peace and justice has become increasingly distant from him. A Jesus enclosed within the walls of temples and churches and stifled by the weight of a deluded human hierarchy. A Jesus victim of organised religions and the poor of the Earth who are victimised by the rich and powerful. A

Jesus defended by the sword and an excuse for making war and a Jesus who is said to be with those who threaten, torture and kill in his name.

Was Jesus afraid of what he felt would happen?

Jesus knew fear because he was a man. He experienced the fear of those condemned to death. Here we are talking about crime and blood.
The just and righteous man died on the cross because he did not come to Earth to redeem sin. Jesus suffered because he gave man his everlasting soul.

At that time, claiming that the soul was eternal and that God lives on in each and every one of us was unacceptable. As far as Rome and Jewish law were concerned, the crime of Jesus was to have spoken the word of God until the very end.

For those in the invisible world, Friday, the eve of Easter will always remain as a day of crime and evil condemnation. It is the responsibility of everyone to redeem sin.

Did Jesus die in front of a crowd?

There were few of us left when the blood began to flow into the chalice. Many had fled, afraid to watch.
It must be understood that they had the choice: to flee or stay to die and be tortured.
Although his friends and followers were few, there were many others, those who wanted to see and watch. They were waiting for a miracle or a final gesture.
Mary fainted. Joseph of Aramathea carried her in his arms Joseph had dared to defy Pilate whom he occasionally invited to dinner. His courage was admired.
The sky grew dark and Jesus cried out "Elie, Elie lama sabactami".
Heads were bowed nonetheless. Jesus died on the cross, as a man, like all men.

Message from a brother of Jesus.

(A question to Jesus)

Did the two thieves supposedly next to you on the cross really exist?

I was not alone on the day I died. The two men you speak of, who were not thieves, were indeed with me and were crucified as I was because they had followed me, because they had defended me, because they were rebels against Rome for the rights of the people of Palestine.

Did your spirit experience turmoil following your death on the Earth?

I shouted at my Father for abandoning me on the Roman cross because I was afraid just as you would be. I did not acquire immediate awareness. My flesh had been penetrated by hatred and I thus acquired the fear of hatred and the turmoil of the spirits.

What is the meaning of the resurrection of Christ?

This is the tangible manifestation of the spirit of Jesus whose unquestionable superiority made many phenomena happen. He knew how to condense matter to briefly recreate the molecular structure that makes the human body seem real to others.
He can not be humanly and physically resurrected. When a human being attains the state of death, an irreversible cellular decomposition takes place.

Have Whit Sunday and Whitsuntide originated from historical facts?

It may be said that Whitsuntide is the celebration of spiritism. Whitsuntide in fact means a mediumnic force. It is witness to the presence of the spirits in the human world. Jesus of Nazareth was a medium. Some of his followers were also mediums but were not aware if this.

Jesus appeared to them shortly after his death to reveal to them the extent of their mediumship. Several apostles were mediums from the same culture but with little education. They were inhabited by superior spirits. When in a trance, the language of these apostles became totally different and Christ's message continued to exist in this manner. Unfortunately, the messages were not remembered or they were very badly interpreted.

Given the considerable power of your fluid, is it possible for you to appear to us?

I have many possibilities but only act when it is really necessary. If, by reappearing I were to create more in love peoples' hearts and more strength in their acts then I could do so. I have appeared to so many people but that has not changed the history of the Earth!

Has Jesus been reincarnated since he was born in Nazareth?

Powerful spirits have been born onto the Earth in order to point to the same path of love, truth and justice. He lived many times on other planets before being embodied on the Earth for the first time.

Father Lenhard's Prayer

I pray for the union of the cross, the crescent and the chandelier
I pray for an end to maternal suffering
I pray for a renewed youth I the light of the sun
I pray for the people of Palestine
I pray for the force of love
I pray for all Man in the very corners of both worlds
I pray for renewed childhood
I pray for man becoming man again
I pray for bread, for life, for roses and jasmine
I pray that the light of truth be found again
For a pope who listens
For an afterlife that makes itself heard
I pray for the awakening of awareness
And for the presence of God in the heart of each and every one of you
I pray
That the light will come

Chamonix January 2001

MEDECINE

If our doctors fail to cure the majority of our illnesses it is because they try to cure the body without tending to the soul.

Socrates

*Illnesses do not come from our physical body
but from our ethereal body.*

Paracelse

Spiritism and Medicine

The world of the spirits remains the world of disembodied human beings. The world of disembodied science is therefore that of disembodied people that were on the Earth in former times. They are here, present in numbers and wish to speak to scientists so that they will not fall into the trap of materialism once more.
Spirits have been visiting for many years to transmit their medical knowledge and their experience in the field of medicine.
This is how a new concept of medicine has gradually appeared as messages have been received.
This concept defines man as having three main elements:

the spirit
the perispirit
the body

The spirit

is an essential part of our nature, the immaterial part of our being and hence the part that will survive after our death.

The body is the carnal envelope for the spirit, an envelope that is subject to the laws of nature and consequently to the laws of matter. The envelope is perishable of course but its behaviour depends on the nature of the spirit inside it.

The perispirit

is between the body and the spirit. It is a sort of double all around the spirit. This semi-material, invisible and impalpable body is the bearer of our senses. At the moment of death, it leaves the body and leads the spirit to the other side. The very nature of the perispirit means that it records all the physical and psychological suffering to which the individual has been subjected. The principle of spiritist medicine consists in dealing with the cause of the problem rather than healing the effects.

Let it be clear here that it is not our intention to discuss the pros and cons of traditional medicine, nor to deny that science has contributed a great deal to medicine and healing. What we wish to say is that therapy and cures continue to neglect the spiritual element in man.

The body is a being that thinks

Cell tissue takes on different forms throughout the body. This has created organs which have particular roles to play.
Intelligent matter will thus play a role at each stage of human development. Thought invades the entire body and locates itself at various points according to a functional body map.
Both the heart and the stomach are thinking entities made up of a collection of micro consciences, apparently guided by an instinct. In fact, they are under the permanent control of the spirit.
The physical body overall is a finely balanced receptacle that is sensitive to the conscience of the spirit inside it as well as to the conscience of those around it. On Earth, stress and aggression are commonplace.
Matter is poisoned by psychological pollution. The health of each and every one of us therefore depends both on us and on everyone else. We must learn to think well, i.e. to have good and positive thoughts.

The spirit organises matter

The result of death is a corpse. What would happen to this inert body if the phenomenon of decomposition were to be accelerated? It would immediately fall into a pile of dust which in any case is the end result of the process.
Seen in this way, we can more easily appreciate the importance of thought with relation to matter. Indeed, if the individual spirit did not exist in the body via the perispirit, matter would collapse.

Let us take the example of someone living alone on a desert island. This person will have built himself a house, made tools, written his own books maybe music or painted. This person will die alone and his body will decompose because the spirit has left it. As for the rest, the house, the tools the painting, music or book they will also rapidly fall into dust simply because their creator has disappeared. Conscience stands out within matter and shows us how effective the spirit is at organising.

A new form of therapy.

One of the advantages of spiritism is that it can help us to design a different type of treatment depending on the nature of our physical ailments.
We are essentially "spirit" above all and this spiritual origin certainly has repercussions on our physical body.
Why is this?
We are not only the product of a wonderful genetic design, but also and above all, the sum of a succession of lives during which our psychology has gradually changed by constantly affecting its surrounding matter, especially the physical body.
Given this, it does not take very long to understand that many illnesses are of psychological origin.

Even though concrete materialism is still the order of the day as far as "official" medicine is concerned, we are witnessing an increasing number of therapists and doctors who detect a psychosomatic origin in our ailments. We can also call this a "spiritual" origin.

Because the spirit is real, a different approach to matter is required. To better understand the problem of spiritual healing, we must begin to redefine man from a spiritual standpoint, constantly insisting on the place of mind over matter.

We are the creators of the flesh as well as being the perpetrators of life and life is part of God.
This divine origin makes us responsible for the architecture of our physical body. It is certainly true that the construction of our physical body will be more or less of a success, depending on the traumas that have been suffered in previous lives. Weaknesses of the soul become weaknesses of the body.

How are people cured spiritually? How can the mind act upon matter? Is it sufficient to believe one is cured to be cured? What part do genetics play in our ailments?
Spiritism can provide us with answers to all of these questions.

Spiritual Medicine

The only medecine that really works is the medicine of the spirit as it accepts the existence of the soul and will act upon the spirit to cure the body.
When we try to cure the flesh by taking only the flesh into account we are dealing with the effect without taking the cause into account. Reaching the spirit and the origins of structured matter means attaining the supreme reason for life.

Allan Kardec

Can you define for us what illness is?

Your personal set of physical ailments is basically determined within your very own psychology. Indeed, the psyche slowly destroys the matter that it has conceived through worry, stress and negative emotions.
A failing psyche will transmit what is required for matter to become weak and resemble it,
 i.e. a failing body.

So are all illnesses in the psyche?

All the illnesses that your body may develop have their origins in the spirit because your ailments are the result of a psychological mechanism that you have created either individually or collectively.

Illnesses are the result of changes of the spirit, changes in behaviour, in one's way of life, way of feeding, daily work as well as previous lives.
Therefore, no illness or form of ailment can be explained without referring to the behaviour of the spirit.

If so many illnesses are of a purely spiritual nature, why do they manifest themselves in precise but different parts of the body?

An illness will manifest itself in the places where matter has changed the most, usually for purely psychological, genetic or hereditary reasons. When the spirit that lives in matter is disturbed, it will go directly to the needy part. This is how it operates within matter.
The physical body has certain weaknesses in its constitution from the outset. These are essentially genetic and therefore hereditary.

What are the major psychological causes of illness?

One of them is the constant physical aggression of life itself. The other lies in the ethereal existence of the spirit before it returned to matter. This pre-existence can exhibit different forms of turmoil that may be responsible for a refusal to reincarnate. Yet this reincarnation has to take place.
These are the two major causes of a possible failing of the physical body at some time or other.

In that case, what is your opinion of human medicine?

The treatment given by doctors is based on a material approach. They should pay more attention to the spirit that is within the body and to the perispirit that transports this spirit.
Medicine on Earth is directed only at the biological exchanges of the organism. It does not take the true nature of man into consideration. The notion of the spirit is ignored because doctors do not believe in it.

Is there an opposition between the medicine of man and that of the spirits?

Most certainly not. Our medicine is complementary to all the research undertaken. And I wish to pay tribute to all the doctors and researchers who have worked to alleviate pain and suffering.

I would like to say that these people have deliberately ignored two components of the fundamental trinity: the spirit and the perispirit.

This has led to certain abuses in the area of medicines as well as in surgery.

> *A new humanity will awaken on the day that the survival of the soul is proven.*
>
> Bergson

Will medicine gradually admit that the spirit exists?

We are sure that there will be a meeting in the future between official medicine and spiritist medicine. In the 21st century there will be a wonderful osmosis between the demands of the body and the spirit.

We are certain that man will become increasingly responsible. After discovering the functions and structure of the body, medical research moved toward the study of extremely minute cellular behaviour.
The arrival of biology was a great step forward. The exploration of the chemistry of the brain and acidic exchanges is a revolution in human knowledge. We admire the advances in the techniques of surgery that have developed over the last few years.

Spiritists do not therefore wish to downplay medical progress or the applications of this progress.

We wish to show man that life is essentially about the perispirit but that this is ignored by a pragmatic medical profession.

It is true that no surgeon will discover the spirit with his scalpel or under a scanner
(Claude Bernard).

In that case, should university education be modified or widen its scope?

From this point of view, rejecting human science is symptomatic of the separations operating in universities. It is vital to call on philosophy, psychology, religious history, spiritist reality, reincarnation and of course a perispirit body to discover the spirit and the way in which it is linked to the body.

There should be an end to the eternal pattern of "science and matter", "spirit and religion". Medicine is particularly concerned by this old fashioned pattern which is still deeply rooted in traditional rationalism.

The medical profession would do well to give credit to many dowsers as the health of human beings is the only rule that should be obeyed.

As we are disembodied humans, we can perceive all that is said, thought and done on the Earth. This very condition leads me to say that general practitioners' medicine is likely to disappear and that specialists will group together. It is within this framework that spiritists will have a role to play (Claude Bernard,1988)[47]

Are illnesses passed on genetically?

In fact, there are three forms of genetics:

- spiritual genetics
- perispirital genetics
- physical genetics

What do you mean by perispirital genetics,

Within your own history and your spiritual genesis there is also the history of your semi-material double, the history of your ethereal body or perispirit.
Due to the nature of its cells, the perispirit has the natural ability to record the sets of events experienced throughout all its reincarnations, as well as between each reincarnation, i.e. life on the other side.

---

[47] *The Allan Kardec Group as a whole (Nancy, Belfort, Besançon, Montpellier, Paris) offers the medical treatment of the spirits via its dowsers. This does not mean that the patient is no longer treated by traditional or official medicine. It helps to relieve the suffering of men and women who wish to receive a different form of treatment that takes account of their spiritual condition.*
This treatment takes the form of herbal medicine, magnetism or hypnosis.

Do this memory present any risks?

As the perispirit is able to record events within its own cells, it will record all the events experienced either very good or very bad.

Sometimes it is very bad, e.g. when people have experienced particularly violent traumas. Theses events will be recorded by the perispirit and will continue to exist on the other side and at the moment of reincarnation.

The memories contained in the perispirit formula accompany the spirit when it returns to the flesh. The flesh then receives all these memories which may be responsible for halting the development of the embryo or the development of the body following birth.

This is what we call perispirit genetics.

Physical Genetics

The third form of elaborate, determined and defined genetics to be studied by biologists is physical genetics.
This is the genetics of the body, the one that passes things on through the genes in families.
We call this type of genetics "physical" and will not go any further than this term.

What part does genetics play in the way it is studied by biologists?

Some modern day biologists make the mistake of trying to link physical genetics to spiritual genetics. We understand this relationship very well for those who are unaware of the spirit, the ethereal body and the nature of the perispirit.

Physical traits can be genetically transmitted from one generation to another. This means that above and beyond spiritual and perispirital genetics, an individual can also record genes that are foreign to him and which are given to him via natural procreation

In what proportion are the two genetics (parental and perispiritual) present in the body at the moment of reincarnation?

This can be expressed as a percentage but is only given as an indication to enable you humans to understand.
The influence of past lives and hence of your intrinsic nature, of your spiritual nature is in the order of 70%. So roughly 30% is genetically acquired, but this figure is still to be defined further.

Genetic inheritance certainly exists but the force of the spirit is the dominant force. A variation on the proportions given above should be established and here we are entering the complex balance between "spirit and matter".

How do you explain character similarities in families between parents and children?

If the similarities in character between parents and children were of genetic origin, this would invalidate the whole of the spiritist theory. In fact, in most cases where there are striking similarities it is because the child and his/her parents have known each other in previous lives or on the other side. These meetings have given rise to natural and explainable affinities.
Concerning resemblances between parents and their children, there is in fact a moral and intellectual set of elements that each person has and that psychology has pointed out as a factor explaining resemblances. This purely spiritist explanation is the only one of its type. The future behaviour of an individual is linked to the education he/she receives at home and in society. Beyond these resemblances, the spirit preserves its own character as it is unique.

How do you explain look-alikes?

Given that perispiritual matter exists before organic matter outside any genetic traits that are passed on, the body that is about to shape itself will bear some resemblance to a past life. These resemblances are printed by the double of the reincarnating spirit.

If look-alikes exist, even though there are very few of them, I can confirm that in a former life they both belonged to the same family. They were twins and time has separated them. Their double, however, has left its mark on their new body.

I can invite you to examine this fact: no person who is the look-alike of someone else bears any resemblance to the other members of their current family.

Does taking account of the three components mean that the pharmacopoeia is modified?

It means that the chemical synthesis with its medical structure must give way to the synthesis of herbal medicine. The latter will become increasingly present.

What will pharmacology and clinical testing be like in the future?

The chemical approach is beginning to wane in favour of herbal medicine. Human nature in the medical profession is such that this gradual transformation will not take place without confrontation.
We will again be faced with the same opposition between conservatives and progressives. Like other new forms of treatment, herbal medicine is a battle.
Chemical remedies are declining but they are still necessary in the short term for man to evolve. I am considering the evolution of the body and the spirit at the same time.

We are witnessing the gradual disappearance of homo-sapiens and the transformation of his metabolism.
In the future, many reincarnated spirits will donate their moral and intellectual powers in order to be at one with Mother Nature.

Are external factors responsible for the development of cancers?

Many external factors are officially put forward as being responsible for the development of cancers: industrial waste, sugar in food, in meats, preservatives that are put into these products as well as such things as tobacco.
All these items taken either together or individually may be responsible for the development of tumours that cause irreversible damage to cells, thereby causing cancer.

It is true that these external factors are sometimes responsible for the development of certain cancers but it is wrong to say that they are the major cause.

This illness existed long before industrial societies even though it was not called cancer.
A cancerous tumour is essentially the result of a psychological imbalance which can reveal itself either consciously or unconsciously.

What do you mean by psychological imbalance?

The real sources of this problem are the burden of anguish, of changing feelings, the weight of your memories that have more often than not been repressed, the transposition of your former ailments, the fear of society and the apprehension of the future.

The spirit is responsible for anarchy in cell behaviour.

How does the spirit do this?

The spirit projects its modified state to the perispirit that in turn passes it on to the cells of the physical body.

In the field of genetics, scientists speak of an extra chromosome that may be responsible for crime. What do you think of this?

Let us thank the Lord! Even though the spirit is not more powerful than genetics as far as physical make-up is concerned, it *is* when it comes to psychological make up. This is why the extra chromosome in question could not turn those that have it into a criminal.
This raises a question, however, to which a negative answer must be given whilst at the same time posing an underlying principle: that of genetics.
Our world is threatened by current thinking in the field of genetics. A number of scientists wish to create a psychological difference using human genetics.
This is nothing new. This was already envisaged several years ago in racist terms. The end result is obviously extremely destructive.
Moreover, a certain number of philosophers also adhere to these genetic theories. This danger must be emphasised and fought against.

What is your opinion on keeping long term coma patients alive so that their organs may be used for transplants?

This can be useful if it saves lives. I believe that a deep coma is in fact a form of death, the stage at which the spirit is separated from the perispirit. What should be understood by the term "deep coma"?
It means artificially keeping an essentially biological entity alive. Keeping a physical body alive has no effect on the spirit.

What do you think about human guinea pigs that are used in medical research?

We believe that all medical activities must have moral and ethical standards. We believe that all scientists and researchers must adhere to these standards. The ulterior motive is the alleviation of suffering and the overcoming of illnesses. Scientific tools, either human or animal, are required if medical science is to advance and if society at large is to benefit from this.

But in this field as with others, we should not play at being the sorcerer's apprentice. Medicine must not turn a blind eye and attempt to justify the unjustifiable. There must be no sadistic torture in the name of science. Unfortunately this exists inside many research laboratories and we strongly criticise it. Having said that, research and experimentation are necessary to acquire knowledge.

It is impossible to avoid certain stages in this field. The demands of society for remedies implicitly require this type of experimentation. It is for this reason that the spirits approve of basic and essential experimentation that will benefit society as a whole.

Why do physical or mental handicaps and illnesses exist at birth, at the moment of reincarnation?

The reasons are as varied as the variety of different paths taken by individuals, the difference in the past and the genesis of each spirit..

Incarnation and reincarnation are difficult processes. A spirit does not enter the flesh in the same way as on object is put back into its case. The spirit prepares its dwelling place before arriving like any "worker". This obviously does not come without problems: mistakes, imperfections, minor disasters constantly arise and can be at the root of problems present at birth.

A better understanding of Downs Syndrome: a witness account from the other side.

My aim here is to speak on behalf of all those who have been affected by Downs Syndrome and to explain how much man is mistaken about this problem in the chromosomes.

When I was reincarnated I was aware of my choice and I knew that this reincarnation was not to the taste of my guide. At that time I wished to return to the Earth quickly.

In my previous life I was struck down by meningitis during an epidemic of this illness in Bombay. The sincere prayers of my family helped me to avoid turmoil but I remained profoundly shocked by this brutal end to my life.

The memory of my double was completely impregnated with this and the role of my guide was to inform me about this. In spite of all the advice he gave me, the only thing I could think about was returning to Earth.
I was willing to take a risk but I took this risk alone because on the other side, as on the Earth, guides respect their protégés freedom of choice.

I was therefore reincarnated. But during the embodiment process, as I gradually came closer to the vibrations of matter, my double forced me to relive the final moments of my previous life. I had violent head pains and I fell unconscious in deep turmoil. I felt like a ball that was about to explode.

When I awoke in the womb of my mother-to-be, my double had become impregnated with images of my turmoil. The process was irreversible.

The meningitis that had previously killed me had been projected into the present not only onto my double but also onto my new genetic map. Downs syndrome had been reprogrammed.

Someone with this condition is therefore responsible for it to a certain degree, even if his history is not the same as mine and it is unfair to make the parents feel guilty.

I remember my reincarnation and the love of my parents. I remember the prison which was my body. I wanted to tell everyone about the "accident" because I remembered it but I was unable to do so.

I wanted to paint, to sing, to write but all this was impossible. When I was happy I uttered high, piercing screams. When I was sad I made raucous noises and thumped the objects around me.

I understood absolutely everything that was said or done around me. I endured the fate of all Downs sufferers: the absence of all logical and lasting expression.

I was lucky to have intelligent and caring parents who were aware how cruel people could be. They did not hide me as if they were ashamed. Instead they protected me.

Society is very unfair. People are afraid of the handicapped. Some of them would even like to eradicate them to prevent the landscape from being tainted.

My life has not been useless. I learned a lot in my family and I gave as much love as I was able to.

In distance healing, how are the mental powers of the therapist received by the patient?

The power of thought is transmitted beyond the flesh by the phenomenon of telepathy. How is this received by the patient?
At the very moment that the phenomenon begins, the patient receives the thoughts almost simultaneously, in the same way as the pulse produced by the combination of your desire and your reason.
We must think about what we desire so that this wish becomes sufficiently intense that it reaches the other person via a nuclein channel on a microwave.

Can all types of thought be received?

Fluid is above all the result of your thought process. If you have good thoughts you will obtain a good fluid and vice versa..

Natural Medicine

Herbal Medicine

The use of medicinal plants goes back to the dawn of time and it is so widespread that all civilisations have their own versions of it.

The pharmaceutical industry has harnessed the medicinal power of plants. Many of their products use plant extracts and vegetable by-products.

Plants are used to cure and maintain a healthy balance in the body.

Spiritist Herbal Treatment

Medicinal plant treatment is suggested by the spirit of various doctors and is the result of research concerning the structure of our double nature (perispirit).

All the treatment suggested by the spirits is in total harmony with the structure of our perispirit.
Plants are used in their vibratory capacity for baths, herb teas, decoctions, or application to the body.
Spiritist treatment means using the vibratory capacity of the plant in connexion with the perispirit of human beings.

What is your opinion of fresh water and sea water therapy?

Water is very good for the equilibrium of the body, the majority of which is made up of water. There is a matching vibration between these two elements.

We wish to encourage the development of fresh water therapy but at the same time we must criticise the high cost of this, making it impossible for the poorer classes of your societies to benefit from it.

For us, water is an element to be studied and should be coupled with medicinal plant therapy in external applications of the vibratory nature of vegetable elements.

Are oligo-elements good for the body?

Nature finds a way into your bodies when things are good for you. You are made up of metals as well as water, with nitrogen, carbon and electricity in your nervous systems. This natural metal will thus find a way to penetrate the parts of your body that need to be healed. These elements are very good for the body, bringing new energy.

Hypnosis is a sleep that awakens

Allan Kardec Group

HYPNOSIS

Hypnosis and its potential.

Hypnosis is still an unborn science. It is a technique that was abandoned by Sigmund Freud at the beginning of the last century because of ideological principles and fear.

Just like spiritism, hypnosis must be recognised for what it is and not be confused with relaxation, auto-suggestion or relaxation therapy. Hypnotic sleep possesses a certain reality that modern medicine refuses to accept.
In a state of hypnosis, the sleeping subject is in complete control of his conscience and body.
The hypnotiser is the guide for this period of sleep during which the spirit freely reacts to the information given to him/her.
If hypnotism were recognised as a science and taught in schools and universities, it could profoundly modify the biological data concerning the definition of man.

The subject is particularly active during hypnosis. The information and suggestions provided go directly to the spirit, which accepts or rejects them.
A simple suggestion such as asking the hypnotised subject to raise his/her arm or open their eyes does not depend on the hypnotiser but on the hypnotised subject.
We can conclude that any physical or psychological transformation of a sleeping subject is the result of the conscious action of the individual on himself via the given information.
This means that hypnosis is a way of learning to control and discover oneself. It also means that it is an experimental method highlighting man's subconscious psychological energy.
From this point, it is easy to cross the frontiers of the body and soul to study all the possibilities inherent in hypnotism.

If hypnosis was a recognised therapy a new approach could be adopted towards the mentally handicapped. Treatment could be given to people who undergo changes in their personality. Each individual would be able to investigate his/her previous lives. There would be a permanent stimulation of one's ethereal body and all of us could journey into our own personal history so as to live in harmony with the present.

What is hypnosis?

Hypnosis is a parallel form of physiological sleep. It helps the subject to awaken his/her subconscious forces to reveal their true nature, i.e. the spirit.
Hypnosis is the perfect encounter of the body and the soul, a soft symbiosis of the subconscious and the values attached to it.
Hypnosis is not aggressive. It is an invitation to liberate potential subconscious energy.

What is your opinion of hypnosis?

We believe hypnosis to be the future of man and largely the future of medicine itself.
Hypnosis highlights the spirit, bringing out the power of thought. It is the essential element for the future of spiritual medicine.

Hypnosis is the science of reincarnation and of the body as it concerns physiology, anatomy, psychoanalysis, psychiatry and spiritism.

In what ways can hypnosis be useful?

The spirit carries the traces of previous lives within it; pain, nightmares and positive or negative images. Human beings need to be able to enter into the depths of the subconscious so as to unlock certain barriers.
Hypnosis remains an excellent tool to reach these depths as long as it is correctly and wisely performed in stages.

Doesn't the hypnotiser influence the patient?

The hypnotiser does not impose anything on the patient. He provides the subject with information that the latter may use as he/she wishes. So, the results obtained during hypnotic sleep are nothing more than the wishes of the spirit of the hypnotised person, carried out in the new consciousness that is offered to him/her.

Can anybody be hypnotised?

Any human being can be hypnotised. Indeed, should the subconscious (which collects the memories of past lives) refuse to be awakened, several sessions of hypnosis will most probably overcome this. The spirit will become accustomed to hypnotic suggestion because it is an invitation to a total freeing-up of the being.

Is entertainment hypnosis bad for therapeutic hypnosis?

Hypnosis has been worked with, studied and experimented with at Nancy in France, in Vienna, in Russia and in the USA.
The school of therapist healers in Nancy including Liebault, Bernheim and Coué has been betrayed. Their research, work and exercises have all been neglected.

Apparently, hypnosis has become a dirty word, a forbidden activity that has been replaced by the notions of suggestion, relaxation therapy and meditation so that the discoveries of the above-mentioned men may be avoided.

The theatrical people who use the science of hypnosis for mass entertainment prevent it from developing and advancing correctly. They try, consciously or unconsciously, to persuade those who have given it up or who refuse to accept it as a simple and natural phenomenon.

Does curing by hypnosis have anything to do with the level of evolution reached by the spirit of the patient?

Has it anything to do with the nature of the perispirit?

I can answer "yes" to your question because hypnosis is an accurate investigation into your true nature and your spiritual nature.
No two people setting out on a journey into hypnosis will obtain the same results. This is because each person has had a different evolution in life.

Strong proof has been provided on many occasions in hypnotic experiments. This is the proof of previous lives.
Some of you will very easily speak about your previous lives when under hypnosis whilst others will not be able to do this. They do not remember or do not wish to remember.
Here, the degree to which the spirit has evolved is very important.

If a person remembers his/her past and can speak about it, this means that he/she is able to accept it.
Not everyone is able to do this. The journey into hypnosis can be a good journey, but may sometimes be limited depending on the person involved.

Can hypnosis help people to stop smoking?

This is a very effective solution as a smoker can be "taught" to hate the taste of tobacco. However, this type of suggestion should be undertaken with care because a compensatory substitute needs to be provided. If the process of suggestion is not well-balanced, then the subject may find him/herself with a physical or psychological imbalance.

SCIENCE

Today's utopia is the science of tomorrow

Paul Valéry

What do you think of cloning? How does the spirit of animals adapt?

What would be the consequences of cloning on humans?

The consequences of cloning on humans would be particularly serious because the desire for life and the perispirit are both affected by genetic manipulation as well as the meaning of life and that of reincarnation.
Cloning is not more acceptable for animals. The consequences of cloning are essentially psychological. It destroys the vitality of the spirit, its consciousness and its balance. These are truly ridiculous experiments.

In fact cloning, as with other current experiments in biology, is due to only a small number of people. The problem is that the product of their research has been jumped on by the media which has broadcast it to the world.
There is a corruption of moral standards in this form of modern day publicity that you should do your best to eradicate.
Creating such artificial beings means eradicating the individual consciousness of the spirit and creating a new form of zombie.

Is atomic energy evil?

Atomic power has the power to put fear in the hearts of the world's population yet it has the potential to provide a great future. It could power cars, aeroplanes, boats and industry. There would be less pollution and fewer economic (and political) problems regarding the sources of production.
There is no doubt, therefore, that further research should be carried out in the field of thermonuclear fusion as *fusion* is the real long term solution in the place of *fission*.

What do you think of the protests against nuclear power stations?

It seems to be very natural for human beings, who are made up of atoms themselves, to base their lives around energy that is at the source of this structure. People are mistaken to protest against nuclear power stations. The only real problem is that of finding a suitable way to convert radioactive waste but this will be discovered in the future.

Man gets closer to the universal vibration, i.e. the spirit, by getting closer to the atom. It remains a little known power force that has not always been put to good use, especially when it falls into the hands of the military. In spite of this, atomic energy must be the future energy of the Earth[48] if the world's population is to be provided for in the future.

How will man live better with atomic energy?

The atom can provide man with a freedom he has never known before, allowing him to work less especially in industries where conditions are hard. It can enable him to develop space technology which will place him at the doors of the universe. With the atom he can create different materials to heal illnesses. In fact, man is in the process of discovering the atom and this is where his fear comes from.

It is a great pity that all the various energy forms discovered down the ages have been used by the military. A code of morals and ethics should be adopted rather than condemning the danger of one form of energy.

Discoveries

Nothing that man has discovered in the past or the things he will discover in the future are foreign to his origins, i.e. to his own creator. As it was stated in *The Book of Spirits*, everything is in everything.
From the most simple, middle-aged physical mechanics to the most sophisticated of atomic powered techniques, all we are seeing is the transformation of natural phenomena by various human minds.

A storm, which is a physical and climatic phenomenon, is a natural representation of our channelled electricity.

---

48 France went from deriving 8% of its electricity from nuclear power in 1973 to 70% by 1997. The fission produced by 1kg of uranium produces as much energy as 2,500 tons of coal. However, nuclear power produces radioactive waste that requires a very special treatment process, in the same way as plutonium 239.

In a volcano or a geyser, we can see a natural image of our energy that is channelled by the human conscience.
All this is simply a version of naturally existing elements that have been exploited by man.

Practicality and Technology

Are micro-wave ovens harmful for human health?

Most certainly. The micro-wave oven is a not a good invention. It is bad for the body and bad for food.
A micro-wave oven gives off radio-activity and this is passed on to the food inside it.
This man-made invention should be thrown away. It is supposed to be handy and quick but we would recommend that everyone should avoid using this appliance. Food should be cooked in a natural way. We are aware that modern man has developed appliances that save time but we are also aware that certain technological development can be bad for the health.

What is the effect on the human body of chemical additives that are put in food (preservatives and hormones)?

Man needs to be more careful. Little by little organic agriculture should take the lead over all other forms of food production that have been developed over the past few years.

Agriculture should become organic, magnetic and divinatory. Man must learn that he can not sow seeds just anywhere. A pendulum should be used to define the appropriate places. Seeds should be magnetised before they are sown. The human organism would greatly benefit from this.
Chemicals in agriculture are certainly responsible for the development of certain cancers. If this type of agriculture is continued over several generations, you will gradually witness the degeneration of human body tissue. Pesticide and chemical fertiliser poisoning is gradual. It takes place over generations and is genetically transmitted

Therefore, it is high time that man changed his approach in this matter.

What is the future of human technology for the 21st century?

In this field, as in many others, the future involves the fundamental notion of evolution. Technology will progress to such a point that man will be able to visit other inhabited planets by 2050.

However, moral standards must be the underlying principle of any technological and scientific development.
This is why we can not guarantee that all forms of technological progress will be of a pacifist nature.
The discovery of nuclear fusion may enable man to visit space, but it will also enable him to create more destructive weapons.

The Environment

What will happen if the ozone layer continues to be damaged?

If man continues to pollute the planet as he is doing now, without paying any attention to the state of the ozone layer, then this layer, which protects man and all living organisms on the planet, will disappear and the planet will be subjected to direct ultra-violet rays. The flora will rapidly disappear, the exchange of carbon in the chlorophyll of trees and plants will fall and your bodies will suffocate.

Extremely dedicated people are working at UNESCO in order to try to avoid this. As I want to believe in the evolution of the planet rather than predict the future, I am sure that the danger of permanent and increasing damage, although real, will be avoided (Gabriel Delanne, 1987).

What do you think of acid rain?

Acid rain exists because there has been insufficient communication between factories concerning their industrial waste. Acid rain is the result of bad organisation and a totally irresponsible attitude.
Ecology has been neglected for many years. Now we are aware that the Earth's atmosphere is increasingly becoming a reservoir for all sorts of gaseous, industrial waste.

The rainwater that falls on the earth has been contaminated by all these gases. The solution to this problem depends on human will power.

SOCIETY

Is it not the goal of society to ensure the well-being of all of its members?

Honoré de Balzac

We learn nothing from words. We learn everything from examples.

François Mitterand

Education

Advice for parents who accept that their child is a reincarnated spirit:

You who have enabled spirits to be reborn, you who will accompany them for several years on the path to adulthood, please be supportive, protective and guiding adults. Above all be loving parents.

Parents should have a love for the truth. If there are never lies or dissimulation, then I am sure the child will grow up in a spirit of sincerity and truth. Teach them the true value of man, that of love. Never give them the idea that they are superior in any way. Avoid flattery as you may awaken a feeling of pride in them that they may have had in a previous life and this would make prisoners of them for the rest of their time on earth.

A child is neither an angel nor a demon. He/she is a reincarnated spirit in a physical world. Never take his dreams away from him/her. Do not project onto your child what you would like him/her to be. Accept your child as he/she is. Love him/her. Be fair and just when necessary, as responsible guides need to be.

Parents, be aware of your limits. Be sufficiently humble as to learn things that you do not know from your child as he/she may be more advanced than you in certain fields.

Remember that a child is not a toy and that a child does not belong to you and you will discover endless moments of joy. You will command his/her respect and respect is also a form of love.

Henri Pestalozzi (03/04/1990)

Henri Pestalozzi

Henri Pestalozzi was born on the 12th January 1746. He was a good and enthusiastic man as well as being a genius. "His generosity led him into poverty", said one of his biographers, as if blaming him for this.
For those of us who know what life on this earth is, it would seem impossible to give more praise to the man who spent his life trying to improve the education of the people. He deserves the title of ***"The Father of the School of the People"*** as he constantly strived to improve humanity through education. He died in 1827 at the age of 81.

On the other side, the spirit of Pestaluzzi remains constantly concerned about children in general. He has informed us of his worries concerning the way in which a certain form of education is progressing in modern day society.

What do you think of the way children are currently educated?

The current education system does not exploit children's natural gifts. It represses the natural and intellectual curiosity of children, giving pride of place to negative tendencies, pride, fulfilment of desires, of domination and violence.

Through your films, games and daily acts you progressively push children into a world where they have to compete with each other. And when you speak with these children you will find they have begun to speak like adults.

Is this type of maturity in language precocious and harmful?

Should people be pleased with the force and power in the language of contemporary children?
Should they be proud or surprised about this cold and rational type of language?
I have come, my friends, to inform you how concerned I am about this tendency to want to suppress a certain form of naivety and innocence that

is peculiar to children. I would like to defend childhood, without seeming to be a softy or over-romanticising it. I believe that parents need to be (re)taught what childhood means. I believe that children should not be projected too violently and quickly into the world of adults, a world of war, of violence, of domination and money.

I am very worried that childhood is being drawn into something bad for children by school initiatives, extra school activities, the media, books etc.

What is your advice concerning education?

If children no longer dream it is because they see dreams on the television screen. If children no longer dream it is because they can not use their imagination to imagine characters or situations based on a single word, sentence or short story.
This is very serious. It is a barrier to the evolution of the spirit.

When the spirit is reincarnated, the past disappears, it becomes a spirit again, the spirit of a young soul in a developing body.

This young soul is prepared to receive knowledge, love and advice from its parents, family, friends and society as a whole. There is nothing easier to influence than a child. A child needs to feel safe with his/her father and mother. He/she needs to grow and develop, moving through a healthy adolescence toward a successful adulthood.

You are aware that even at a very early age, money distinguishes children from one another at school. You are aware that this money has the power to give children complexes or make them proud.
Do not push children towards a world of inhuman competition. Do not push them towards a cold world that is devoid of dreams or passions.

Do not strive to create genetic geniuses. I am certain that the future of the planet is in need of loving souls that open like flowers in the spring.

What should very young children be taught?

Children should be taught the beauty and the simplicity of drawing, of singing, of music, of painting and of nature.

They should not be exposed to philosophy, morals, politics or religion in this very young period of their reincarnation. Influencing a child in this way is not the role of a parent. A reincarnated spirit wishes to evolve rather than hear things that he has already heard previously.

What do you think of today's education?

Western society has given pride of place to secondary education following the Second World War. This was a serious mistake and is being felt today.
Fifty years ago when a child completed his/her primary school studies he/she had general knowledge that was far greater than that of today.

What knowledge should a child entering the first year of secondary school have?

At the age of 12, a child should know how to read, write and count. He/she should know syntax and how to spell in his mother tongue. He/she should be aware of the important events in his country's history as well as that of the planet. He/she should know about geography as well as the world of animals and vegetables.
A child of 12 should also be aware of the civil rights and duties of the society to which he/she belongs. All this knowledge should form part of a basic education that the child will need if he/she is to fully appreciate the society in which he/she lives.
The adult world would do well to take a close look at the current level of knowledge of a twelve year old child entering secondary school. The result is a disaster.

Should we give all children a secondary school education?

The current policy of getting all children through the baccalauréat at the age of 18 is a major error as it is not suited to the natural evolution of all individuals.

The great drama of the latter half of the 20th century was that of pushing children towards a type of education that they had not chosen whilst at the same time lowering the value of manual jobs. The result has been the appearance of generations of children with no formal qualifications and this has led many of them to be inactive and unproductive. Whilst claiming that you are giving everyone access to culture and learning, the opposite is in fact happening. A manual worker who has received a good, basic education can pursue his training and learning outside the traditional areas of the classroom when he feels it to be appropriate.

What advice would you give?

You should reintroduce Victor Hugo and a sense of what is well written and well spoken, a chronological teaching of history, logic, mental arithmetic and correct spelling. In this way primary school will produce children who will be able to make a positive choice afterwards.

SOCIETY

Is the family structure really necessary?

The family is a support and not an end in itself. If family links continue on the other side, this is due to the nature of spirits that love one another rather than to the circumstances of their family thinking.

What do you think of marriage?

Marriage is an institution set up and imagined by man. It is the result of the organisation of society, of different civilisations and histories.
Given this, the union of two people within the institution of marriage has certainly contributed something to the logical and intelligent organisation of your societies.
In current society, marriage has no logical reason to exist but it should be maintained for those people who wish to enter into marriage. It is a question of freedom. It is the choice of two individuals who wish to obtain a *civil* (and I insist on this word) recognition of the love that is between them.

What do you think of polygamy?

Polygamy is more a question of civilisation than of morals. What is accepted in one place is not acceptable in another. In absolute terms, we will not pass judgement on this. We will only state that what is important is the notion of happiness in love and that in this respect everyone is free to act as he/she wishes.

It is to be noted that the answer to this question is different from that given in *the Book of Spirits*. Since that book was written, things have considerably changed in western society, showing that love can not be locked inside strict monogamous rules. There are indeed too many examples of this.

Feelings should not be institutionalised. If polygamy was an institution it would not be better than marriage.

It is possible to serve God and Mammon

Jesus

Is it an advantage to have money in life?

Quite the contrary. Having money should be considered as a test because a person who has a lot is 100 times more responsible than a person who has nothing and owes 100 times more to his neighbour.

What do you think of money?

Money is at the root of wars and struggles. It creates hatred and racism.

What is wealth?

I see wealth in the physical and intellectual side to all people and all nations. I hear the hammer falling on the anvil. I see the plough cutting through the earth. I congratulate all the workers on the Earth, all those who have managed to escape from the slavery of the past. I celebrate all the humble and obscure people – those about whom nothing will be written or said.

I praise all those without whom the right to food, to clothing and education would be nothing more than a pipedream. I praise all those who have worked for God without realising it.
Hands, chapped by the cold, work on materials to overcome their brutality. Hands blackened by coal or cut by the press, hands that do not have the right to life because of their colour, the hands of the artist that has been silenced because he spoke too much of freedom. Man is the true wealth.

(Louis Aragon)

What do you think of prostitution in our society?

Certain thinkers and philosophers believe there are necessary evils on Earth. Should we confirm that this is true?
As far as prostitution is concerned, I do not think so. Prostitution is a form of slavery. It is more of a necessity than a truly deliberate choice. It is a consequence of your societies and of renunciation.
Apart from one or two exceptions, I do not believe that a human being can take great pleasure and joy in being a prostitute. It would be good if prostitution disappeared.
We do not bring any form of moral judgement here but we feel sorry for those who suffer from it.

What do you think of people that live on the fringes of society such as tramps?

No-one can say that they will never be a tramp. I think that this type of life is totally useless and that those who claim that they wanted to be like that are mocking as they are unable to admit they are morally in distress.
Being a tramp seems to me to be a form of suicide, a person pushed to his/her limits by the indifference of people around him/her.
It is not money that a tramp needs to be able to stand on his/her own two feet, but the love that people need to carry on living.
The extent to which a society has evolved can be measured by the number of beggars it has.

What do you think of euthanasia on animals?

This question is raised in 1857 by the *Book of Spirits* but it concerned human beings. The answer of the spirits at that time was a categorical "no" to any form of euthanasia. Since that time, medical science has considerably progressed. In 1857 there was no prolongation of life by medical means. Nowadays this exists and it is why the answer given by the spirits today is more subtle. We disapprove of artificially prolonging life and therefore approve of euthanasia where it can be medically proved that the subject will die in the near future. This is also the case for animals. There is no reason to view the animal world in a different way in this respect.

Has man progressed more in countries of advanced technology?

Man has evolved in different parts of the globe but evolution does not necessarily mean technological progress.
This is why simple and uneducated people wherever they are and whatever they do, should not be considered as being ignorant about everything. They are often closer to the truth and the essence of life.

Changing the future. A message from Henry IV (incorporation in 1986)

Change is not a utopia. Those who adamantly say that the world will never change are in league with those who do not want it to change.
Rich and poor, race against race, those who dominate and those who are dominated. This is what happens when indifference and a lack of love take over.
My social ideal is not utopia but simply what may be possible. Let us briefly define it: it would take only a few months to totally change the political face of the Earth by eliminating all nuclear weapons, by converting all military installations into useful and productive premises and by deciding to irrigate the dry lands in Africa and certain countries of Asia.

The United Nations could take on the role of organising all this. All financial operations on Stock Exchanges would stop and there would be a great programme to develop vast areas of the Earth instead.

There could also be an environmental plan to save rivers, trees and oceans from the threat of pollution which will be the peril of this millennium.

All this would be possible if man followed the principles of Christianity and humanity.

Do concentration camps still exist and if so where?

My friends, human beings live on an inferior planet. This is the result of the inferiority of the beings that live on it. The main trait of this inferiority is the refusal to understand the truth, however hard it is to accept. He who witnesses crime and refuses to see and denounce it is no different to he who commits it.

There is no continent that does not have some form of concentration camp.
In this world, men, women and children are oppressed and tortured every day. This is a well calculated and obscure reality on all continents. The reasons for this are the differences in ideas, in race, in social class and in culture.

The people who have created, who control and run the different forms of concentration camp are servile, base and low human beings. More serious still is the attitude of the leaders of the countries who are fully aware of what is going on. They do not denounce such places because they derive benefit from them.
We can put forward the figure of 30 million people who are currently victims of the world of concentration-like camps.

> *The death penalty is contrary to the noblest thoughts*
> *and dreams of humanity over the last 2000 years.*
>
> Jean Jaurès

What do you think of the death penalty?

We are obviously against the death penalty. No-one has the right to decide whether someone should live or die, either through capital punishment, euthanasia or abortion.

Sexuality

Is it possible to live without sexuality on the earth?

Man truly needs to live out his sexuality. If not he runs the risk of becoming unbalanced because something is denied within him.

Should sexuality be given a moral definition?

The answer from the spirits is "no".
Why define what comes naturally? Let us not define something that is inherent in your embodied spiritual reality. Let us avoid placing sexuality within rigid rules and laws that have no connection with this entirely human phenomenon.

Why is there a certain perversity linked to sexuality?

Perversion is not something natural in man, but it can become a human phenomenon when society is badly organised. It is not difficult to see that love is not always present in sexuality in the way it is presented, explained or analysed by various people.

So what is this sexuality that is reduced to an instinct, an urge with the notion of violence?

All sexuality should take place in accordance with the noblest and most righteous of feelings: that of love.

Abortion

What effect does abortion have on the returning spirit?

Abortion will stifle and suffocate the spirit that wishes to reincarnate. The spirit that is forced to return to the ether will find itself in a state of turmoil similar to disembodiment, a turmoil that is unnecessary. It will also foil the plans of the spirit that will then have to wait to be able to reincarnate, perhaps for a long period of time.

Are there any instances when abortion is acceptable?

Life should never be sacrificed on the Earth.
However, there are circumstances that force certain mothers to be separated from their child. This is rare and is the only exception we would make to our principle.

It is very serious to interrupt the process of incarnation at any moment because doing so represents a crime towards life itself, toward evolution and toward the sincere choice of a spirit to continue widening and deepening its awareness and conscience.

Suicide

Each year 600,000 human beings die in this way. Suicide has therefore become a serious and real social problem that can be summed up in a very simple manner.

What are the causes of suicide?

The main causes are the following:

A lack of love, mainly in the family but also friends who are not true friends
Wasting away in a job that is boring, uninteresting and repetitive
A feeling of being useless in an unequal society.
A feeling of inferiority marked by social hatred and narrow-mindedness
A sudden awareness of a previous suicidal life. This can lead to a neurotic obsession with suicide itself

Your answer is different from that given in *The Book of Spirits*

Yes, because societies have changed. Since the pioneering days of spiritism, the Earth has known nothing but war, social hatred, a disdain for life and a greed for money. Science and technology have developed on Earth. This is good as the gradual control of energy has demonstrated the genius of man. Unfortunately, the moral inferiority of the spirits on the Earth is dominant. Not everyone has benefited from technical progress. It has not been used to help and relieve poverty but has been restricted to a relatively small number of consumers of "progress" with no regard for the laws of nature, for the notions of *love and sharing*.

Does man have the right to do what he wants with his life and end it if he wishes?

No-one has the right to end life itself. Such an attack on life will stifle the spirit when it is reincarnating (abortion) or when embodiment is suddenly ended (suicide).

Will the spirit experience turmoil after events such as suicide and abortion when it returns to the other side?

The spirit will experience turmoil similar to that of disembodiment. This turmoil is unnecessary.
The spirit that wished to reincarnate in order to live out a new existence will see its plans thwarted by those who do not want it to return.
A spirit that commits suicide, whatever the reasons, will feel guilty of having contravened a fundamental divine law.

Does a spirit that commits suicide reincarnate more quickly?

Such a spirit indeed feels the need to return. Hence, having realised the error and futility of the act of suicide the spirit will decide to come back and continue an existence that ended too early.

Message from a spirit that committed suicide at a young age (received 13/06/93)

(The group helped this spirit, as we have helped others following this type of death. Our help came through prayer and a spiritual chain. In this way we were able to project it toward the light of its guide.)

I did a bad thing and if you had not been there I would have been in a serious state of turmoil.
I wish to give a message to all those who are thinking of committing suicide, to those who want to go faster than time itself, to those who wish to get around

the trials of life by giving up, to those who are afraid of suffering, to those who think they will find peace, paradise or eternal rest.

I wish to tell them that they must live on the Earth because they ARE on the Earth, that they must do their duty on the planet, that whoever they are whatever they do, they always have the opportunity to do something good and to do things well. Committing suicide means forgetting to do good and I forgot.

I know what will happen to me. I have met my guide thanks to you and I am aware that I can not remain for long in the condition in which I am. I must continue so I must return. I will not start again but continue where I left off. My act has caused me to waste a lot of time. I am not here this evening to judge or condemn. I am not the only one responsible for my act but it was nevertheless I who knowingly committed it.

Life must go on. It must go on with full force. Do not seek death, it will come soon enough. If we live in a body on the Earth, I believe it is a divine law.

I can feel God. I had already had this feeling. I had forgotten Him when I committed suicide.

Freedom is a cage as long as a man remains satisfied

Albert Camus

*Freedom goes hand in hand with responsibility.
That is why men are afraid of freedom.*

George Bernard Shaw

Freedom

Whatever his social condition, every human being feels like a prisoner in his spirit.
No person on Earth can ever claim to have lived and experienced everything they would like.

What is freedom?

Freedom can not be proclaimed. It will appear little by little.

Some people thought they would follow their own individual paths, paying little or no attention to their fellow countrymen. They thought they would become free before the rest.
This is a serious mistake!!
No living person can claim to be totally independent without any intellectual or emotional input from those around him. This is the way of the world and it is a good way. Each and every one of us, whatever his condition, needs other people. This means that freedom only becomes possible collectively.

How does one become free?

Freedom does not arrive, it needs to be built. Many of God's architects have presented a plan suggesting love and justice but they went unheard. Man rejected them. He even crucified them.

What prevents freedom from existing?

The great problem for the inhabitants of the Earth and many similar planets is that relationships are always seen in a context of the dominant and the dominated.
The strongest person in a tribe will become the leader because leadership is obtained by force. The richest person in a society will become the leader because he is the richest.

Should the value of a man be measured by is muscles or how much money he has?
No!
But unfortunately man continues to live with these values.

If there is no freedom on the Earth, can it be found on the other side?

As death appears to be the only thing that all people have in common and in front of which they are all equal, it was decided that a better life would be offered to those who did not find this life to their liking. Many people were taken in by this and naively believed that they would attain freedom after their death. It was therefore pointless to seek freedom on the Earth.
A second error!!

The afterlife is built in the present. Life on the other side depends on the life one leads here.

God gave freedom, man created slavery

André Chenier

How is freedom built?

"Take up arms!" some will shout.
A serious error!
Vengeance and destruction only bring tears and disillusion. The path that leads people out of slavery is paved with love, not the passive and complacent love of religious adoration but that of conscious love. If each person sees others as being children of God, then love will wipe death away and our two worlds will be united in osmosis.

When will man become free?

Man will be free when he has understood that the notion of freedom implies being committed and responsible.
The only way to become free is by realising that we are alive to free ourselves

(Diogene 10/04/1986)

The evolution of man

In a country where living conditions are particularly difficult, will the reincarnated spirit find it as easy to progress and evolve?

A reincarnated spirit will find it difficult to evolve in particularly difficult conditions given that it may be deprived of emotional and material stability.

This planet is not just or fair, nor is it well-balanced. All the bad things you see around you should push you to do your best to improve the situation.
There are no chance meetings, they are all planned

Paul Eluard

The future seems to be planned if we consider certain events. What happens to free choice in this case?

The future is not written down somewhere, it is there to be built. No event in a person's life is written down as the determinists believe.

The premonitory aspect of certain clairvoyance should be linked to telepathy and especially what is called universal telepathy.

What has prevented spiritism from expanding since the death of Allan Kardec?

The birth of metapsychics and parapsychology has largely betrayed the spiritist movement.
It became the norm to speak about the unknown mechanisms of the human subconscious rather than about the fundamental force that is within each and every one of us, i.e. the force of the spirit.

No-one spoke about the survival of the soul or the way in which it manifested itself to man. Spiritism has been rejected by those very people who were afraid of the word, by those who were afraid of death.

> *Depending on whether you are powerful or poverty-striken,*
> *the verdicts of the courts will make you white or black*
>
> Jean de la Fontaine

Justice

What is a criminal?

Human beings have a rather narrow definition of crime. For you, crime essentially consists in taking another person's life. Consequently, he who takes away another person's life will be seen as a criminal.

For us, this is a form of crime, one image or view of crime. In our opinion, there are many more criminals than that: there are criminals in thought and in act even if they do not take other peoples' lives.

There are people who have never held a knife or a gun but who are real criminals. Taking advantage of other peoples' pain is also a crime. In this case your so-called judges would find it difficult to decide whose head to cut off!

Is a criminal always totally responsible?

Who was the thief? Who was the murderer?
The question is often well worth asking, especially as the person committing an act is often the victim of those who have remained silent. They are often the true criminals.

Will crime ever disappear from the Earth?

Yes, when humanity has evolved to such a level that there is love in everyone's hearts.

The laws and institutions on Earth are directly linked to the overall level of evolution on it.

What can be done to stop a criminal being a criminal?

For each human being to have the right to dignity and respect, the destructive force of pride needs to disappear from people's hearts.

How can this pride be made to disappear?

Pride can be eliminated by the will and with the help of everyone. Do not refuse to look your enemy in the eye and when you have done this correctly, when you have seen both his eyes burning with hatred and when you have penetrated his soul with love you will have shaken his heart. He will fall.

What do you think of justice on the Earth?

Man's system of justice is based on a system of class, race, religious morals and individual or collective hatred. As such it is not always for the good of humanity.

What is your idea of true justice?

True justice can only be spiritist. I would like to see reincarnation and the phenomenon of possession finally recognised. What you have is a parody of justice, a materialistic system of justice that considers the accused as someone passing through. Only spirituality can give justice its true meaning.

If man is not condemned in the spiritist philosophy then he should not receive a more serious sentence in human justice. A new system of justice needs to de defined, a system that is based upon love for one's fellow beings, on the ability of a society as a whole to admit its mistakes and to help the accused whatever their offences might be.

So should those who commit serious offences be punished?

Punishment should not mean destroying, nor should it mean killing. The only true "punishment" for the guilty is to turn them into an innocent person again.

How can we gradually open the doors of our prisons?

For the doors of prisons to be opened, all the members of a society need to open the door to their hearts.
This subject should not be treated as secondary. There is a simplistic argument saying that old people and children should be looked after first before turning to common law prisoners. This is a ridiculous argument. There should not be a hierarchy in misfortune. Evil must be fought in whatever form it appears.

Are prisons a necessary evil? Are they good for man and society?

Prisons are not the right answer. They represent the rejection of one social group over another.
People who steal, attack others or kill are rarely free when they act. You must help them understand, help them to feel free. Prison will certainly not help these "criminals" to understand.

Why are prisons unsuitable?

Hatred will never be vanquished by hatred. Only love can win out over hate. Excepting capital punishment, you lock people away between walls and behind bars. These "prisoners" are only bad for a small number of people, not for the majority.
They suffer and think just as you do. But you prevent them from thinking. They can not evolve any more, they stagnate. And because of their close proximity to others they will be very likely to commit similar crimes again.

In fact, your prisons are the symbol of the repression of the bad conscience of society.
Prisons are the subconscious of society as a whole.

In fact, it is not indifference, ignorance or the penitentiary system that will help your fellow human beings.

WHAT THE SPIRITS SAY AND THINK

Only art and science can help man attain divinity.

Ludwig van Beethoven

Concerning art

We do not like the modern day interpretation of our work. It is more than tactless. It is an encroachment and an insult to our creative minds.

"Nabucco" has become a pop song. I do not see any musical evolution whatsoever in this type of adaptation. When people are asked about the opera Nabucco, they will say "oh yes it's a nice song!"

We are working on the other side to help creative works on Earth aspire to something higher. Copying is unbearable, as is mediocrity in overall musical expression

(Antonio Vivaldi 1987).

I am disgusted. I have just witnessed the sale of "The Romanian Woman", my work, my creation and all for the sum of 41 million francs. I find this disgusting. I fought against all the schools and academies. I would not have got a penny for this painting and now I am obliged to witness the awful bartering over my work of art by people who know nothing about art.
My God, if only the money could benefit the poor!
All deceased artists are disgusted by such events. It is high time man understood that the value of a work of art is not in its market value.

(Modigliani)

The history of art is the history of man, of his civilisation, of his fears, the history of the planet. Human nature has always felt the need to express itself through art. Understanding art means understanding the meaning of life.
Art must not be given a hierarchical value. The art of one civilisation is not superior to that of another. All art forms complement each other in a wonderful overall harmony.

Shapes have an important role and remain on the other side where they are delivered from matter. The curves and straight lines that have come from the artist's imagination become the direct transposition of his thoughts.

Poetry is a superior form of human expression because the poet directly expresses feelings with words.
The poet observes nature and feels the elements. He can penetrate everything around you and transforms it into words and sentences. The poet transforms words into a spoken form of music.

The artistic sense is a spiritual vibration that meets the needs of the soul. No work is truly finished in the eyes of the artist because when he creates he is seeking infinity. When seen in this light, no limits should be imposed on art.

The Earth has all too often stifled the creative spirit through business, money and ridiculous laws that prevent the creator from giving his best.

Concerning incarnation and life

Happy are the reincarnated spirits who have understood that life is a struggle. Happy are those who combat all forms of injustice.

You must not be indifferent or immobile. You must not be unaware of how your brothers all live on this planet.

He who walks nonchalantly, observing the tears, the blood, the pain and the hunger should beware of himself.

Concerning spirituality

It is fashionable, in good taste and modern to broadcast all sorts of ideas and thoughts that come directly from the Far East. The aim of this is to demonstrate to man that good living and well being consists in ceasing to see and to hear. It would appear better to hide inside one's physical envelope and pay no attention to the outside world or to other people.

If meditation means that people live a life of constant abnegation with regard to the physical reality around you, then love no longer exists, love is dead.

Mahatma Gandhi

We can not say that the world must change without accepting to change with it. The spiritual concept of the world involves applying the realities of the earth which are the opposite of crystallising and unchanging forms of thought.

Hence, the world is infinite and life will never cease. The spirit outlives the body and evolves constantly, not having to fear the judgement of God. Material goods do not show a person's value.

All things require thinking followed by action. Can one stand before the spirit whilst approving capital punishment, whilst being racist, whilst pretending poverty does not exist, whilst approving (through fear) the oppressive forces on the world? It is not possible!

An Earth will be born where there is solidarity between incarnated souls throughout the world.

Allan Kardec

I call upon all families not to shut themselves off from others. Feel for the children who die, as they are also your own. The Earth must become more human so that it can become more spiritual.

Victor Hugo

The spirit has no homeland. Neither is it bound by frontiers. The spirit knows only the absolute.

It upsets and angers me here on the other side to hear people use my words, saying that the 21st century will be religious or will cease to exist.
Let it be clear that this sentence was never expressed by my spirit and certainly not written.
Yes, I thought and I said that the coming century will be **spiritual** *or will not be and I am sad to see the way in which this expression has been used for religious ends.*

André Malraux

It is much easier to believe in heaven and in God's forgiveness than to believe in happiness through work and effort. On the other side, there are no dodgers. The naked truth is before us.

Concerning spiritism

It is good to communicate with the spirits to know that death does not exist as such. Léopoldine and Charles are all with me. It hurt me so much to lose my child that I wish here to give testimony for you and for all who read me.

It is said of Victor Hugo that spiritism was a consolation for him. It is thought that it was a consolation for a mad old man who refused to accept death, taking refuge in "talking tables" to counteract it.
This does not bother me at all. My dear friends, the mad old man is observing their ignorance and stupidity from the other side. When the old man died he was very far from the funeral organised by the Republic that had forgotten him for 30 years when he was in exile. I was so far from this ceremony. I was already in the company of my true, spiritual nature.
People should listen to old madmen who begin communicating with the spirits.

A timely death reunited me with my children. Oh dear death, my supreme exile, freedom at last, God's way of thanking me. I was able to praise him in poetry and he rewarded me with the bright light that shines for all those who meet again in the afterlife.
So, long live madness and now here I am with men and women who are spiritists and who assert it out aloud

I, Victor Hugo the poet wish to testify to my survival, my eternity, my rights, my life and the freedom to visit you. Long live spiritism.

Victor Hugo

I wish to come before you to testify about the help that spirits provided in the resistance to defend France during the Great War.
One night, lost despite our maps, several officers and myself were anxiously trying to stop the German lines advancing. Having examined the

problem from every angle, we always arrived at the same conclusion: we did not have enough material.

About 2a.m and to the stupefaction of all those around me, I decided to call upon the great medium Madame Fraya. She arrived at the Elysée about 3a.m and we began to examine the problem. She seemed relaxed and half asleep. A spirit began speaking through her, constantly repeating the words "the taxis, the taxis".

We understood that we were being told to use all the utility vehicles in Paris. It was in this way that a message from the spirits brought the taxis of the Marne into the history of the Second World War.

Georges Clemenceau

The spirit must not be ignored in favour of technical progress that owes its relative intelligence to the very same spirit. It is this spirit that I had always fought against, believing it to be a source of ignorance whereas in fact it is a model of evolution.

I systematically associated the Kardec movement with religion and fought it actively.

Since this period, we have met again and I must add that he has given me great comfort.
I must describe this meeting as extraordinary.
My name is Larrousse

Pierre Larrousse

We witnessed the extraordinary arrival of spiritism in France. Eugénie and I were great believers in spiritualism and we met Allan Kardec on several occasions.

It is difficult to imagine how important this person was at that time. He had over one million followers in France and his books were reprinted each year. It is hard to grasp the philosophical and social importance of the spiritist movement in the 19th century.

Allan Kardec did not agree with my policies and accused me of having used the urns of the Republic to put the Empire back in place. He was right. Eugénie always thought that I should abdicate and the spirits gave me the same advice. I refused to follow their messages and one year after the

death of Allan Kardec, the drama of 1870 took place as well as the disaster of Sedan.
My greatest error was to send Hugo into exile but he forgave me for that a long time ago.

I would love to see modern day France recover the power it had at that time in a spiritist renaissance. I encourage you with all my energy.

Napoleon III (1985)

We can not base the idea of owning property on other peoples' poverty.

Vincent Auriol

Concerning capitalism and money

You must learn to reject all forms of economic dominance through the use of money.

Opulence exists and certain great financiers get rich on the naivety and labour of the poor.

I am thinking about the miners of South Africa, about their chained ankles, their numbered bracelets. I am thinking about the owners of these mines, about the capitalist diamond dealers who exploit them because they are black. They are forced to do only one thing: crawl on their hands and knees in the mines, holding their tongues and dying of hunger. (Martin Luther King)

No problems will really be solved until money ceases to be the foundation of your societies.
We are horrified at the gigantic fortunes of the princes of the desert that have become a sort of shameful challenge to widespread poverty.
Beyond the peoples, races and all the quarrels of the past, beyond all things that have opposed people the spirit must come together as one with man. I will never understand any spiritual aims and claims that are not closely linked to the combat of humanity, however sincere they may be.

Whoever lays claim to his father in his God, whoever lays claim to the survival of their soul and to their spiritual future must also lay claim to their need for social justice, for political thinking in a world divided by money. They must continually protest.

Money! What happens to you in the face of this ocean? Oh you poison of humanity, what happens to you in eternity? You are nothing. You are just cheap and short-lived rubbish that can sometimes make weak minds dream.

Louis Aragon

My friends, it is indeed time for this planet to change if possible. We must counter all the pessimistic views claiming that the power of money can not be altered. I believe in the profound force of human nature, I believe in the awakening of consciences, I believe in socialism and from the other side I observe those who say that the old and worn out capitalist formula will always be credible. I have always been placed in opposition to General de Gaulle. What a mistake!
We are working together on the other side. So many politicians would be disgusted by this. I am with you to bring you my version of the truth.

François Mitterand (1997)

In the absence of time, I dream of another world
As I look at the Earth I implore the Mona Lisa to
stop smiling at hunger stricken children and to offer
them life, offer them help

Concerning hunger in the world

There are people dying on this Earth because of injustice, misunderstanding and unbearable conditions. I am thinking about all the children in India, Africa, Asia and Brazil who reincarnate on the Earth for a few days or a few months only to die again of hunger in terrible pain.
The spiritual condition and the law of the spirit in paliangenesis are not responsible for this. Man is guilty of this because of his anti-social behaviour.

One of the abominable human realities of your Earth is that it is certainly rich and big enough to feed all who live on it.
This does not mean giving charity. It means having a conscience, being responsible, aware and caring.

Because I defended the weak and the humble, because I wrote the truth, because I defended Dreyfus I was murdered along with my wife. We choked on the carbon fumes from our fireplace and chimney that had been purposely blocked.

That is all in the past. Now I constantly watch the Earth evolve with all its contradictions. It is high time the existing injustice between the North and South was put to rights. It is high time you started feeding all the children of the planet because the Earth is capable of feeding everyone. Man must agree to put an end to the domination of money. It is time that the people were told they have been misled, that heads of state are but puppets in the hands of high finance. It is time to reaffirm that politicians are nothing without economic power.

Good intentions have never given food to the starving and the financial wizards of the northern hemisphere can be compared to the Nazi butchers of the Second World War. I know that everyone wishes to do something and I am not accusing good-willed people. But I am well aware that the Lords of finance need to be taken down from their pedestal so that men can live and children will no longer cry of hunger like wolves howl to the night;

Emile Zola (1985)

Are spirits that reincarnate into poverty aware of the difficulties they will have in life?

These spirits have not all made a deliberate choice to return. They have reincarnated in an instinctive turmoil in countries where food is not available.

What is it like for them on the other side after suffering from hunger?

Children who die of starvation suffer from a profound turmoil in the afterlife. After suffering from hunger, they suffer when they return to the world of the spirits as they constantly feel the hunger they had felt during their lives, despite no longer having a physical body. This awful and unfair state of affairs must be changed and you can all help them.

Concerning politics

One thing that could accelerate the evolutionary process for human beings would be to move towards spiritual socialism. This is a form of utopia that could quickly be put into place.

The proof that governments are inefficient can be seen in the growth in the number of charity organisations. They only have short term solutions, unfortunately and poverty is in need of something more than short term.

Neither France not Europe should smile or make fun of the neo-fascist movement that is reappearing at the present time. Previous generations discovered the price that had to be paid for letting such a movement grow.

Hope for a better and different world lies more in the hands of the inhabitants of the Earth than with its leaders. The same idea is beginning to appear in all nations, especially amongst young people. They are now refusing:

The massive stocking of weapons

Racial hatred

Hunger and poverty in the southern hemisphere

A lot of individual or collective action has been undertaken to make people aware just how fragile their states are and how stupidly their institutions appear.

Concerning the policies of America

The domestic policy of the USA is a mafia type policy based on money. It is not a real and deliberate policy as it is based on the individual, on ambition and climbing the social ladder.

The United States of America certainly believed that they had conquered the world when the Berlin wall came down. This was a serious mistake. What is more, this country is slipping increasingly deeper into intolerance and barbarity, into racism and poverty. It is sinking into corruption and a total lack of any form of social justice.

America is no longer the great nation that Jefferson or Lincoln dreamed of. It is a collection of different situations, based essentially on the domination of money.

Concerning Palestine

I come to you again my brothers with a thought that is continually haunting my spirit and for which I struggle. The people of Palestine need a homeland. Things have improved but there are still serious problems concerning the existence of this region that should become a country, which should become the homeland of those who have been forgotten, sent packing, ignored and abandoned. They have often acted in despair committing acts that have been condemned by man and by universal morals. But it is understandable.
Bloodshed should not avenge bloodshed, pain should not avenge pain. Justice should awaken peoples' consciences for a Palestinian people in the country of Palestine.

Anouar El Sadate

The people of Palestine are dying, suffocated and assassinated. In this message I declare myself wholeheartedly in support of the cause of Yasser Arafat.

Those who continue to criticise and blame the desperate acts of a people asking for nothing more than their own identity, are refusing to see the reality of things. It is very easy to take this attitude.

What would French or English people say if one day the highest instances in their countries decided that they were no longer clearly defined and that they had no frontiers with other counties nor civilisation and that they would be annexed by another country?

Each ethnic race and all people have to live on this Earth, the Jews as well as the Palestinians. If anyone believes that the ideas of a spirit can go against the people of Israel, then they have not understood a word I have said.

Anouar El-Sadate

In former times they were a nomadic people. Today they are on the defensive. They have money, power and domination.

We must not refuse history. We must examine it and give it its true meaning. Now they must embrace their neighbours and respect their request to be liberated.

I pray with you this evening for a just and real Palestine. I honour the spirit of Yasser Arafat.

Evil is often the absence of good. Evil often means forgetting because times passes for man and if the Jewish nation forgets then Palestine will die.

Jesus

Concerning fascism

This country is under serious threat. The danger lies in the extreme right wing with a real threat of fascism. The whole planet is undergoing an upheaval in civilised society. There is a crisis concerning values and morals.

Moral values are based on beauty, goodness, passion, sharing, love and all the urges present in each individual who today appears to be stuck in a social position.

Disappointed citizens will let things go, paying no attention to a ghost-like government that takes no initiatives, simply fixing the holes as they go along but not really governing.
The extreme right wing is not only growing in popularity in this country but in other European countries.
Does the future of Europe lie in extremes of all kinds? A so-called national front would threaten the future of the whole of France.
This is a serious situation. All of you are threatened. The threat is to put a muzzle on the country, to censor everything, to control the whole country in a reign of shameful racism.

Charles de Gaulle

The human race must stop fighting and reject vengeance aggression and the spirit of revenge. Love is the way out of this spiral.

John Fitzgerald Kennedy

Hatred always kills. Love never dies.

Mahatma Gandhi

Concerning racism

It is correct to say that the Earth belongs to no-one. It is incorrect and unfair to claim that it could be the property of one race.
Who can say that a blade of grass or a tree is Mexican or American? Who can say whether an ocean or a piece of land is French, English or Canadian? These are purely human inventions that set countries against one another.

There is no superior or inferior race. There is only one race and that is the race of divine human beings.

I do not want the black, the Arab or the Armenian to be tolerated because tolerating means being seen as different from the others. Other people are the same as you and I, and I am the same as all other people.

All the facets of racism must crumble without exception. This concerns the colour of the skin as well as other conditions. I mean that the handicapped should not suffer from racism, that negative social attitudes should not develop towards those people who work very hard at basic tasks on a daily basis.

We shall pray for Tom…..we shall pray for all the Toms of this world. We shall pray that none of them has a meagre cabin.

I had a dream and I told the American people about it. I still have this reoccurring dream. I dream that one day all people will take each other by the hand, the blacks, the browns, the whites, same blood, same flower, same life, same God, same love, same mother and same heart.

I still dream of that day. I am still waiting for that day. I am still waiting for the day of dignity. I await the day of my God and my Father. I await the end of bloodshed. I am still waiting for the day of smiling and laughter. I await the day that men and women will dance on the Earth together.

I am awaiting the end of man and the beginning of the soul.

Martin Luther King 1982

Before reincarnating I had not foreseen such a brutal end to my life. Terrorist fanaticism was the cause of my death. I did not want to leave. There is so much to be done.

I joined those who are working for peace in the invisible world and I wish to work on the other side to further justice on the Earth between the north and the south. I will fight against all racial hatred, work to see wealth spread more evenly over the planet and promote respect for life in general. This is my only goal.

I observe men. I know both their political and spiritual frontiers and along with so many other spirits I am saddened to witness this desire to stand out from the others by a social status or by a geographical location on the Earth.

Why think that one race should dominate another?
Why believe that one caste should dominate a whole people?
Why wish to dominate through torture and martyrdom?
Why fight?

The future of man lies in his awareness at a planetary level. The future of man on the Earth lies in a total society, in the absence of any frontiers.
Everyone should be able to keep their history, their character, their race and anything that shows who they are in this short-lived incarnation. But no-one should cultivate their differences in the hatred of others.

One planet amongst millions, humanity amongst a multitude of life, stardust in the Universe amongst the stars, you must grow in order to find your God and live according to his law in love.

Which man, which party, which caste or which power has ever included love in its social programme?

Mahatma Gandhi

Message from Martine Luther King (1983, incorporation)

We have the same blood, the same flesh, the same bones, the same life and the same death.

If you have wounds on your body they hurt you in the same way as they would hurt me.

We love at the same time, we live at the same time, we die at the same time, we watch the same stars, we have the same sky and we crawl on the same Earth. We are from the same tree.

Nature made our bodies different and she created this difference in the name of harmony. You are what I am not and I am what you are not. As we are different we are bound to meet one another, to live together and to love one another.

Is my child more innocent or guilty than yours? Does the pigment of his skin justify that he be judged?
And because hatred was the justification for spilling my blood, we must no longer speak of our differences but of our wealth and the beauty of being different.

The most powerful answer to what I am saying is called reincarnation.

We return to the flesh and flesh differs depending on our country and on our mission. Our thoughts become stupid if we continue to behave differently depending on our race.

There is only one race and it is called the Spirit.

> *Money can always be found to create war but never to create peace.*
>
> Albert Brie

Concerning peace

Peace on Earth is based on the notion of a balance of military power. This concept is absurd and inefficient. If arms exist there is a temptation to use them. All the weapons built must be destroyed and we are alarmed that certain politicians do not wish to disarm the world. Peace can not be envisaged as long as this balance of war power exists. Peace can only come from universal disarmament.

Evil lives side by side with good. Beauty lives in the presence of ugliness on the same planet where all people should have the right to the same dignity.

A book is a letter written to all the unknown friends we have in the world.

Lingrée

CONCLUSION

Death has been able to "express itself" through this book with no barriers whatsoever. Some people have been named but they are only a very small proportion of those who come to visit us.
Why is this? Because death manifests itself where it can be received, where it is expected and listened to in conditions suitable for total and real expression. It then becomes obvious that the aims of these visits will take on many different aspects through the diversity of the messages received.
Spirits are nothing more than the souls of the dead and communicating with them means remaining within the realm of humanity. This means that the afterlife represents a population of spirits that are very different from one another, given the differing levels of culture, education, ignorance, evil or goodness.

This is why death calls out to life as a survivor, from the most humble to the greatest, from the sufferers to the serene and from the most vile to the best.

Hence, astral suffering has been given a way to act. Evil and hatred have also been given this.
People faced with the absence of loved ones and who suffer because of this are brought comfort and certainty.
The spirits have therefore answered all the questions put to them.
Hence, the spiritism that appeared over a century and a half ago continues to reveal that death does not exist.

Spiritism is the only philosophy on Earth that has not resulted from the thinking of one man or a group of men, but has come from the thought and knowledge of the deceased. Spirits are free from the chains of matter and are no longer weighed down by material concerns. Their perception is clearer, their knowledge wider and their judgement more precise. The afterlife is also a vast learning place where everyone can continue to learn if they so wish.

Man is continually trying to improve his living conditions and be at peace. He continues his quest for the absolute, seeking answers to the fundamental questions in life. Faith is no longer sufficient, he requires knowledge. In this context, spiritism has its place if it is dusted down and cleared of the negative beliefs, harmful clichés, bad practices and old superstitions.

No, they have not left for all eternity. They have not disappeared, taken away with a decomposing body. They are here, proclaiming their survival and opening the tombs of uncertainty so that the song of the spirit can make itself heard in the conscience of all people.

It is true that the dead speak to the living. But they do not come to reveal lottery numbers, the location of a treasure trove, a future marriage or how many children we will have. There are more important preoccupations on the other side and the vocation of spiritism is different.
The simple fact of being able to communicate with the afterlife has serious and far-reaching consequences.
It is a new world that is opening up and it is especially important because each and every one of us without exception will go there.

"We'll have plenty of time to think about death later", many people say. When they say this they are forgetting that death is the continuation of life. Reflecting on death is as important as reflecting on life.
This book will perhaps prompt others to be written and these will also praise those in the heavens who are proclaiming one basically simple truth: **death does not exist.**

One day the eyes of the spirit will go beyond the eyes in the body and everyone will see God in the mantra of the Universe.

Jesus

BIBLIOGRAPHY

Already published in the collection: "Allan Kardec Spiritualist Group"

(in the French language)

Two collections of mediumnic poetry (1992-1998)

A la Rencontre des Esprits   (1997)
by Jacques Peccatte

La Délivrance des Mondes   (2000)
by Olivier Fauvel

Le Nouveau livre des Esprits (2002)
By Karine Chateigner

Ecce Homo (2007)
By Karine Chateigner

Entre Ciel et Terre (2008)
By Karine Chateigner

Les ombres de l'Histoire à la lumière des Esprits (2017)
By Claudine Camus

Le Journal Spirite-The Spiritualist Journal - a magazine created in 1989 (one issue in English)

This journal is published in French every 3 months. (subscription from abroad possible).

This book was translated from the French version into English by David Eckersley

LINKS

Webside in English: http://www.spiritisme.com/en/

In the French language:

Site internet Spiritisme.com:
http://www.spiritisme.com/

Biographies:
http://www.spiritisme.com/biographies/

Forum "Au-delà des mots":
http://www.le-forum-du-spiritisme.com/

Medium Art's:
https://www.facebook.com/M%C3%A9dium-ArtS-1439272336333425/

Cercle spirite Allan Kardec Facebook:
https://www.facebook.com/Cercle-Spirite-Allan-Kardec-113335318778247/

Vidéos Cercle Spirite Allan Kardec:
https://www.youtube.com/user/CercleSpiriteAK

Thérapies spirites:
https://www.therapies-spirites.com/

Site internet antenne de Lyon:
https://www.spiritisme-lyon.com/

Site internet antenne de Paris:
http://allankardec.paris.free.fr/index.html

Site internet antenne de Toulouse:
http://www.spiritisme-toulouse.com/acceuil/index.html

CONTENTS

MY JOURNEY TOWARDS THE DOOR INTO THE AFTERLIFE 7
PREFACE 11
FOREWORD: ALLAN KARDEC 13
    The Passage of Allan Kardec 14
    The Grave of Allan Kardec 16
WHY "THE NEW BOOK OF SPIRITS" WAS WRITTEN 19
    The creation of our group 19
GOD 23
    The initial cause: God 25
    The Intentions of God 29
GENERAL ELEMENTS OF THE UNIVERSE 31
    Concerning the universe 32
    The universe 33
    The Comets 36
SPIRIT AND MATTER 39
    Matter 42
    The Spirit 45
CREATION 49
    The Formation of Worlds 50
    Creation and birth of the Earth 52
    The history of Man 57
THE THREE KINGDOMS 61
    The Mineral Kingdom 63
    The Vegetable Kingdom 64
    The animal kingdom 67
INHABITED WORLDS 75
So many inhabited worlds 77
    Inferior planets 80
    More developed Planets 83
THE PERISPIRIT 87
THE SPIRIT 95
    The genesis of the spirit 96
FROM LIFE TO DEATH 101
    Death 102
    Trouble 105
THE OTHER SIDE 113

THE AFTERLIFE	114
A General Description of the Afterlife	115
The afterlife of evil spirits	124
The activities of the spirits in the afterlife	133
REINCARNATION	139
Reincarnation:	141
Conclusion	157
EVOLUTION	159
The Evolution of the Spirit	160
The Evolution of Worlds	164
THE MANIFESTATION OF SPIRITS IN THE PHYSICAL WORLD	167
MEDIUMSHIP	173
What is mediumship?	175
Art and mediumship	181
Poetry	181
Medical Mediumship	182
THE EMANCIPATION OF THE SPIRIT	183
Consciousness	184
Sleep and Dreams	185
Telepathy	190
Thought chains or fluidic chains	192
Dowsing	193
Psychometrics	196
Black Magic	197
The astral journey	198
Alchemy	200
Levitation	201
Occult practices	202
ANCIENT CIVILISATIONS	205
The Druids	206
Atlantis	211
Enigmas	213
PHILOSOPHY	217
Land of the future	218
PHILOSOPHY	219
RELIGION	223
Spiritism, the third revelation of God, is not a new religion	224
RELIGION	227
Mahomet	238
Buddha	240
Moses	243

- Jesus 246
- MEDECINE 265
  - Spiritism and Medicine 266
  - Natural Medicine 281
  - Hypnosis 283
- SCIENCE 287
  - Practicality and Technology 290
  - The Environment 291
- SOCIETY 293
  - Education 294
  - Society 299
  - Sexuality 304
  - Abortion 305
  - Suicide 306
  - Freedom 309
  - The evolution of man 311
  - Justice 313
- WHAT THE SPIRITS SAY AND THINK 317
  - Concerning art 318
  - Concerning incarnation and life 319
  - Concerning spirituality 319
  - Concerning spiritism 321
  - Concerning capitalism and money 323
  - Concerning hunger in the world 324
  - Concerning politics 326
  - Concerning the policies of America 327
  - Concerning Palestine 327
  - Concerning fascism 329
  - Concerning racism 330
  - Concerning peace 332
- CONCLUSION 335
- BIBLIOGRAPHY 337
- LINKS 339

www.ingramcontent.com/pod-product-compliance
Lightning Source LLC
Chambersburg PA
CBHW050241170426
43202CB00015B/2876